The Theory of the American Romance
An Ideology in
American Intellectual History

The Theory of the American Romance
An Ideology in
American Intellectual History

by
William Ellis

U·M·I Research Press

Ann Arbor / London

Produced and distributed by
UMI Research Press
an imprint of
University Microfilms Inc.
Ann Arbor, Michigan 48106

Library of Congress Cataloging in Publication Data

Ellis, William A. (William Albert)
  The theory of the American romance : an ideology in American
intellectual history / by William Ellis.
    p. cm.—(Nineteenth-century studies)
    Bibliography: p.
    Includes index.
    ISBN 0-8357-1984-7 (alk. paper)
    1. American fiction—19th century—History and criticism—Theory,
etc. 2. American fiction—19th century—History and criticism.
3. United States—Intellectual life. 4. Romanticism—United States.
5. Realism in literature. I. Title. II. Series: Nineteenth-century
studies (Ann Arbor, Mich.)
PS374.R6E45   1989
813'.309—dc20   89-5139
                                                                         CIP

British Library CIP data is available.

The paper used in this publication meets the minimum requirements of
American National Standard for Information Sciences—Permanence of Paper for Printed
Library Materials, ANSI Z39.48-1984. ∞ ™

To Louis Contant

Contents

Acknowledgments

I wish to thank Donna-Lane Nelson, Natalie Novak, and Michel Langella for their help in the preparation of the manuscript, Prof. Julian Markels of Ohio State University for careful reading and disinterested criticism of several chapters with a perspective different from his own, and the personnel of the beautiful English and American libraries in the center of Vieux Toulouse, and of the various libraries of the University of Toulouse, for making their facilities so readily available to me.

Introduction

An introduction is a pleasant exercise: it allows the writer to speak informally of his subject. Mine is the idea of American exceptionalism, as found in the most ambitious of attempts to explain the classic American novel—the theory of the American romance. Because its historical and intellectual background is the subject of the next chapter, I wish to speak here of the motives for my discussion, which is at once an outline of the development of the theory and a criticism of its ideas.

I do this because, at first glance, my critical intention may appear peculiar; for the theory, at least in its original form, has been removed from critical attention for some time. Why disinter a body of ideas if the purpose is not to revive the corpse, but to bury it once again? The short answer has two parts: first, in my opinion, the theory lost its hold for reasons unrelated to merit; second (and as a possible consequence of this) there are signs that it is being revived, although in a guise so altered that some of the revivalists may be unaware of how traditional their ideas are. Therefore, I want to help prevent revival by examining the theory's demerits in detail. At the same time, I want to do justice to the valuable concerns, now largely neglected, that the theory brought to the study of the classic American novels—the novels of Cooper, Hawthorne, Melville, Twain, and James.[1]

But first, a word about the theory itself. Under its influence, perhaps a majority of critics, for more than a generation, agreed that the American novel of the nineteenth century, because it had the form of the romance, was very different from its European counterpart. In its most influential version, the theory maintained that the formal difference arose from a difference in concern. The European novel was absorbed with society, and by studying manners, told truths about social life. In contrast, the American romance, at once archaic and proto-modernist, took the human condition as its subject, and by dramatizing mythic and symbolic situations, told truths about human nature. The novel was empirical and realistic; the romance metaphysical and often fantastic. The novel was substantial and concrete, with a wealth of detail; the romance, less ballasted by social fact, was more abstract, but more profound. Because all literature refers, although not always directly, to the social conditions that nurture it, the explanation for the alleged differences was sought in the societies that nurtured the two forms. America and Europe, it was claimed, did not really share a common civilization: America was exceptional among the nations of the West. European society was class-based and divided by class conflict; this, with the weight of ancient traditions, riveted the attention of European novelists upon society itself. America, knit by consensus and relatively traditionless, offered little to the social observer. Its social texture was thin, but, to the extent that class and cultural struggle had been avoided, it was happily and harmoniously thin. Precisely because of this, the American novelists looked beyond society to existential situations of metaphysical import.

This view, first stated in Lionel Trilling's *The Liberal Imagination* (1950), was the dominant view for over thirty years. It never went entirely unchallenged, but the early challenges were infrequent and generally ignored.[2] The exceptionalist claim was weakened when A. N. Kaul, with *The American Vision* (1963), persuaded many readers that the American novel had a social side that had not been allowed. But Kaul agreed that, in form, the American novel had exceptional features. In this at least the theory was maintained, so much so, that by 1969 Joel Porte could write:

> Thanks to a series of major critical studies that have appeared in the past decade and a half, it no longer seems necessary to argue for the importance of romance as a nineteenth-century American genre. Students of American Literature—notably Richard Chase—have provided a solid theoretical basis for establishing that the rise and growth of fiction in this country is dominated by our authors' conscious adherence to a tradition of non-realistic romance sharply at variance with the broadly novelistic mainstream of English writing.[3]

In the seventies, however, the situation changed; the theory began to sustain attacks. These were numerous enough that by the beginning of the eighties, as Michael Davitt Bell observed, the "cliché" that the American novel was romance had acquired "plenty of detractors."[4] Bell went on to outline their detractions: that the difference between the American romance and British novel had been exaggerated, that Lionel Trilling's idea of reality, upon which his definition of the novel depended, was naive, and that the distinctions between the romance and the novel were only spuriously distinctions of genre. As a consequence, Bell acknowledged, "it might appear that a student of nineteenth-century American fiction would be wise to avoid the term 'romance' altogether." He had used the term, he was careful to add, only because the American novelists had used it, and not because he was "concerned to revive or redefine the distinction between 'romance' and 'novel' . . . a distinction . . . far less important than the more general distinction between all fiction and what conventional thought took to be fact."[5] Not that the orthodoxy had been overturned; its truth, however, could no longer be assumed—a result perhaps inevitable once Kaul (and Porte after him) had shown the American novel's social concern. And although Bell himself sidestepped the debate, its very existence seemed to promise that the eighties would bring the question of romance (and the question of exceptionalism) to the center of critical attention.

Surprisingly, this did not occur. After a few articles published in the wake of Bell's *The Development of the American Romance* (1980), the subject has aroused little controversy. The result, I believe, has little precedence (although, in a time of critical fashions, it may be becoming the rule): a major influential theory, at the very moment when persistently challenged, suddenly dropped out of sight—taking with it the challenges themselves. The only possible surmise is that the issues it raised had ceased to be of interest—but its former prominence raises the question of why this should have occurred. Despite the risks of drawing an inference from silence, the reasons seem to me at once obvious and inadequate. By taking them up briefly here, I shall expand upon my comment that the theory deserves, if not a renewed influence, a renewed attention.

The first and most important reason, although only incidental to the theory itself, is that the advocates and opponents of the theory practiced a criticism that became unfashionable. I mean the humanistic "old criticism"[6] (as George Steiner calls it), whose origin is Aristotle's defense of poetry—that is to say, of literature itself—against the Platonic charge that literature is merely a rhetoric, and a dangerous one at that.[7] In its modern incarnation, which dates from the thirties, some of whose exemplars in the English-speaking countries were Lionel Trilling, F. R. Leavis, Edmund Wilson, and Philip Rahv, the old criticism was committed to a position between the "sociological criticism,"[8] often populist or Stalinist, that flourished and died out with the depression, and the formalist new criticism, which rose to prominence at the same time and became an academic orthodoxy—in the criticism of poetry at least—in the fifties and sixties. Against the new critics, who tended to treat literature as Plato did—as a rhetoric (but a benign one), valuable because it created objects of formal beauty through the intense organization of language—the old critics held that literature is in large measure a criticism of life, including but going beyond the boundaries of literature and language itself. From their perspective, literature is valuable for its referential content and for its ideas; it *is* a beautiful rhetoric, but it is also a mode of knowledge, hence a source of ethics and, distantly, of politics.[9] This opinion was held, moreover, whatever the philosophical loyalties that divided the old critics themselves. So diverse were these among the early romance critics that they spanned the (then) philosophical spectrum—from the rationalism of Lionel Trilling, through the Lawrentian romanticism (via Leavis) of Marius Bewley, to the partial existentialism of Richard Chase.

At the same time, against a narrowly politicized sociological criticism, the old critics upheld, although not with the intensity of the new critics, the importance of form. Trilling and Bewley rejected Dreiser partly on formalist grounds; Dreiser's language, they argued, because it was ugly and inchoate, undermined Dreiser's ability to achieve any significant insight or expression.[10]

Nevertheless, the old criticism denied that rhetoric can compensate for poverty of insight. It maintained that insight and rhetorical efficacity—truth and beauty—are allied in two senses: in a minor sense, because the beauty of an expression is enhanced if true, while insight is more persuasive when poetically expressed; in a major sense, because of the difficulty in separating intensity of language and form from the significance of a work's insights. The old critics usually accepted (although not always—Edmund Wilson, I think, did not) the dictum that form and content are one, but if the new critics placed the emphasis on form, the old critical emphasis was on content. As F. R. Leavis put it: "it is true . . . of the . . . great English novelists that their interest in their art . . . is brought to an intense focus, an unusually developed interest in life."[11] Although the old critics often differed, they all, even the Lawrentian Leavis, followed the Aristotelian notion that formal success is contingent upon the quality of a writer's vision, chiefly his moral discernment, which includes his ability to distinguish the essential from the accidental and the universal from the particular in the activity of the world to which his work refers.[12] Art, in other words, is the philosophical companion of logic in the quest for knowledge, and approaches, as Geoffrey Thurley puts it, "a realm of Truth . . . through images and allegories."[13] The images and allegories of literature, which we admire because of our intense response to them, are a vision of reality. As a result, form cannot be ultimately separated from the value of the interests and the knowledge it embodies; and knowledge, because it cannot be separated from values, has an ethical import. It remains to be said that the old criticism conceived of criticism itself as an enterprise similar, but subsidiary, to literature. Hence, just as literature evaluates experience, so should criticism largely evaluate literature on its ability to do this task well.[14]

In the light of these principles, it is easy to see why the old criticism and its works, such as the theory of the American romance and the detractions of its opponents, should have fallen into disregard. First, the new scientism in literary criticism, represented by Northrop Frye's *The Anatomy of Criticism* and the work of the structuralists, added its voice to the formalist argument, although, unlike the new critics, Frye and the structuralists opposed the judgmental dimension of critical activity such as the ranking of texts (now "discredited" if we can believe Robert Scholes).[15] Second, and with far more effect,the postmodernist theories that came to dominate the criticism in the eighties disseminated assumptions, historicist and relativist throughout, that were diametrically opposed to those of the old criticism.[16] This was especially true of deconstruction, which denied the possibility of either insight or form. Insight is impossible because literature does not refer to anything outside itself—not, however (as the new critics believed), because literature is a language unto itself, creating self-contained "verbal icons," but because language itself is non-referential. Form too is an illusion, because the figurative power of language subverts every attempt at coherent expression—again, not only in literature, but in discourse as such.[17] The ideological energy of postmodernism, then, shifted the spotlight from old critical concerns. So far as the postmodernists agreed with the new critics that literature is not referential, the idea of literature as a criticism of life was further discredited; so far as the idea of form became the focus of critical debate, the idea of form held by the new critics obscured the one held by the old—especially since the remaining old critics lent their support, sometimes self-effacing, to the new-critical defense of form.[18] As a further consequence, the debate between the theorists of the American romance and their opponents disappeared. What attraction could this debate, which saw form as a function of contents given by the intersection of history and the quest for truth, have for critics who denied the significance of content, and sometimes the existence of truth as well? Even Bell's book, although alive to the relation of the novel to history, declines to discuss, as a matter of minor importance, the merit of the distinction between romance and novel, or to raise the issue of American exceptionalism, in order to speak of the American novel's relevance to postmodernist concerns.[19]

Nevertheless, it must be admitted that the rise of structuralist and postmodernist criticism does not entirely explain why the theory of the American romance has received little attention in recent years. After all, not everyone was swept away by the "textual revolution." There is contemporary criticism, chiefly political in intention, from Judith Fetterly's old-left, feminist view of the American novel to Sacvan Bercovitch's and Myra Jehlen's studies of the effect of nationalist ideology upon American literature, that assumes literature's referentiality and that speaks an evaluative language reminiscent of—even when finally different from—that of the old criticism.[20] But here too the theory, although acknowledged, is rarely acknowledged as a major influence.[21] Probably this is owing to inattentiveness—for, as we shall see, some of the implicit but nevertheless important ideas of the theory have been rediscovered by recent critics. Perhaps these critics, in glancing over the more than thirty years during which the theory was advocated (and then intelligently, if inconclusively, attacked) simply assumed that there was little left to explore or to add. This certainly seems to have been the attitude of Bell when he set aside, in *The Development of the American Romance,* the debate between the theory and its opponents; his voice betrayed a weariness of tone.

Obviously, since I have written this book, I do not agree. I believe that a revival of the theory's intention—to find the relations between the form, the insights, and the historical context of the American novel—would be a good thing, especially since the revival of the theory's larger, old-critical concerns is actually underway.[22] This has happened in part because the postmodernist movement, after its initial success against formalism, appears to have lost some steam. This has occurred for several reasons, among them entropy, a rejection of postmodernist jargon, and the revelations of Fascist involvement on the part of Heidegger and Paul De Man. Perhaps most important in the long run, post-modernist theorists have not really answered the challenges of their critics. No convincing reply, for example, has ever been made to the charge by M. H. Abrams, first laid against deconstruction but applying to most postmodernisms (including some elements of structuralism), that its polemics are self-refuting.[23] That is, by promoting their own discourse, postmodernists lay claim to that very truth and coherence of expression which they deny is possible. At the least they have never been able (as Derrida himself allows)[24] to escape the propositional nature of language, which presumes both truth and coherence. In addition, as Robert Scholes and J. G. Merquior have argued, the deconstructionist belief that language is non-referential, based in part on a misreading of Saussure, is untenable.[25]

Not that the postmodernist enterprise has been completely unsuccessful, but the very nature of its genuine successes has enforced the need for a revived old criticism. The postmodernists have shown (as the old critics before them) how a narrow formalism goes wrong. Once a text is isolated as the new critics and structuralists often isolated it—from its "biographical, historical, or ideo-logical content and matter,"[26] its signifiers really do begin to float, just as deconstruction claims. Meaning becomes indeterminate because the reader has built a wall around himself, rendering ambiguous the declarations that come from the other side.[27] He is less uncertain, however, from the perspective of the old criticism precisely because the meanings of words, read in their "referential content and matter," are stabilized. As an ironic consequence, the old criticism, which does not privilege form (and so can appreciate writing without much unity), is perhaps better placed to defend form than is formalism itself. Perhaps this reason, as much as the apparent dead-end of the postmodernist enterprise, has led to the defection of formalist critics familiar with recent critical theory, such as Tzvetan Todorov, to the old-critical camp.[28]

Hence the theory of the American romance, as an old-critical enterprise with an admirable project, deserves to be reexamined, but not because it drew the right conclusions. If this were the case, the matter could be left alone, because the arguments for its conclusions really have been, in my opinion, exhausted. It is because the project was and still is important, was intelligently argued and yet miscarried, that the theory deserves our attention—this and the failure of the critics who opposed it to go far enough, usually because they limited themselves to practical criticism. That is, they simply reexamined some of the major American novels and indicated how these are novels, not romances, or if romances, not more so than the European novels from which they allegedly diverge. But the opponents of the theory did not attempt either a historical or a logical criticism: they did not address the issue of American exceptionalism, and they did not show how and why the theory arose or how and why it went wrong.

This is important for two reasons. First, it would add a remarkable chapter to critical history to show how a number of critics, despite great talent, developed a body of opinion that misled not only themselves but most students of the American novel for a very long time. Now this is important not only for its own sake—which provides the second reason for my study. Had the defects of the theory been spelled out before, some of the revivalist efforts of contemporary criticism might have been forestalled. I am thinking of contemporary ideological criticism, which has gone astray, despite its real merits, for some of the reasons that ruin the theory in the older form studied here. This is evident in the writings of Sacvan Bercovitch, Myra Jehlen, and the critics who, under their direction, have composed the recent and highly praised *Ideology and Classic American Literature,* a work whose importance can hardly be overestimated, not only because of its own power, but because its conclusions will certainly inform much future criticism, including the new *Cambridge Literary History of America,* under the editorship of Bercovitch. Because the work of the ideological critics, especially that of Bercovitch and Jehlen, is the subject of my final chapters, it need here be noted only that the ideological critics have revived the central idea of the old theory: that America was exceptional because of consensus, and that, as a consequence, the classic American novel was romance.

These then, are the two tasks I have set myself: to unravel the development of a formidable theory and, by indicating its errors, to tell a cautionary tale—one that continues to tell against some contemporary scholarship. My criticism of the theory, however, is an inner criticism. I accept the humanistic, old-critical assumptions of its authors and their opponents—hence my disregard for structuralist and for extreme postmodernist readings—although, with ideological criticism, I do discuss an interpretation that is in some measure (and to its detriment, I believe) postmodernist, despite its similarity to the old criticism. Like the deconstructionist J. Hillis Miller, I believe that recent critical trends and other kinds of criticism have little to say to each other, and critics must choose between them.[29] My choice, however, is the opposite of Hillis Miller's: the arguments against most postmodernism (and formalism too, whether new-critical or structuralist, so far as the novel is concerned) seem to me to be convincing. Therefore, like most of the critics I study, I assume that literature undertakes a criticism of life. Regarding the novel, the question of form is largely answered by the life it examines. For example, when a novel directly examines society it is a traditional novel; when it neglects society to examine the human condition it is not, and another term, such as "romance," might well be needed.[30] I agree with most of the critics I study in the further assumption that the interests of novelists are usually shaped by social and cultural tensions, and that, in the nineteenth century, the central tension of the traditional novel was that between classes and strata in "bourgeois society"—either this, or tension between societies, such as we find in the novels of Melville and Conrad. Having followed the romance critics so far, however, I believe that they misread the American novel largely because they misunderstood its social and cultural environment. In order to demonstrate how the theory of the American romance (before its recent revival) failed, I discuss four important books: Lionel Trilling's *The Liberal Imagination,* Marius Bewley's *The Eccentric Design,* Richard's Chase's *The American Novel and Its Tradition,* and A. N. Kaul's *The American Vision.* These are not the only examples that might receive attention—Charles Feidelson's *Symbolism and American Literature,* Harry Levin's *The Power of Blackness,* and Joel Porte's *The Romance in America* are also important books—but taken together the four I have chosen offer a survey of the theory's curious development and permit a detailed critique. I then turn in my final chapters to ideological criticism, especially as it appears in the essays of Sacvan Bercovitch, Myra Jehlen, and in the collection *Ideology and Classic American Literature,* and show how the ideological critics have revived some of the major elements of the theory without, unfortunately, amending its fatal defects.

My argument is a simple one. The theory of the American romance was based upon the consensus interpretation of American history—which ripened, during the Cold War, as a consequence and (minor) cause of an emerging national identity. As a result, the American novel (and American culture and society as well) was misunderstood. Two emphases deserve to be noted here. First, I believe that the theory was persistently contradictory. Second, I believe that the theory's basis in consensus history led to the neglect of the similarities between American and European society. As a result, the theory ignored what common sense would suggest as the social origins of the classic American novel. The same failure, it seems to me, is evident in ideological criticism, and for the same reason.

Having invoked common sense, I had better explain what I think it says. Just this: in the nineteenth century, America and the European nations were part of a single civilization, class-based and divided by cultural tensions between classes, subclasses, and other formations. The tensions within this civilization, or between it and others, are the dramatic substance of both the American and the European novels. In other words, American and European novelists had the same interests, and American and European novels usually had the same form. This I am often content to call realism, while adding that I use the term loosely, as a label for typical practices and not as a term defining loyalty to a narrow verisimilitude. Much of the best "realism" is less interested in verisimilitude, and contains more elements of "romance"—if by this we mean a certain expressionism (of which more in a moment)—than the theorists of the American romance believed.

I do not deny the Americanness of American literature—any more than I deny the Frenchness of French literature, but I am aware that by rejecting the idea of an exceptional American tradition I am also rejecting the idea that the American novel has exceptional virtues. It follows that I believe that the American novel has been overrated. Perhaps not by much however; the revival of Edith Wharton's work has added weight to the canon.[31] Nevertheless, I do believe that what Leavis claimed about American criticism thirty years ago is still true today: it is "inflationary in tendency [while] at the same time it shows an indifference to the real American achievement."[32] And I agree with Leavis again in his claim that the American and the English achievement were one:

> In the nineteenth century the strength—the poetic strength—of the English language went into prose fiction. . . . I will merely offer the proposition that in Jane Austen, Dickens, Hawthorne, Melville, George Eliot, Henry James, Conrad, D. H. Lawrence we have the successors of Shakespeare.[33]

The collocation remains telling, and suggests that as we move from *The Scarlet Letter* to *Adam Bede,* from *Oliver Twist* to *Huckleberry Finn,* from *Middlemarch* to *Portrait of a Lady,* from *Benito Cereno* to *The Heart of Darkness,* we are not moving from one singular tradition to another. Few literatures, as Nicholaus Mill has shown, offer so many cognates among their novelists, both major and minor, as the English and American.[34] One reason for this was the interdependence of English and American novelists: the influence of Scott upon Hawthorne, of Hawthorne upon James and Eliot, of Eliot (also influenced by Scott) upon James, and so on.[35] Another was the affinity, rooted in similar societies, of experience and concern—without which the interdependence would never have been important.

But if this is common sense, why did talented critics argue against it? There are two answers to this question; the first directs us to the theme of consensus again. I have already mentioned my belief that in the nineteenth century the United States was not a society unified by consensus. (Or, if it was, it was one whose consensus was ruptured periodically.) The reverse is true, however, in the twentieth century, which has been, as Lionel Trilling long ago noted, a period singularly ideological in its essence:

> What would have pleased the social philosophers of an earlier time has come to pass—ideological organization has cut across class organization, generating loyalties and animosities which are perhaps even more intense than those of class.[36]

In our time, when ideology has partially replaced class as the basis of social and cultural life, the United States possesses a unique consensus: alone among the democratic nations, a very large majority has a single ideology. This is, as the ideological critics call it, the "American ideology,"[37] which is also, as older critics such as Trilling knew, a variety of liberalism, one so archaic that traditional factions refer to themselves as conservative, although they do not resemble genuine conservatives, with an aristocratic ethos and attachment to the life of rooted collectivities. Rather, American liberalism's archaism stems from its extraordinary nationalism (with quasi-religious overtones), its continued respect for the ideas of laissez-faire political economists, and the fact that it has made fewer compromises than liberalism elsewhere with community values, civil public planning, and the developed welfare state. Thanks to the triumph of this liberalism, most Americans, as Trilling noted, have "the same notion of life" and indeed share in "a single way of life."[38] The same notion of life is defined by their ideology's values, especially the primary one of acquisitive individualism, and the rejection (for all that the state is democratic) of the kind of public planning that might create a civil order. Their single way of life is defined not only by American manners but also by the suburban environment—itself a product of twentieth-century consensus—in which the manners are nurtured.[39]

It is evident that I disapprove of the liberal consensus. However, my disapproval is not entirely to the point since a different perspective could restate my description in an approving way. My point is that, because of ideological partisanship —sometimes unexamined and unintended—modern historians, the theorists of the American romance, and contemporary ideological critics have projected the liberal consensus of the American present into the past, when it did not exist—or if it existed at large, it did not exist in the subjects that animated the classic American novelists. The result for the interpretation of the American novel has been unfortunate. That novel has been seen as issuing from consensus, although in fact it examines cultural conflict, and an illusory form— the romance—has been imagined for it, although its interests and formal virtues are typical of the best novels of the nineteenth century.

The second reason why the romance critics were led astray suggests another justification for reexamining their work. They tried to solve a genuine problem, experienced by many readers of the classic American novels, whose resolution in the theory, was one of the foundations upon which the edifice was raised. The problem is this: the classic American novel, when compared with the European, often seems to be a short-winded, insubstantial affair, one that neglects the significance of social portraiture, especially the study of manners. Where is the great American study of the provincial community, the American *Middlemarch?* Where is the great American novel of the city, the American *Little Dorrit?* Why do they not exist?

The answer given by the early romance critics had the beauty of simplicity:

because of America's exceptional consensus, the American novelists were interested in the human condition, not society, hence they wrote not substantial novels but romances, in which the study of society would have been beside the point. If this answer is wrong, as the theory's opponents have claimed—rightly, in my opinion—then it must be admitted that no entirely convincing solution to the problem has yet been proposed.

Although the major substance of this book is the criticism of the theory itself, in the last chapter I do sketch a solution to this problem. Indeed, the solution depends in large measure upon the criticism the book undertakes. For if the classic American novelists wrote novels of the same kind as their European contemporaries, then we need to look again at the circumstances that directed their attention, that abetted their successes, and that, by frustrating their efforts, were responsible for their novels' insubstantiality—which now must be seen as the failure it actually was instead of the incidental byproduct of a form separate from, but equal to, the traditional novel. Here the solution has been indicated, although in an incomplete way, by a number of old critics, some, such as James and Van Wyck Brooks, even earlier than the critics I study, and some, such as Lionel Trilling, A. N. Kaul, and Sacvan Bercovitch, among the romance critics themselves. I confess that my own solution can claim neither completeness nor great originality, and I offer it with some hesitation, but a person who criticizes the solutions of others is obliged to lay his own cards on the table.

Another solution that I believe has some merit may be dealt with briefly here. At least two contemporary critics, Gerald Graff and Michael Davitt Bell, have indicated their belief that the insubstantiality of the classic American novel has been overstated.[40] To an extent I agree; the romance critics, if they did justice to Howells, often downgraded Dreiser and Norris (with some reason, I admit) because of their poor style and the limited quality of their insights, and ignored (without good reason) Wharton, as well as lesser, but still interesting novelists such as Stowe and Henry Blake Fuller. Of the novelists they did not ignore, James of course (as they acknowledged) is a very substantial novelist, not only in his novels set in Europe, but in those with an American setting as well: *The Bostonians,* certainly, but also *Washington Square,* which is as substantial as its French model, *Eugenie Grandet,* and *The Europeans,* which is as substantial as some of the novels of Jane Austen, with which it may be usefully compared. I believe that Twain is a more substantial novelist than he often appears, and not only in *The Gilded Age. Huckleberry Finn* and *Pudd'nhead Wilson* are much shorter, say, than the novels of Dickens—who is certainly Twain's English cognate—but as Bernard De Voto observed, this is largely because of Twain's remarkable economy of means. In *Huckleberry Finn,* "Old Man Finn . . . seems to fill the first half of the book, yet he appears in only a few pages. Mrs. Judith Loftus lives completely in a single chapter."[41] Rewritten by Dickens (in his early phase at least) *Huckleberry Finn* would have been twice as long, but with no more substantiality than it actually has. Cooper is often a substantial novelist, as in *The Pioneers* and *Satanstoe*. Of the major American novelists, then, only Hawthorne and Melville remain "abstract," and with both qualifications have to be made—Melville especially, remembering *Omoo, Redburn, White-Jacket,* and the first third of *Moby Dick*. Nevertheless, even granting the partial truth of this argument, I think the perception of insubstantiality is valid, perhaps not so much for individual novels as in the careers of the American novelists themselves. If we set aside Dreiser and Wharton (a large and questionable undertaking) because their greatness has been disputed, and because their careers began only very late in the nineteenth century, then we find it is true, as Trilling claimed,[42] that in the heyday of the traditional novel no American novelist except Henry James made a body of work that can be set, in quality, quantity and kind, beside the work of Dickens and George Eliot. And most of James' novels take place in Europe. For the American scene, there is no comparable body of work by anyone. The result, I believe (here departing from Trilling, who believed there were compensations) is that the United States, in fiction, stands midway between England and France on the one hand, and Germany and Italy on the other—countries that failed to mirror themselves adequately either in literature or philosophy and so remained politically immature and unstable in the twentieth century.[43]

The problem that the romance theorists tried to solve, in short, was genuine and lasting, especially since the term "romance" is not a modern fabrication. American writers of the nineteenth century, notably Hawthorne and James, did indeed employ the term and attached it to some of their works. Moreover, the characteristics they imputed to it are some of those noticed by modern critics, such as thinness of social detail and a tendency toward abstraction. However, their own use of the term was not like that of modern critics: it was not celebratory. Whenever the term appears in his prefaces, Hawthorne adopts an apologetic tone, and when James wrote that Hawthorne "was not in the least a realist—he was not to my mind enough of one,"[44] he was not making a category distinction. Although James was willing to call Hawthorne's novels romances, he did not intend to indicate that Hawthorne wrote in a form separate from, but equal to, the novel. Rather, he was criticizing Hawthorne for failing to maintain the highest standards of his age. Although I think that Hawthorne was more of a "realist" than James allows, James nevertheless strikes the right critical note. If we speak of romance at all we should not think we are referring to a distinctive and distinguished genre, at least not in America. What then should we mean? In fact, setting aside as irrelevant pure gothic romance and historical romances like *Ivanhoe*—because these have existed in all countries in all times since the eighteenth century—I think the term is confusing and ought to be retired. Nevertheless I am willing to admit three possible uses for it, though none supports any version of the theory of the American romance. First, we can by "romance" simply indicate a type of mainstream novel with a heightened coloring, often owing to utopian themes, the treatment of romantic love, or the expressionistic creation of character, i.e., that "romantic realism" practiced especially but not exclusively by early nineteenth-century novelists in both Europe and America. It is in this sense that Hugo and Sand can be called writers of romance, that James called Stendhal "the most powerful . . . of romancers,"[45] and that a contemporary critic has argued that the Russian novel is largely romance because it usually grafts an aristocratic love plot, of quasi-feudal origins, upon its portrayal of a seething but arrested Tsarist society.[46] However, if the classic American novel is romance because it lives in the company of *The Charterhouse of Parma, Consuelo, Les Misérables, Anna Karenina,* and *Father and Sons,* it is certainly not the singular creation it has often been held to be.

There are, of course, fictions so metaphysical, fanciful, or fantastic that they are certainly off the beaten path of realism—however loosely that term is defined—and some are among the greatest written, such as *Gulliver's Travels.* Here we do find some legitimate American counterparts, most obviously *Mardi.* However, this comparison raises two insurmountable objections. First, the proportion of romances of this kind is probably no higher in American than in English literature. Second, the American examples of the genre are usually inferior to the English. If we contrast *Gulliver's Travels, Rasselas, Vathek,* "Wandering Willie's Tale," *Frankenstein,* and *A Christmas Carol,* to *Mardi, The Monikens,* and *The Marble Faun,* the American romances cut very sorry figures (in fact, they are usually regarded as among the worst things their authors wrote—setting aside the excellent, because realistic, first hundred or so pages of *Mardi*). Among full-length efforts, only *Moby Dick* and *A Connecticut Yankee* have strong claims to be this kind of romance and also works of genius; but two such dissimilar fictions (even if we add some distinguished *nouvelles,* such as *The Mysterious Stranger*) do not a great, or any, tradition make. Moreover, *Moby Dick* is partly realistic; at least one critic (Martin Green) has argued—rightly, in my opinion—that the best sections of *Moby Dick* are precisely those that are *not* "romance."[47] In short, so far as the American novel is concerned, "romance," in this sense is usually merely a compendium of bad visionary or fanciful writing.

Finally, there is the American novel's insubstantiality itself. We can, if we like, call insubstantial novels romances, on the condition that we are indicating not a genre, but simply novels that fail to live as fully as they should. (We are making, in other words, a distinction of quality, not of kind.) Here, I believe, we find *The House of the Seven Gables, Typee, The American Claimant,* and parts of many of the novels in the canon. I should add that this sense of romance slides into the one just mentioned; very often American novels fail to be substantial because when they ought to be developing credible characters, settings, and actions they veer off into bad visionary or fanciful writing. It seems to me that this is the major flaw of *Moby Dick,* the Chillingsworth sections of *The Scarlet Letter,* and the melodramatic passages dominating some entire novels of the Leatherstocking Saga.

Fortunately, the best American novels are not ruined by romance in either of these latter senses, but it does seem to me to be undeniable that these are defects from which American novels suffer. Yet this is just what the romance theorists and, with ambiguity, contemporary ideological critics do deny. The theory of the American romance often focused on the defects of the American novel, pronounced these to be virtues, inflated their importance, baptized the result "romance," and then announced the discovery of a great new genre.

The writers and critics of the nineteenth and early twentieth century, such as Henry James and Van Wyck Brooks (until *The Pilgrimage of Henry James*), knew better. They knew that the American achievement in the novel fell short of the English, the French, or the Russian. James, because he spoke of the absence of certain traditions and institutions in America, is often thought to have believed that America was not suitable for realistic treatment. This, however, was not the case. Had it been so, James' criticism of Hawthorne's lack of realism would have been pointless. Nor would he have emulated Balzac in *Washington Square,* or have urged Scribners to confine Wharton to her New York subject matter. It is true that James had a lively sense of the difficulties facing American writers, but to speak of difficulty is precisely to speak not of impossibility but of challenge. In the eyes of men like James and Brooks, the American artist should confront his difficulties and overcome them. His major difficulty was simple and massive: with the exception of a cultivated minority that suffered from a squeamish gentility, the majority of Americans possessed a very great materialistic appetite and (hence) a very crude social, intellectual, and artistic culture. This led to (and was reinforced by) coarse manners and unsubtle, often raw (although not yet suburban) towns, cities, and landscapes. As a result, the American novelist was caught in a paradox. While his sensitivity was what qualified him to observe the American scene, that very sensitivity was bound to recoil from its crudeness and prompt him to look away and succumb to the temptation to write romance in the bad sense mentioned above. As Van Wyck Brooks put it:

> Hawthorne was right with regard to the society of his day, but consider what he lost and what we have lost by it . . . if Hawthorne held aloof from everything that stood for movement in his time that was the price of being sensitively organized in an age of rude, vague, boisterous, dyspeptic and incoherent causes.[48]

The revulsion felt by writers such as Hawthorne was entirely natural and deserving of sympathy, but the extent of their success could be measured by the extent to which it was surmounted. That it could be surmounted there was not the slightest doubt in the minds of men like James and Brooks. America was amenable to realism; hence their similar criticisms of Hawthorne.

For in their view America was not a separate civilization requiring separate artistic forms, but the cadet—often, but not always, provincial—of a civilization that included the European nations. True, America was comparatively crude, but its crudeness required no elaborate explanation and certainly no hypothesis of American exceptionalism. It was the simple result of the populism fostered by democracy, the materialism fostered by the opportunities for profit, the complacencies grounded in prosperity, and the inhibitions of the genteel tradition. In light of this, the task of the American writer, as James and Brooks conceived it, was to record, to explain, and to criticize—that is, to contribute to civilized standards by observing American society, acknowledging its virtues, and criticizing its defects—often through comparison with other societies. While twentieth-century scholars such as Daniel J. Boorstin would accuse intellectuals like James and Brooks of attempting to import European standards into a virtuous America, these writers saw their efforts in a different light.[49] They simply wished the United States to become more civilized; and for them civilization was a universal quality, as much potentially American as European, for all that the Europeans had acquired more of it. To reject civilization by attempting to relativize it—on the grounds that it was "European"—this they would have regarded as provincial defensiveness, indeed one of the difficulties that American artists continually had to face. It was a defensiveness, moreover, that was in any case misplaced, for in the comparison with European nations the United States was not always at a disadvantage. James and Brooks, for example, always endorsed the generosity of the democratic spirit, in which the United States was preeminent in the nineteenth century.

While, as I have mentioned, their understanding is in my opinion incomplete, one reason I have written this book is to help in the revival of this older understanding of the American culture. At present the classic American novels are both overrated and underrated: overrated because they did not possess the valuable originality that the romance critics attributed to them. They *were* original, perhaps, in their principal defect: they could not sustain the substantiality of European novels. We can call this failure, or, if we like, "romance." The classic American novel is underrated because, as Leavis argued, its real achievement is ignored. It was a heroic enterprise (whose heroism is obscured if we deny its many failures) because it sometimes transcended the provinciality of its cultural origins. In this it is unlike the modern American novel, which has a tendency to remain trapped "inside the whale." To take just one popular example, in *The World According to Garp* a tone of manic and violent absurdity is vividly struck, then sustained throughout six hundred pages. The latter fact accounts for some of the book's popularity, but it is a defect. For *Garp* is a novel with a variety of settings and a large, cosmopolitan cast of characters.

Either of these ought to entail significant dramatic conflict and a wide emotional range but *Garp,* despite its violence, never develops dramatically, and its absurd note never varies. This is because the absurd action does not arise naturally out of the characters and their contexts, as it might have if Irving, in his handling of character and place, were like Waugh, whose manic characters actually create their absurd world. But too often in *Garp* the absurdity is merely imported into a realistic context, with little relation to the characters. Hence one finds oneself waiting uneasily not for what the characters will do, but for what the author, gratuitously, will do to them. *Garp* effectively projects an absurd mood, but this mood is too-little accounted for. As a result, the novel's recommendation of a witty stoicism in the face of absurdity is unconvincing. In this *Garp* is typical, and its weakness suggests that contemporary authors, despite their talent (John Irving is very talented) are possessed by, instead of possessing, their experience, which has been generated by social and cultural circumstances that the authors are sensitive to, but do not understand. As a result their books, although sometimes striking, are provincial in that they are unable to transcend the subjectivity of the world that has produced them.[50]

The classic American novels, at their best, are not as limited. Their authors were not always victims of their experience. Despite the provinciality of their origins, they were not, at their best, provincial in their visions, in part because they understood (although sometimes only fitfully) that their immediate experience and their immediate circumstances often *were* provincial. Accordingly, they looked beyond these—it is no accident that they developed the international novel (here, perhaps, we do have an American originality) and that Europe and European society is a significant presence in the work of all of them. And not only Europe: despite the view of the early romance critics that the classic American novelists were not interested in society, we find in their novels a large social inquiry that extends to the Puritan oligarchy (Hawthorne), to tribal peoples (Cooper, Melville), and to "anomalous" classes and groups in American society such as the slaves (Melville, Twain), the landed aristocracy of patroons and slaveholders (Cooper, Twain, James), the urbane, bourgeois patriciates (James, Wharton), the working poor (Hawthorne, Wharton), and the radical reformers (Hawthorne, James). Although often unsuccessful, this inquiry was a part of their attempt to broaden their personal vision and their society's vision of civilized possibility. Probably all of them, even Twain, would have endorsed Henry James' assertion:

> I think that to be an American is an excellent preparation for culture. We have exquisite qualities as a race, and it seems to me that we are ahead of the European races in the fact that more than either of them we can deal freely with forms of civilization not our own, can pick and choose and assimilate and in short (aesthetically, etc.) claim our property wherever we find it. To have no national stamp has hitherto been a regret and a drawback, but I think it not

unlikely that American writers may yet indicate that a vast intellectual fusion and synthesis of the various National tendencies of the world is the condition of more important achievements than any we have seen.[51]

The casualness of James when he invokes "the various National tendencies of the world" indicates how cosmopolitan the classic American novelists could sometimes be. This in turn indicates how little their novels' virtues are to be explained by the constraints of an American consensus—the explanation offered by the theory of the American romance. I believe it has been the critics who have been constrained by the modern consensus and, whether from partisan acceptance or rejection of it, have been unable to see beyond it, thus fashioning an image of the classic American novel that misses much of its interest, downplays its failures, and fails to do justice to its real, if modest, achievements. As a critical analysis of the theory of the American romance, this book is offered as a contribution to a debate.

1

Culture and Society: An American Exception?

To understand the theory of the American romance, we must consider the consensus interpretation of American history upon which it was based. The consensus interpretation, itself not an isolated thing, was an offshoot of an intellectual movement of the late thirties that Alfred Kazin has called "the new nationalism." This movement broke with a common assumption about American history and American culture, namely that in culture America had been dependent upon or inferior to Europe. "Suddenly," as Kazin observed, "as if it marked a necessary expiation of too rapid a disillusionment in the past, American writing became a swelling chorus of national affirmation and praise." Although neither the theory nor the consensus interpretation can be quite contained by this description, both emerged from the new nationalism's desire to recover "America as an idea," and this "in the light of a new—if frantically enforced—sense of responsibility."[1] This sense was directed, in the thirties, against the threat of a rising fascism, but it shifted in the forties and the fifties to oppose the new threat of communism. One result was that the consensus interpretation, as an expression of the new nationalism, achieved its widest currency—although it is with us still—at the height of the Cold War.

By the consensus interpretation I refer, of course, to a body of historical writing that interpreted American history in the light of two assumptions.[2] The first was that Americans had been throughout their history remarkably successful in avoiding ideological conflict and had, as a consequence of consensus, developed a society remarkably free of significant class conflict.[3] As a result, the United States was seen to have succeeded—where all European nations had failed—in the creation of a unique society in which the unchecked expansion of capitalism had been accompanied not by—as in Europe—revolutionary or counter-revolutionary responses, but by unparalleled ideological and social stability. By this account the United States, unlike European countries, did not develop a typical bourgeois society.[4] From this followed the second assumption: that because it possessed a unique historical dynamic the United States had developed a civilization radically different from that of Europe, where ideological and class conflicts had been constant factors in social life. Not only was America severed from Europe, but the European nations were considered to be a unit. As a result (which this book will deplore throughout), the idea of Western civilization as a family of nations including the United States was obscured in the new opposition of the United States to "Europe." As Max Lerner, in *America as a Civilization,* put it:

> I am not arguing for a chauvinist view of America as the source and center of Western civilization. But it is worth asking whether we must deal with America always as a fragment of a larger civilization unit whose creative center is assigned elsewhere. It is unfair even to Europe to make something called the "West" the great isolable unit: for as the initiative in technology and in economic and military power shifts steadily across the Atlantic, there is danger of Europe's being dismissed as only a tributary of American civilization. Malraux rightly argues for the concept of "European man," although he recognizes the ties of Europe with America; similarly, recognizing the ties of America with Europe, one can argue for America as a civilization. For good or ill, America is what it is—a culture in its own right, with many characteristic lines of power and meaning of its own, ranking with Greece and Rome as one of the great distinctive civilizations of history.[5]

Nor was this all. In some versions of consensus history American independence from European influence was so far asserted that it was seen to have extended even to the colonial period, and not to have included any connection with the Enlightenment. In this spirit, Daniel J. Boorstin claimed that the ideas of the "Founding Fathers" were of "local lineage," not of "a cosmopolitan philosophical ancestry." Hence the philosophers of the Enlightenment, often considered "putative fathers of the Revolution," were, in relation to that event, "irrelevant."[6] While the European "past, and therefore the future, seems a grab bag of extreme alternatives . . . the [American] past is a solid stalk out of which our present seems to grow." Indeed, "why should *we* make a five-year plan for ourselves when God seems to have had a thousand-year plan ready-made for us?"[7]

By this token American civilization could be seen as a historical fulfillment, its consensus marking an appropriate end to the historical process, contributing to the myth of a "people outside history, uniquely favored by fortune, faced with no difficulties that could not be resolved by goodwill, physical hardihood, and technological virtuosity."[8] In the sense that any claim to privilege supposes a sense of superior worth, this view, however qualified, tended to advance a belief not only in cultural singularity, but in cultural superiority as well. In any case, the United States was assumed to be exempt from the intellectual and cultural standards of Europe. About this Boorstin was explicit, claiming that "our virtues, like our ills, are peculiar to ourselves; that what seem to be inadequacies of our culture, if measured by European standards, are nothing but our differences and may even be virtues."[9]

As for the first assumption—that America had always been guided by consensus—this was present at the inception of consensus history, which was marked by an attack upon the school of Progressive historians represented by the Beards and by V. L. Parrington, whose work represented the flowering of radical and agrarian populist ideals as grafted upon a methodological root of economic determinism.[10] What came under special attack was the Progressives' belief that the social conflicts of capitalist development had been the motor force in American history. If true, this meant that American history had followed a course like Europe's. Beginning in reaction to this belief, the consensus historians developed a comprehensive theory of American experience.

So successful were they, as a hostile critic, Barton J. Bernstein, has observed, that "the Progressive synthesis . . . seemed to fall apart under the sustained assaults of the postwar years." The homogeneity of the national past, its consensus and continuity, instead of the "convulsive movements and deep economic cleavages emphasized by the Progressives," became the dominant themes of American history. Apart from the Civil War, no significant discontinuities were admitted in American history. The further consequence was "to erode what was distinctive in the historical experience and even to blend it into categories such as myth and paradox which minimized or embraced conflict."[11] Americans, throughout their history and whatever their ideas, their social, regional, or ethnic origins, began to be perceived in terms of a stereotype:

> As sharers of a common ideology (presented by Professor Daniel Boorstin in a slightly different form as "givenness") and as "men on the make," Americans, according to Professors Richard Hofstadter and Louis Hartz, operated within a narrow framework in which even the dissenters usually accepted the fundamental tenets of the liberal tradition. Jacksonian democrats, despite their nostalgia for a vanishing agrarian age, were incipient capitalists. Populists, by this interpretation, were frustrated and baffled capitalists. According to this general view, protest was understood frequently as sour response to thwarted capitalist expectations, even as evidence of irrationality.[12]

Now the consensus historians not only described this stereotype, but often celebrated it, doubtless because they believed that the nation was, and was to be, both prosperous and egalitarian. Many affirmed, confusedly, the triumph of liberalism and the success—in the New Deal—of non-ideological reform. Finally, as Bernstein again observed, their history, fortified by this affirmation, "frequently supported those who proclaimed the end of ideology in the Western world and sometimes called for the defense of national values against the Communist threat."[13]

One motivation behind consensus history then, as some of its practitioners candidly acknowledged, was political, and was adjusted to the contingencies of the Cold War. As Daniel J. Boorstin testified before the House Un-American Activities Committee:

[One form of my] opposition [to the Communist party] has been an attempt to discover and to explain to students in my teaching and in my writing the unique virtues of American democracy. I have done this partly in my Jefferson book [*The Lost World of Thomas Jefferson* (New York, 1948)] . . . and in . . . *The Genius of American Politics* (Chicago, 1953).[14]

Boorstin's reference to communism was entirely sincere and also understandable in the circumstances of his testimony, but we should recall that, in principle, the economic determinism of the Progressive historians, not communist politics, had initiated the consensus assault. Nevertheless, although the methodology of the Progressive historians was not that of Soviet dialectical materialism, it appears that the common emphasis upon economic factors led scholars such as Boorstin and, as we shall see, Lionel Trilling, to link the Progressives with the communists.

My concern is with culture, with culture as a way of life and with culture in the Arnoldian sense, as the best that has been thought, said, and done by a way of life. For cultural theory the implications of consensus history were significant. In order to see how significant they were, let us turn to a familiar contrast between conservative and feudal civilization on the one hand, and liberal capitalist civilization—bourgeois society—on the other. I should add that my use of the term "bourgeois society" is descriptive, and not at all intended to be doctrinaire. As will be plain by the end of this book, I retain an old-fashioned affection for this civilization, born from the decay of feudalism and dying in course of our own century's upheavals—to be replaced, in the West, with a civilization still capitalist but not very bourgeois, for its *homo economicus* is no longer the individual, competitive entrepreneur.

It is generally conceded that the feudal civilization of the Middle Ages had been sustained, at least in part, by its religious perspective and by its face-to-face estate relationships, both of which had tended, however unevenly, to create a common culture that encompassed the entire social order and expressed the aristocratic and religious ideal of society as an ordered whole. This is not to say that feudal civilization was bereft of social conflict; the numerous peasant revolts remind us that the reverse was true. But until the catastrophe of the Black Death, social strife was not usually accompanied by a cultural challenge to the values fostered by the Church and the aristocracy: discontented peasants demanded traditional "justice" instead of revolution. And not only the peasants but, as Max Weber and Marx both observed, the commercial bourgeoisie identified itself with the feudal regime.[15] Only when the Black Death had created a severe labor shortage, social, occupational, and geographical mobility, and a competitive job market were patriarchal bonds substantially loosened. Even then it took another great historical "accident"—the discovery of America, whose conquest pumped capital and self-confidence into the life of the English and Dutch bourgeoisie—to complete the erosion of the social foundations of clerical and aristocratic cultural hegemony. Before the Black Death, such cultural divisions as occasionally emerged from the tightly woven fabric of feudal civilization were caused by the sporadic eruption of heresy or lawlessness. But heresy was quickly and savagely put down, and the outlawed, along with anomalous groups, remained in the position of social pariahs. In other words, regarding feudal civilization we may speak of cultural revolt and repression, but not of the persistent alienation of a social group important enough to sustain a coherent and critical "counterculture." Because it possessed coherent cultural values in rough harmony with its social relations—and to which all the estates paid more than lip service—feudal civilization had an "integrative ideology" and was, in cultural terms, an "integrated civilization."[16]

With the destruction of feudal civilization and its replacement by a capitalist one, it was assumed by social observers that the possibility of a common culture embracing all social groups had disappeared. The relation of culture to society henceforth had to be a *critical* one, and not only because capitalism reduced art to a commodity. Once capitalism and the bourgeoisie had created a civilization of relations defined by the impersonal market, large-scale industrial production, and the material antagonisms of class (as distinct from estate), very few believed that a cultural expression could, without incoherence, assume and express the cultural values of society as a whole—as could, for example, the *Commedia* of Dante. For bourgeois society was not a whole; it had no unity in values or in its wider culture. Liberalism might be its prevailing political ideology, but liberalism's accent on the primacy of the individual and the market as a model for relations ensured that bourgeois society would be "distinguished by its ability to dispense with unifying faiths."[17] It was, as both its critics and defenders recognized, a peculiarly "open" society, such as had not been seen before, that developed not a common culture interpreted and sustained by an integrative ideology, but a cultural pluralism. That is, bourgeois society engendered subversive social formations (either classes or strata) whose culture was not bourgeois, whose political ideology was not liberal, and whose continued existence represented a challenge to bourgeois political, social, and cultural hegemony. Working-class socialism was only the most obvious challenge to the bourgeoisie; nor was all significant opposition on the left. As historians as philosophically different as Stanley Elkins and Eugene Genovese have shown, the expansion of capitalism resurrected in slavery "an archaic mode of production at the very moment of the ascendancy of [the] more advanced [capitalist] mode."[18] Genovese, discussing Elkins, noted the paradox in the history of bourgeois society, i.e., that "the liberal bourgeois institutional and intellectual inheritance . . . provided the perfect framework within which the slave regime could work out its own imminent tendencies, which were anti-bourgeois in essence."[19]

That subversive social formations—which in their cultural manifestations

fully deserved, as later movements did not, to be described as "countercul-
tures,"—were not immediately crushed as they would have been in a feudal
society, was ensured not only by economic considerations, but also by the
"contradiction" (as Boorstin put it) in the liberal "idea of freedom . . . which
affirms a value but asserts it only to allow a competition of values."[20] All of
this, I insist, was traditional wisdom; it was the peculiar nature of bourgeois
society that (apart from local communities doomed by industrialism and urbanization) it had little or no cultural unity. It was rather a Pandora's box containing
(barely) the competitive visions and claims of classes. As a result, in the literature of bourgeois society the "problematical"[21] novel replaced the epic and the
romance, those forms appropriate to earlier, integrated civilizations. In the
words of the young (and still pre-Marxist) George Lukacs:

> The epic and the novel . . . differ from one another not by their authors' fundamental intentions
> but by the given historical-philosophical realities with which the authors were confronted. The
> novel is the epic of an age in which the extensive totality of life is no longer given, in which
> the imminence of meaning in life has become a problem, yet which still thinks in terms of
> totality.[22]

Because of capitalism and bourgeois society, it was impossible, whatever the
intentions of the author, for a work of literature (except the lyric poem) not to
make a critical social comment. Even indifference to social problems (and to
social reality itself) could not transcend these problems, for behind indifference
was a tacit rejection of some element of society. In achieving its unity of
meaning and form a work would have to be selective in its values; its import
would always reveal a social and cultural bias. Even its unity of purpose was a
rebuke to liberal capitalism's anarchy of production, alienating conditions of
work, and social antagonisms, for all of these had been traditionally assumed—
even by sophisticated defenders such as Mill, Spencer, and Schumpeter—to
exist necessarily at the core of capitalist development. As M. S. Wilkins, in a
review of Raymond Williams' *Culture and Society,* pointed out:

> The earliest ideas on culture . . . developed in opposition to the laissez-faire society of the
> political economists. As the ideas on culture took shape, on the one hand, they became
> identified with a "whole way of life," on the other hand . . . culture became a court of appeals
> where *real* values could be determined.[23]

From its inception as a response to the conditions created by liberal capitalism,
the modern conception of culture has had attributed to it, in its relation to
society, a critical content. Culture had become by its nature critical of society,
and implied social reform. Accordingly, the *raison d'être* of the novel, perhaps
the major form of bourgeois literary culture, was also seen to be the criticism
of society.[24]

The consensus interpretation of American history implicitly challenged this traditional view. For if it were possible that the United States had been, throughout its history, a society without capitalism's usual problems—anarchy of production, the alienation of labor, and severe class conflict—and had put an end, as it were, to ideology (i.e., all forms of non-liberal political thought) then one could conceive of a culture that would not, by its very nature, have to stand in critical relation to a society with a capitalist base. For the social contradictions that had, in Europe, initiated critical culture would in the United States have been resolved. These possibilities were taken up by American scholars in the late forties and throughout the Cold War, and in light of consensus assumptions they systematically reinterpreted the American past. Culture and society in America were seen to be as integrated as they had been in Europe before the triumph of capitalism. Although its denigration of ideology as an agent was somewhat atypical, a representative and distinguished example of this perspective was provided by Daniel J. Boorstin's *The Genius of American Politics* (1953). In Boorstin's view, because "opportunity [in America] was real . . . the whole American experience has been utopian."[25] From this it might be inferred that there had been no critical response to society in the United States because social mobility had forestalled the emergence of class interests and of cultural pluralism based upon class.

As a result, Americans have had a tendency "to see things as wholes," a sign that in the United States there was "seamlessness of culture,"[26] itself the product of a

> "seamlessness of experience." Aspects of experience which are elsewhere sharply distinguished here seem to merge into each other: the private and the public, the religious and the political . . . the "is" and the "ought," the world of fact and . . . of morals.[27]

The merging of "is" and "ought" is of course the negation of criticism, and to say that Americans have merged "is" and "ought" is to say that American culture has been "seamlessly" uncritical of its atypical society. Boorstin went on to add that "this sense of wholeness" was expressed in two elements: in an "organic concept of time," representing the "continuity of institutions," and in an "organic concept of space," representing the "organic nature of [American] society."[28]

Let us set aside both the unexceptional idea of the continuity of institutions and the conceptual difficulty raised by the image of the "organic concept in space." With the "organic nature of society," we meet the language of romantic conservatism in general and of Burke in particular, to whom Boorstin acknowledged a debt. The "organic nature of society" is a concept with a various pedigree, but it is certain that when Burke and the other conservative romantics thought of it they had in mind, to a great degree, the cultural integration of feudal civilization. It was the argument of Boorstin and other consensus historians that the United States had actually realized the Burkeian concept of an organic society. This was true even in the "contradictory" ideal of freedom, non-existent in feudal society, for "our unique history has thus offered us those benefits which come [in Edmund Burke's words] from considering our liberties in the light of an inheritance."[29] In short, the society of the United States had achieved, in an unprecedented way, the condition of an integrated civilization.

In literary criticism the implications of this belief were quickly felt. Nineteenth-century American writers, alone among the writers in the West, were thought to have been without the critical relation to society that had become inescapable elsewhere. Accordingly, they were thought to have gained access to experiences and to corresponding artistic forms that, with the rise of capitalism and bourgeois society, had in Europe become obsolete. For example, it was claimed that Whitman had largely succeeded in his attempt to write a modern epic.[30] In the novel, according to the theory of the American romance which began to take hold at this time, it was claimed that American novelists had been writing romances, "following distantly" as Richard Chase put it, "the medieval example."[31]

Because American culture was thought to be "seamless," we are not to suppose that it was also thought to be without dichotomies. The existence of cultural dichotomies does not in itself refute the concept of "seamlessness." The culture of feudal civilization, after all, contained serious dichotomies: for example, the simultaneous celebration of chastity and illicit courtly love. Most of these, however, did not point to a rupture between classes or lead to a radical criticism of society. By analogy, nineteenth-century American culture was sometimes allowed to have been divided against itself, but without implying sharp social divisions. By a recourse to myth, students of American history, as Bernstein put it, "minimized or embraced conflict." In a sense this was true even in books that spoke of debate, such as R. W. B. Lewis' enthralling *The American Adam,* the subject of which was an American mythology embodied in this image. Many Americans, Lewis argued, believed that the prospects of their nation held out a new hope of mortal felicity. It was believed that in the United States history was beginning afresh, without connection to the tainted European heritage; Americans were to be happy Adams in a new Eden. However, as Lewis observed, not everyone was persuaded of the virtue of innocence. Opposed to "the party of Hope"—the partisans of the Adamic image—was "the party of Memory," while beyond both lay "the party of Irony"—those who were "skeptically sympathetic toward both parties and . . . confined by neither."[32] As Cecil Tate has pointed out:

> This debate, Lewis maintained, is the highest level of culture because a culture actually achieves identity through the emergence of its particular dialogue. It is not the dominance of

one set of ideas or convictions that distinguishes a culture, but the ideas which are held in tension through the dialogue.[33]

In other words, the ideological debate that Lewis examined did not point to a European-like cultural struggle with a profound dimension of social conflict, even though Adamic figures in the poetry of Blake and Shelley and in novels such as *Wilhelm Meister* might have suggested an analogy. Instead, the debate was taken to indicate a cultural "identity" of ideas "held in tension." (One is bound to ask: held in tension by what?)[34] Through such logic the "seamlessness" of American culture continued to be affirmed, and the cultural identity of the United States, as it emerged in works such as *The American Adam,* had little to do with a divided American society or the criticism of it. Indeed, in the minds of our nineteenth-century writers, their actual society was apparently present only as a reference for society as such—or the universe. That beneath the extravagant speculation of much nineteenth-century American literary culture there might have been social criticism at work was a possibility that did not dawn on many of the scholars of the fifties.

There are, of course, qualifications to be made. Some dissatisfaction with American society on the part of important figures of American culture was allowed. In the case of Emerson, for example, his belief that all institutional structures would become outmoded (and be continually replaced) implied that American society, as constituted in his day, would have to give way to something else, a prospect that did not disturb his equanimity. As might be expected, such attitudes ran counter to the wisdom of consensus history. As Boorstin put it:

> America has thus been both the laboratory and the nemesis of romanticism. While the American experience would surely dishearten a visionary like Thoreau, it could actually encourage a Puritan or a Jeffersonian. The belief that man could change his institutions at will and that from such changes Utopia would flow was perhaps the most basic of the romantic illusions to dissolve in America.[35]

It is not surprising, then, that the fifties saw a devaluation of the Emersonian strain in American culture.[36] It is important to notice how the devaluation was made. By making "practicality" in social affairs synonymous with the way of society in the United States, one did not have to take seriously Emerson as a social critic, despite (or perhaps because of) his support of feminism, abolitionism, John Brown, the Liberal European revolutionaries of 1848, his sympathetic interest in the condition of the Irish-American working class, and his kindly, if skeptical, glance at Utopian socialism. Along with Thoreau, Emerson could at once be valued as a "visionary" in the world of the spirit and be condemned as an optimistic "utopian" full of "romantic illusions" in his social vision.[37] In effect, it could be denied that his ideas had any social dimension at all—

although he stood for nothing if not the belief that commitments should reflect principles. As a result, to the extent that Emerson was a social critic he could be disregarded; to the extent that he was allowed to have made a contribution to American culture, this contribution could be relegated to the world of spirit. It needn't be seen to imply a criticism of American society.

This indicates why, despite their belief in the benefits of consensus, consensus historians and literary critics began to value highly that part of American culture alleged to have been troubled by "powers of blackness," "a romantic nihilism, a poetry of force and darkness."[38] This part was supposed to have been the contribution of those who had rejected the optimism of Emerson. The problem here was to square the consensus perspective with the expression, in American literature and especially in the novel, of a fair amount of agony. As Harry Levin put it in the opening chapter of *The Power of Blackness,* entitled "The American Nightmare":

> Taking for granted the obvious American thesis, the cheerfully confident trend of practical and prosperous culture, it is the antithesis that we find in our greatest writers. Visionaries rather than materialists, rather symbolists than realists, the vision they impart is not rose-coloured but sombre.[39]

But if writers such as Hawthorne, Poe, and Melville (Levin's subjects) were not complaining about American society, what were they talking about? Levin's answer was typical. The "American Nightmare" was not generated by the malfunctioning of a specific society. On the contrary, "when we refer to the American way of life" (as it emerged in the pages of our darkest writers), "we simply mean the human condition, accelerated, amplified, and projected on a wide screen." Levin quoted with approval W. H. Auden, to the effect that "most American novels are parables; their settings, even when they pretend to be realistic, symbolize settings for a timeless and unlocated (because internal) psychomachia."[40]

The blame, in other words, was laid upon old Adam. The black experiences recorded by pessimistic American writers reflected not upon society in the United States, but upon human nature. And if human nature was black at the core, what could even the best of societies do about it?[41] When this perspective is supplemented by Lewis' claim that the Adamic hero is "*the* hero of American fiction,"[42] and we recall that the Adamic hero embodied the Emersonian strain of American culture, we can see how the pessimistic strain of that culture was held to support Boorstin's belief that the United States had been the fitting burial ground of "utopianism." The darker side of American literature, in short, recorded the shipwreck of "romantic illusions." For this American society could not be condemned: romantic illusions about politics and social theory deserved to be dispelled. It might even be held that thanks are due the society that had made the disillusionment possible. This is precisely what Boorstin, for one, did maintain: the note of triumph in his discussion is unmistakable. The real initiators of the catastrophes recounted by American literature were, in this view, those Adamic innocents who, like Emerson, had an exaggerated estimate of humanity's capacity to transcend established social relations. That this interpretation harmonized well with the politics of the fifties goes without saying; more to the point is that American writers, even when pessimistic, could be thought unconcerned with social criticism.

This view could be turned to account even when it had to be allowed that American writers had indeed practiced social criticism—and criticism of a very astute kind. Henry James, for example, drew high praise from Lionel Trilling for his sharp treatment of anarchism in *The Princess Casamassima,* and the social pessimism (as distinct from pessimism about the human condition) that James was thought to have shared with Hawthorne, Melville, and other distinguished American writers won a general endorsement.[43] An amount of social pessimism is of course compatible with pessimism of a more metaphysical variety, and it is equally compatible with a liberal perspective when seen to be directed against those who—like the anarchists of *The Princess Casamassima* or the utopian socialists of *The Blithedale Romance*—would move beyond the terms of established society. It is even compatible with a neoconservative liberalism when directed against those who, like Emerson, embodied liberalism in its more radical and egalitarian forms. But to speak of social criticism in this sense is, once again, to reduce it to a secondary activity whose target is no longer society itself, but those who protest, at the margins of a society, against its continued existence. The upshot was that in its literary as well as its wider culture the uniqueness of American society continued to be affirmed.

2

Lionel Trilling:
Social Origins of the Novel and the Romance

In literary criticism, the consensus interpretation was expressed in the theory of the American romance. The remarks made in the previous chapter about bourgeois society and its divided culture have their application here. Typically, we recall, this society had been culturally pluralist, and cultural pluralism had been synonymous with cultural struggle between classes. The theorists of the American romance, as we shall see, accepted the traditional view that the development of the novel "in its classic intention," as Lionel Trilling put it, was attendant upon the rise of bourgeois society and that the material of the novel was provided by cultural struggle or tension, either within that society or between it and some other. In addition, cultural tension gave the novel not only its matter, but its form. But consensus history asserted that a unique society had developed in the United States, one whose culture had been "seamless," that is, devoid of cultural tension between classes. The question then arose: how did that affect the form of the classic American novel? The answer, when it came, was provided by consensus history: the American novel had been, in its form, as unique as American society.

The classic contributions to this idea were published chiefly in the fifties, beginning with Lionel Trilling's *The Liberal Imagination* (1950). They may fairly be said to have concluded with A. N. Kaul's *The American Vision* (1963), in which certain departures were made. The theory of the American romance, as it emerged, can justly be termed a collective effort, although in saying this I do not imply that it was the result of a collaboration. Yet it is true that a common perspective unites the books that developed the theory. The perspective was defined by the premises of consensus history, and by the fact that the critics who made the theory had similar politics, belonged, in most cases, to the same generation, and breathed the crisp air of the intellectual climate fostered by the Cold War. And their work was interdependent. To see this, let us turn to *The Liberal Imagination*, and some passages where Trilling drew contrasts between the American and the European novel, and American and European society:

Now the novel as I have described it has never really established itself in America. Not that we have not had very great novels but that the novel in America diverges from its classic intention, which as I have said is the investigation of the problem of reality in the social field. The fact is that American writers of genius have not turned their minds to society. The reality they sought was only tangential to society. . . .

. . . In this country the real basis of the novel has never existed—that is, the tension between a middle class and an aristocracy which brings manners into observable relief as the living representation of ideals and the living comment on ideas. . . .

. . . [The great characters of the American novel] tend to be mythic because of the rare fineness and abstractness of the ideas they represent; and their very freedom from class gives them a large and glowing generality.[1]

Very soon, I shall relate these remarks to the idea of consensus, and show how they were of the essence of the theory. At present, I want only to mention their influence. They were quoted by Marius Bewley in *The Eccentric Design* (1959), the first essay of which is a commentary upon them. Bewley's discussion (from an earlier essay) was in turn used by Richard Chase in the opening of *The American Novel and Its Tradition* (1957). Chase was critical of Bewley, but not of his argument as derived from Trilling, and later in his book Chase himself drew from *The Liberal Imagination* for his discussions of Twain, Fitzgerald, and Faulkner. Charles Feidelson acknowledged with "special thanks" the personal help he had received from Trilling in writing *Symbolism and American Literature* (1953); while A. N. Kaul, in *The American Vision,* after acknowledgments to R. W. B. Lewis and Feidelson in the preface, began his opening chapter with the passages from Trilling that Bewley had cited.[2]

It is to Trilling, then, that we must turn if we are to find the ideas common to all of these critics. This is true for a number of reasons. Trilling was the first critic, after D. H. Lawrence, to develop systematically the idea of the exceptionalism of the American novel, and he did so in two short essays—"Manners, Morals, and the Novel" and "Art and Fortune"—that still remain, by virtue of their lucidity, the best introduction to the theory of the American romance. His influence, as the preceding remarks indicate, was immense, and deservedly so. Moreover, Trilling stated the political context from which the theory emerged more explicitly than anyone else. This is notable because, in an era that was soon to declare (a little prematurely) the end of ideology, Trilling insisted on the continuing relevance of politics to literary criticism. The politics of the critic, he said, should not to be extraneous to his judgments. For the connection between literature and politics is a close one, and literary criticism involves political considerations: "It is no longer possible to think of politics except as the politics of culture, the organization of human life toward some end or other, toward the modification of the sentiments, which is to say the quality of human life."[3]

The political considerations of *The Liberal Imagination* and by extension the theory it adumbrated, were most clearly stated in a lecture given in 1974, a part of which is now the foreword to newer editions of the book. There Trilling spoke of the book's "polemical purpose." This was its opposition to "the commitment that a large section of the intelligentsia of the West gave to the degraded version of Marxism known as Stalinism"[4]—although, as a matter of fact, nowhere in *The Liberal Imagination* is there mention of Stalin or Stalinism, while Marx, Engels, and Lenin are mentioned only in passing. The intellectuals most sharply criticized were in fact V. L. Parrington, Charles Beard, F. O. Matthiessen, and Granville Hicks. In opposing these men, then, Trilling meant to oppose Stalinism. Yet only Matthiessen, as a fellow traveler, might be thought fairly to deserve the Stalinist label; Hicks perhaps, as well, although he had resigned from the communist party because he was not a Stalinist. Parrington and Beard, however, were Progressives. At the least, Parrington's death in 1929 fairly acquitted him of a Stalinist affiliation, yet it was he who drew Trilling's heaviest fire.[5] Trilling's actual criticisms, as we shall see, were responsible. But, in associating a native radicalism with a foreign despotism—as did the consensus historians—he helped to initiate an intellectual movement in which not only the limitations but the insight of the Progressives—their sharp awareness of social and cultural conflict—were forgotten.[6] And as part of this movement, the theory of the American romance was born.

It is tempting, then, to judge the theory in terms of the political virtue of Trilling's enterprise. Yet despite the insistence of Trilling himself on the close connection between politics and literary criticism (and despite my own general agreement with this), it is a temptation that will be resisted until a fair consideration of consensus history and the theory of the American romance has been made—although I think I should say that I agree with Trilling about Stalinism, but think him wrong to have associated the blameless, if limited, Parrington with it. But this is not the point. The truth of an idea cannot be reduced to the motives that lie behind it, although even virtuous motives may be fairly charged if an idea is found to be false. This is why I mention Trilling's virtuous motives here.

Something similar can be said about the consensus interpretation itself, although here too the issue is clouded by the common assumption that the interpretation and neoconservatism necessarily go hand in hand. Yet as both the distinguished consensus historian Richard Hofstadter and Eugene Genovese have pointed out, this is not the case. Hofstadter was quite explicit on this point: "the idea of consensus is not intrinsically linked to ideological conservatism," adding "the historian is not required to endorse what he finds."[7] In a similar vein, Genovese, speaking as a Marxist, offered the comment that the consensus interpretation, the Civil War aside, was unobjectionable in principle: if true, it would have only described "the process by which the American bourgeoisie established its hegemony."[8]

The point made by Hofstadter and Genovese is quite simple: once we have agreed on the meaning of "consensus," the question of the United States as a product of consensus is an empirical one, and its answer neither validates nor invalidates any particular political position. It is only because historians often have not grasped this that the consensus idea has triggered irrelevant polemical thunder.

But it must be said that the consensus historians themselves, and the intellectuals who agreed with them, such as Trilling, were responsible for much of the thunder and laid their work open to error through excess of zeal. Their confusion was probably owing to their very emphasis upon consensus, which led them from the idea of an organic society to the idea of "organic holism."[9] In this conservative notion, to which even historians on the left have unwittingly subscribed, the traditions of any society constitute a unity, even when their relations are dialectical. As a result, these traditions are held to determine a society's future, and traditions not already present are presumed incapable of taking root, or blighting, should they gain a foothold. As a further consequence, historians of all political persuasions have tended to ransack the "American experience" for a "usable past," in order to give to their politics a traditional sanction. The enterprise rests on a misunderstanding of both social development and tradition. For traditions are chiefly historical, not organic: old ones may collapse and new ones be established. Even were it true that American society had hitherto adhered to consensus, this would be no guarantee against the future; conversely, even if American history in the past had been rent by conflict, this would not mean that in the future a consensus could never be fashioned. In any event, although Trilling himself did not make an adequate distinction between political questions and questions of literary theory—especially with respect to the intellectuals who drew his critical fire—we must be careful not to repeat his mistake when evaluating his treatment of the American novel. For this was indeed a *tour de force,* and employed the consensus interpretation with a great deal of flair. Even more to the point, Trilling's understanding of the novel was profound.

The theory of the American romance, as first defined in "Manners, Morals, and the Novel" and "Art and Fortune," was based not only upon Trilling's understanding of the novel as a genre, but upon his sense of the relationship of literature and reality; that "all literature is concerned with the question of reality—I mean quite simply the old opposition between reality and appearance, between what really is and merely seems."[10]

His sense of this was traditional, and reflected not only that "old ethos of liberal enlightenment,"[11] whose spokesman he was, but the old-critical position of humanism, which not only liberals may share. Literature, in this view, is valuable chiefly because of its insight into reality: by distinguishing "what really is" from "what merely seems" its first purpose is to enlighten. By implication, literature that does not increase insight into the nature of things traffics in false consciousness and is inimical to art. But reality is large, and we must not assume that any genre takes the whole of it for a subject. Even the reality of the novel, although large, is specific: "the field of its research being always the social world, the material of its analyses being always manners as the indication of the direction of a man's soul."[12] This too was a traditional observation. The novel stands at the opposite extreme from the lyrical expression of the self.[13] By analyzing "manners as the indication of the direction of a man's soul," it penetrates "the illusion that snobbery generates"—that merit is a function of social place, or social place a function of merit—and so distinguishes "illusion and reality as generated by money and class."[14] The result is that the novel offers us (within the context, as we shall see, of the rise of bourgeois society) a criticism of the *social* world. This is not, however, to say that all societies have lent themselves to this criticism. The contrary is true, we recall, in America, where writers of genius, Henry James aside, "have not turned their minds to society," with the result that American society did not produce the novel in its classical form. Moreover, this was owing not to the personal failures of American writers (for there have been, Trilling allowed, American writers of genius) but to social circumstances that separated American from European society. Two questions immediately arise: (1) what *was* the social basis of the novel? and (2) why did American society not provide this basis, despite its similarities to the European societies that did? The answer to the first question, and a partial answer to the second, were given in the following discussion:

> In [America] the real basis for the novel has never existed—that is, the tension between a middle class and an aristocracy which brings manners into observable relief as the living representation of ideals and the living comment on ideas. Our class structure has been extraordinarily fluid; our various upper classes have seldom been able or stable enough to establish their culture as authoritative. With the single exception of the Civil War, our political struggles have not had the kind of cultural implications which catch the imagination . . . despite a brief attempt to insist on the opposite view, the conflict between capital and labor is at present a contest for the possession of the goods of a single way of life, and not a cultural struggle. . . .
> . . . It is impossible to suppose that the novelist [who is not able to treat a cultural struggle between classes, with a conflict of ideals] will be able to muster the satiric ambivalence toward both groups which marks a good novel even when it has a social *parti pris*.[15]

The thesis of consensus history—that both American society and the culture it brought forth have been exceptional—was here stated clearly, yet it must be said that the logic of Trilling's argument is by no means self-evident. On a first reading, indeed, his assertions raise as many questions as they presume to answer. To begin, it is unclear why, if the novel investigates the social world through the critical study of manners, this study depends upon (1) manners being brought into "observable relief" and (2) a "satiric ambivalence" on the part of the novelist. Cannot manners be studied without these preconditions? Nor is it clear why manners in observable relief and satiric ambivalence depend upon the existence of a "cultural struggle" or "tension" between classes. Are not manners always available to be observed, and may not satiric ambivalence be achieved without this stimulus? Most important, even if we accept the account so far, it is also unclear why it was the tension between the aristocracy and the bourgeoisie (or "middle class" as Trilling put it here)[16] in the eighteenth and nineteenth centuries that first brought forth the novel in its classic intention. After all, there had been earlier cultural struggles between classes, even between these classes. The period of the Reformation, for example, had been particularly rich in them, for instance the struggle between the aristocratic, Catholic Spanish and the bourgeois, Protestant Dutch. Why did not the novel become the major literary form then? *Don Quixote* is there to remind us that novels *were* possible in the sixteenth and seventeenth centuries, and certainly there was plenty of talent. Finally, in what sense, following Trilling's definition, can the novel be distinguished from the epic and the romance? For do we not find, at least occasionally, in both the epic and the romance the study of manners from a satiric perspective, and tension or struggle between classes as well? On all of these questions Trilling was silent, yet they must be answered before we can turn our attention to the idea that the United States, in the nineteenth century, did not produce the novel—or at least not the novel in its classic intention.

The difficulties, though real, can be overcome through inference, and Trilling's account remains impressive if we allow a few unstated assumptions. First, we must not take him too far. His understanding of the novel was historical, not historicist; he would have never denied that satiric ambivalence and the representation of manners were in principle possible before the novel was born. His point was rather about conventions—of thought and emotion and of writing itself. With the rise of the society that made the novel the dominant form, satiric ambivalence and a sense of the importance of manners were more typical than they had ever been before. Second, we must assume that Trilling accepted the traditional conception of bourgeois society, a partial account of which has already been given. Finally, the term "satiric ambivalence" should be taken at its widest measure of significance, as the developed consciousness of bourgeois society—a critical consciousness, in other words, arising out of cultural pluralism.

The necessity of these assumptions is evident when we realize that satiric ambivalence—here understood as a relentlessly critical, but questing consciousness—along with the attention to manners that ambivalence entails, is an element that ordinarily separates the novel from the epic and the romance. The obvious distinction between these genres—the difference between prose and verse—is of little account if we allow that much of the verse of the epic and the romance is formulaic, while the finest novels, as the Leavises and their students have shown, can be regarded as examples of dramatic and poetic form.[17] But, however these genres may be comparable in the intensity of their language, a difference in perspective usually remains. In the epic and the romance manners may be studied, and studied with a satirical intention, but the attitude of the author is rarely ambivalent (that of the characters is a different matter). For even though manners in the epic and the romance (as Trilling himself pointed out) indicate, much as they do in the novel, "the direction of [men's] soul[s]," the direction that the souls of men *ought* to take is not usually in question. Usually, the epic and the romance embody the transcendent ethos of the integrated civilizations—classical and feudal—whose literary forms they were. The concept of a "transcendent ethos" is not a difficult one: it is the moral dimension of an integrative ideology. Within an integrated civilization the estates share— not only in their consciousness, but implicitly, in their relations—a common culture such as that provided by feudalism and Christianity in the Middle Ages. This entails an integrative ideology, which in morals sets down a clear code. When a culture is so actively shared, its ethos, accordingly, is rarely regarded as the property of any one estate. Of course, because the cultures of integrated civilizations have differed, so have their ethics—from the heroic and primitive ideals of *Beowulf* to the elaborate gradations of virtue and sin in the Thomist doctrine that informs the *Commedia*—but the effect of a clear ethos upon the epic and the romance is the same: it usually excludes ambivalence on the part of the author. I do not, I insist, want to press this distinction too far—Homer and Chaucer, for example, are often ambivalent[18]—but in the loose terms of generalization, in the typical epic or romance, manners (indeed, the behavior of entire societies, such as the Burgundians in *The Nibelungenlied)* may be criticized, but usually from the perspective of values uncritically believed, even by those against whom the criticism is directed. Adherence to values is a problem; the values themselves, rarely so. This is another way of saying what has been said before, that within an integrated civilization social conflicts are rarely cultural in the sense that a cultural struggle implies an indeterminate clash between different systems of value. Of course there were in both classical and medieval times conflicts between different kinds of integrated civilizations. Yet, however much these may provide subjects for satiric ambivalence to modern minds, to the minds of the participants they usually did not. Greek versus Persian, Christian versus Moslem, Catholic versus Protestant—these genuinely cultural struggles did not give rise to the novel, even when, as in the case of the Reformation, cultural struggle involved class conflict as well. For within each society engaged in such a struggle the transcendent ethos to which the society subscribed was so entrenched (and the simple need for self-defense was so compelling) that it usually precluded the development of a genuine ambivalence about its own ideals. Just as important, the very fact that the attention of men was fixed upon transcendent values—which in the case of feudal society were religious as well—entailed that manners alone did not occupy center stage in the literature of integrated civilizations. The transcendent ethos, against which the behavior of the characters of the epic and the romance is measured, is as much before our regard and is given as much serious attention as are the characters themselves. In *this* sense it may then be said that in an integrated civilization manners are usually not seen by the writers of the epic and the romance in observable relief—at least not to the extent that they are by the novelists of bourgeois society. For manners, in integrated civilizations, do not make a claim upon our undivided attention as they do in bourgeois society. In the epic and the romance, as much as in the novel, manners embody values, but both values themselves and the ideas that express them may also be treated with a directness that is alien to the novel's method of social observation. In the epic and the romance the objective correlative is often dispensed with, and the import of these forms is often conveyed by disquisition and by allegory.

It must be said at once that this by no means counts as a necessary disadvantage to the writer of the epic or the romance, no more than the uncritical acceptance of a transcendent ethos precludes complexity of emotional response. It is a commonplace that the metaphysical scaffolding of the *Commedia,* for example, is not merely scaffolding. That Dante was able to embody the tenets of Thomism in his descriptions of Hell, Purgatory, and Heaven, that he was able to illustrate these tenets by means of the punishments and rewards he describes, and that he was able to write quite directly of the philosophical meaning of his experience without a lessening of interest—all of this rendered his work more profound than if he had, in the manner of a novelist, relied upon manners alone to convey his meaning. At the same time, he was still able to communicate an extraordinary range of feeling. For example, when in canto 5 of the *Inferno* he confronts Paolo and Francesca, his sympathy for their love and pity for their damnation do not suggest to him that they have been unjustly damned. In canto 31 he is made to kick (accidentally) the head of the traitor Bocca degli Abbati, and then, when Bocca refuses to divulge his name, on the reasonable grounds that he does not want his infamy to be publicized, Dante abuses him savagely. Yet Virgil, as Dante's mentor to the etiquette of the underworld, does not here restrain his pupil, and his approval of Dante's actions informs us that the damned deserve just such rough treatment. As a reader touched by an ambivalent consciousness, I recoil from this idea, yet my shock at the callousness Dante displays is in some sense my difficulty, not his. We may think, justifiably I believe, that in such episodes Dante's sensibility partakes of the limitations of his age, yet grant that Dante's perspective is coherent on its own terms. The point is that, despite the complexity of emotion, the complexity is not tinged with a novelist's ambivalence. (I speak of Dante now as an author, and not as a character in his poem.) By having assimilated the

Thomist (and Aristotelian) conception of hierarchies of experience with different kinds and degrees of value at each level—the authority of which resided in the circumstance that it harmonized with the social experience of medieval civilization—Dante was able to register, without contradiction, a variety of responses that in a bourgeois context (often, let us grant, to its advantage) might well be the mark of emotional confusion, let alone of satiric ambivalence.

We can now understand more clearly why the novel developed with the advance of bourgeois society. The novel is most possible when the common culture of an integrated civilization is shattered, when the ultimate values of life, rather than the ability of men to conform to them, are clearly called into question. When men have the consciousness that the proper direction of their souls is a problem—indeed *the* problem of existence—a cultural struggle or tension can readily be viewed with ambivalence, that satiric ambivalence upon which the novel depends. It is then that men turn their attention to manners with the single-minded purpose the novel requires. For in an ambivalent world, where the existence of a transcendent ethos is doubted—because the elements of a common culture have vanished—men engage in a quest of moral discovery for values that are not already known. Manners, which indicate the directions that men's souls are actually taking, then assume an unprecedented importance. They come into observable relief, for it is through them that men become aware of what their cultural alternatives and moral possibilities are.

This was not often the case as long as men lived in societies with a common culture and an integrative ideology. Men might fail, whole societies might pass away, but about the validity of a society's ethos there was little doubt. The study of manners might be important in order to determine who conformed to the moral code, but there was little thought that social relations, of which manners are the visible manifestation, might give the clearest indication of moral possibility. The very idea of moral possibilty would have been itself a little alien. Hence the observation of manners did not have the importance it would have later, when it became easy to suspect that values might not descend from a mandate authored in heaven.

It was bourgeois society, once it had shed the fervor of the Reformation (a fervor that sustained among the believers a sense of a common culture) and had revealed its secular and relativist bias—once, as Marx put it, "Locke drove out Habakkuk"[19]—that shattered the confident belief in the existence of a transcendent ethos. The challenge that bourgeois relations presented to feudal society was different from that any integrated civilization had ever faced before. Even the struggle between Catholic and Protestant, although cultural and connected to class, had been for its participants a struggle for power; the existence and necessity of a common culture and a transcendent ethos were everywhere supposed. But bourgeois relations, because they had grown in the interstices of feudal society itself, could not be exorcised as alien, although they were indeed subversive of the values that feudal society held dear. The challenge of bourgeois society was that it had no integrative ideology, no transcendent ethos; that its social relations spawned cultural pluralism instead of a common integration; and that even its values—such as the ideal of freedom, often regarded as its contribution to civilization—were asserted as Boorstin has already reminded us, "only to allow a competition among values." With the rise of this society, whose openness was often genuine, yet also often a welter of philistine cross-purposes, cultural struggle or tension between classes—that is, the aristocracy and the bourgeoisie—was indeed something new on the face of the earth. The aristocracy, the guardian of feudal society—of its common culture, its integrative ideology, and its transcendent ethos—was confronted by a class that represented not another such culture, ideology, and ethos, but the marketplace. The struggle was compounded by the paradox that the liberation from aristocratic bondage that was offered was altogether genuine, yet grounded in a cultural pluralism that pointed to moral relativism—for how, in a society where values competed in the marketplace, might true values be distinguished from false? The reply that the valuable is whatever is desired simply begged the question, the more so when, as was the case, there was no unanimity of desire, and desires clashed. The paradox was that moral relativism, born of cultural pluralism, and denying transcendent values in the name of liberty, could point to the ultimate bondage of nihilism: a paradox that was not lost on Balzac when he created Rastignac, Lucien de Rubempré, and Vautrin. Once these new social relations had sown the seed of doubt regarding ultimate values, cultural struggle could, for the first time, be easily viewed without partisanship—that is, as something different from a clearly defined struggle between good and evil. Satiric ambivalence, the critical study of manners as the tangible evidence of culture and value, and, in short, the novel itself—"the epic of an age in which . . . the immanence of meaning in life has become a problem"—could come into being. The novel, then, is a dissonant form, in contrast to the epic and the romance, and has a moral dimension that is often absent from them. As Trilling justly observed: "The novel has had a long dream of virtue in which the will . . . learns to refuse to exercise itself upon the unworthy objects with which the social world tempts it, and either conceives its own right objects or becomes content with its own sense of its potential force."[20] In the epic and the romance, the ethical code of society, descending, as it is supposed, from a transcendent mandate, is usually unquestioned. In the novel, it is precisely an ethical code that the characters, through their dramatic conflict, are seeking to create—a code of values, once it is conceived, that cannot harmonize with the "unworthy" totality of contradictory values that exist in bourgeois society.

The society in which the novel, as a distinctive form, is a possibility is a society that has what Trilling called "the reality of class." For in such a society class assumes an importance for literature it has not had before. Without an ethos that people can, without reserve, believe to transcend the ways of particular classes, the classes themselves become the carriers of culture, and hence of value. Their conflict is a conflict between mutually exclusive conceptions of value that embody alternative visions of civilization: a conflict, therefore, because it touches the foundations of social life and extends into the ideological sphere, that calls into question the whole of society as it actually exists. The reality of class, it must be noted (for Trilling made much of this) is not to be confused with the existence of class conflict as such, but always refers us to class conflicts that involve a cultural dimension as well. A further attribute of a class society is that it possesses what Trilling called "substantiality,"[21] a term that appears vague and is likely to make us think, when we first encounter it, of either over-population or a proliferation of institutions. Yet Trilling's notion of substantiality was serious and precise, and can be indicated by his paraphrase of a passage by Henry James, where James describes what the United States, in contrast to England, lacks in the way of it:

> There is a famous passage in James' life of Hawthorne in which James enumerates the things which are lacking to give the American novel the thick social texture of the English novel—no state; barely a specific national name; no sovereign; no court, no aristocracy; no church; no clergy; no army; no diplomatic service; no country gentlemen; no palaces; no castles, no manors; no old parsonages; no thatched cottages; no ivied ruins; no cathedrals; no great universities; no public schools; no political society; no sporting class;—no Epsom; no Ascot! That is, no sufficiency of means for the display of manners, no opportunity for the novelist to do his job of searching out reality . . . James Fenimore Cooper [also] found that American manners were too simple and dull to nourish the novelist.[22]

Now one point of this passage, perhaps not grasped often enough, is that most of the things James mentioned are conservative institutions of aristocratic origin. Trilling, however, seized upon this, which leads us back to his original argument, that it was the cultural struggle between the aristocracy and the bourgeoisie in early modern Europe that created the novel in its classic intention. Nineteenth-century Europe, Trilling went on to say, is the very paradigm of a substantial society: one in which different classes, in behavior and ideas suggesting different civilizations, live side by side, carry on relations with one another, and also strive for spiritual supremacy—even when, politically, they are at peace. Substantiality then, as much as the reality of class, is the "product of a class existence." That is to say, "the conscious realization of social class produces substantiality."[23] The "reality of class" and "substantiality," in other words, add nothing essential to Trilling's idea of a "cultural struggle" or "tension" between classes. The three terms refer to the same reality, and stand or fall together. A society without cultural tension between classes is without the reality of class and without substantiality as well.

We can now see why, in Trilling's view, the United States failed to develop the novel, although American society was bourgeois to the core. Trilling saw the society in consensus terms. It had never had the tension between a middle class and an aristocracy, and its conflict between capital and labor was only for the goods of a single way of life. The lack of a cultural struggle between classes and the failure to bring manners into observable relief was part and parcel of the circumstance that the reality of class had not been a reality in the United States: "American fiction has nothing to show like the huge, swarming crowds of the European novel, the substantiality of which is precisely the product of a class existence." As a further consequence, American writers, despite their best efforts, had been handicapped in advance whenever they attempted to write novels. For, as Trilling assured us, "the diminution of the reality of class . . . seems to have the practical effect of diminishing our ability to see people in their difference and specialness."[24] In short, American society, for its novels and their characters, has lacked substantiality—that is to say, a class existence. There has been relatively less for a writer of fiction to observe here than in the more substantial societies of Europe. As a result, the best American writers have not turned their minds to society. For neither the satiric ambivalence of the novelist nor the critical analysis of manners that it renders possible are qualities attainable through an act of will. They are predicated upon a kind of society the United States has not had: a substantial, class-based society riven by cultural tensions between classes—a struggle that simultaneously brings manners into observable relief and that generates satiric ambivalence in artists. By contrast, American culture has been seamless. Therefore, the United States has not produced novelists of manners—except when its novelists have looked outside American society, as did Henry James.

Trilling's case rested upon two assumptions about American history: (1) America has never had a conservative tradition, because, unlike Europe, it never had an aristocracy to offer a conservative alternative to the liberal culture of the bourgeoisie; and (2) the American workers, unlike European workers, have never offered a cultural alternative to bourgeois society either. The first point seems evident enough; the United States indeed has never had a titled nobility. Yet I shall argue in later chapters that on this point Trilling, despite his profound understanding of the novel, was mistaken. If we do not take "aristocracy," "class," and "cultural struggle" in a parochial way, we will find that the social basis of the classic American novel *was* provided by cultural tensions, hence the insubstantiality of American novels cannot be explained by the absence of these factors. The classic American novel contains both the representatives of bourgeois society and the representatives of pre-bourgeois, conservative, and "aristocratic" social formations. In short, the social basis of the American novel was, in its tensions, essentially the same as that of the European novel. Like the European novel of the same period, the classic American novel was a novel in its classic intention—not of "manners" in the narrow sense (nor was the European), but because it was critical and "realistic." In the next chapter, by taking up Trilling's second point I wish to show where his argument was at once contradictory, and nevertheless influential.

3

The Consensus Interpretation
and the Theory of the American Romance

Although unremarked at the time, Trilling's brief discussion of the American novel came to grief when he described the relations of class, culture, and manners. We have seen that his account of the novel supposed that culture and values in a bourgeois society are functions of class: different cultures correspond to different classes and their strata. Trilling was explicit about this in a comment on a famous, if apocryphal, exchange between Fitzgerald and Hemingway (a story he thought important enough to tell twice). In "Manners, Morals, and the Novel," he wrote:

> Scott Fitzgerald said to Ernest Hemingway "The very rich are different from us." Hemingway replied "Yes, they have more money." I have seen the exchange quoted several times and always with the intention of suggesting that Fitzgerald was infatuated by wealth and had received a salutary rebuke from his democratic friend. But the truth is that after a certain point quantity of money does indeed change into a quality of personality: in an important sense the rich are different from us. So are the very powerful, the very gifted, the very poor. Fitzgerald was right.[1]

In his essay on F. Scott Fitzgerald he referred to this story again, with the observation "that the novelist of a certain kind, if he is to write about social life, may not brush away the reality of the differences of class."[2] Fitzgerald and Hemingway of course were American novelists, and in "Art and Fortune," as we have seen, Trilling had underscored his belief that in this respect—the link between class and culture—American society has *not* been exceptional: "our various upper classes have seldom been able or stable enough to establish their culture as authoritative." The reference to "our various upper classes" and "*their* culture" leaves no room for doubt, just as Trilling's belief that these same classes have seldom established "their culture as authoritative" leaves no room for doubt that he also believed American society had been culturally pluralist. Yet how could this be? For we have just seen that his account of American exceptionalism supposed that American culture has been seamless. It is not simply that in America the various classes, with their different cultures, have lived in peace. For, by Trilling's account, America never had an aristocracy, while its bourgeoisie and its workers have shared "a single way of life," that is to say, a common culture. If this is true, where, then, *are* those various upper classes with their various cultures, and where are those various lower classes, with their various cultures, upon whom the upper classes have failed to impose? The candid answer must be: nowhere. Trilling simply broke with his own theory in order to assert American exceptionalism. His confusion is not uncommon. Anyone who knows the United States has at some time met the patriot who, in reply to one criticism, affirms American cultural variety, and who, in reply to a different criticism, affirms that everyone in America, whatever his class, is pretty much the same. We are not, however, accustomed to finding these sentiments expressed simultaneously by a distinguished literary critic. Here is evidence, I believe, that Trilling's polemical purpose interfered with his perception.

His confusion was compounded by the statement that in the United States "the conflict between capital and labor is at best a contest for the possession of the goods of a single way of life and not a cultural struggle." There are two things to note about this. First, Trilling allowed in principle that a conflict between a middle class and a working class *could* be a cultural struggle, and hence provide a basis for the novel in its classic intention: the qualifying "at present" is clear. And of course it is true that middle- and working-class conflicts have done so: we need only think of Zola's *Germinal* or Lawrence's "The Daughters of the Vicar." Second, by mentioning the present conflict between capital and labor, Trilling allowed that there has been conflict between the bourgeoisie and the working class in the United States—his point was that this conflict has never been cultural. The statement seems reasonable, but it is not, in the light of Trilling's conception of manners.

Although the basis of the novel is cultural struggle or tension between classes, the novelist can observe this critically only through manners, which indicate the directions of men's souls, the directions taken by cultures based upon class. What, then, are manners? In fairness to Trilling it must be said that he has sometimes been misunderstood. Trilling himself remarked that certain critics (meaning Delmore Schwartz) acting from "political assumptions of a pious sort" had taken his interest in manners to mean that he was "interested in establishing a new genteel tradition in criticism and fiction."[3] This, as Trilling rightly maintained, was not the case. His account of manners remains convincing. Manners, first of all, express culture in social behavior as "a culture's hum and buzz of implication," its small "expressions of value," as in "dress or decoration, . . . tone, gesture, emphasis, or rhythm, sometimes by words—the things that for good or bad draw the people of a culture together and that separate them from the people of another culture."[4] Second, beyond culture, manners express "class traits" as " modified by personality," the notation of which "makes for substantiality."[5] Now, if manners are class traits, different classes have different manners. And if manners also express culture, then classes with different manners of necessity have different cultures.

We are back, in other words, with the traditional view that Trilling endorsed, and with which I agree, that in a bourgeois society culture is usually a function of class. This view, moreover, squares with the idea that only through manners does the novelist become aware of the cultural dimension of social behavior. But notice how this relation of culture and manners to class subverted Trilling's attempt to distinguish between class conflicts that are cultural and those that are not. For if culture is a function of class, then *any* class conflict is going to involve tension between cultures—even if of a trivial nature. From the perspective of the novelist there is every reason to believe that manners, expressing the cultures of classes in conflict, would be brought into sufficient relief to be observed. Supposing a conflict to be trivial, why wouldn't its very triviality further rather than inhibit the novelist's necessary satiric ambivalence?

These points can be illustrated if we turn to the United States where, according to Trilling, the bourgeoisie and the working class have struggled only "for possession of the goods of a single way of life." By "goods," it is not certain that Trilling meant money alone, but among the goods he meant, money is certainly one. And no one can deny, remembering that the slogan of Samuel Gompers was "more," and that whatever else they have struggled over, capital and labor in the United States have struggled over money. Now we have it on Trilling's authority that questions of money *are* questions of culture. For, we recall, "quantity of money does indeed change into quality of personality: in an important sense the rich are different from us. So are . . . the very poor." Therefore, since the bourgeoisie and the working class in the United States have struggled over money, they have also engaged in a cultural struggle. Yet this is precisely what Trilling denied.

We may seek a way out of this difficulty on Trilling's behalf, but to do so entangles our steps still further. We might argue, for example (and Trilling seemed to imply this at times), that the pursuit of money is a cultural trait of the bourgeoisie and not of the working class because, when workers pursue money, they are behaving like the bourgeoisie. But this explanation is clearly inadequate: in Europe, where workers also pursued money, they created a distinctive culture just the same. There is, of course, the important truth that those who have been materially exploited face the danger of losing their humanity and, with it, their culture. To believe otherwise is to have a complacent view of exploitation. But to argue that workers have failed to develop a culture because they have been exploited is really to argue against Trilling: one cannot easily associate the idea of an exploited working class with that "old ethos of liberalism" which Trilling rightly claimed as his own. Nor is it likely that Trilling, writing in the forties, with the depression a recent memory, believed the reverse to be true—that American workers had been so comfortable as to have been virtually bourgeois. Nevertheless we are left with the assertion that the bourgeoisie and the working class in the United States have shared a single way of life. But if this is true, then the workers already have the culture of the bourgeoisie without its money—in which case, Hemingway was right, Fitzgerald wrong.

(There is a further point, historical instead of theoretical. Trilling's belief that the conflict between capital and labor had not provided a social basis for the novel in the United States is not true. There *is* a distinguished tradition in the American novel based upon this conflict. To this we shall return.)

Trilling was inconsistent. The question to ask now is this: did he make sense in other ways? The answer, I believe, is that his argument can be extended, provided we are willing to reconstruct it, and set aside his statements to the effect that culture is a function of class, and that both are expressed in manners.

For, regarding America, this is what Trilling in practice did himself. To say that class conflict is not cultural is to say that class does not determine culture. And if, in the United States, the struggle for material goods has not been a cultural struggle, then the basis of American culture, whatever it has been, has had an immaterial nature. What then, is this immaterial basis of American culture and manners? One answer, which Trilling strongly implied, is political ideology.

That political ideology *can* determine culture is a point Trilling did make when he affirmed the connection between politics and literature, and of the modern necessity to think of politics as the politics of culture. What we want to know, however, is if he believed that class conflict in America had never had a cultural dimension because the culture of the various classes had been determined by a shared ideology. Certainly had this been so the United States would indeed have been exceptional in the West. In a brilliant passage preceding the statement that in the United States "the real basis of the novel has never existed" he wrote that

> money and class do not have the same place . . . they once had. They [do] not exist as they did in the nineteenth century or even in our youth. . . . As for class, in Europe the bourgeoisie together with its foil the aristocracy has been weakening for decades . . . its nineteenth-century position as ideologue of the world has vanished before the ideological strength of totalitarian communism.[6]

In bourgeois society, which has recently passed away, the chief realities were "money and class." Ideology played a secondary role, as the reference to the bourgeoisie as the former "ideologue of the world" makes plain. In bourgeois society *classes* are the subjects; ideology is made by a class to further its ends.

But a change in the modern world is indicated by the "the ideological strength of totalitarian communism." Here no class accompanies the ideology named; ideology has become an independent force. Indeed, Trilling went on to say that, in our century, "ideological organization has cut across class organization, generating loyalties even more intense than those of class."[7] In other words, when bourgeois society gives way to what Trilling would call "ideological society," political ideology becomes the basis of culture.

This has been, in general, a very recent development. However, in a discussion of the relation of the novel to political ideas, Trilling implied an exception. Following Balzac, Trilling observed that while Stendhal's political novels exemplify "the literature of ideas . . . represented by character and action," it was possible "to claim for the novel the right and the necessity to deal with ideas [without] the 'objective correlative,' to deal with them . . . directly."[8] He claimed for the novel, in short (and this is the crucial point), the same "right and necessity" that had previously been the privilege of the epic and the romance. The present, Trilling believed, is especially appropriate for the "literature of ideas," because bourgeois society has dissolved and been replaced:

> Ideological society has, it seems to me, nearly as full a range of passion and nearly as complex a system of manners as a society based on social class. Its promise of comedy and tragedy is enormous, its assurance of relevance is perfect.[9]

In principle, then, the environment of the epic and the romance (a culture common to all classes), could be recreated in a society organized by a single ideology. But if a society organized by ideology provides the perfect basis for a literature of ideas, is there reason to believe that Trilling sometimes thought that nineteenth-century America was such a society? I believe there is, for in his discussion of the American novel he claimed that "the great characters of American fiction, such, say, as Captain Ahab and Natty Bumppo, tend to be mythic because of the rare fineness and abstractness of the ideas they represent;" they have "freedom from class" and lack "substantiality."[10] This, I submit, is precisely what we should expect from a literature of ideas—whose origin is not a class-based, but an ideological society.

There is another indication of this. It was given in Trilling's passionate interest in the future of American politics, from his belief that in "the United States at this time liberalism is . . . the sole intellectual tradition . . . [while] nowadays there are no conservative or reactionary ideas in general circulation."[11] Although "at this time" and "nowadays" are qualifiers, we already know that Trilling believed that the United States has never had an aristocracy, and aristocracies, as we also know, are the sources and repositories of conservative ideas. Nowhere in *The Liberal Imagination,* in fact, did Trilling suggest that there had *ever* been a conservative intellectual tradition in America. From this it is possible to infer—if not quite a belief, yet a consideration—that the society of the classic American novelists was based not on class, but on liberal ideology.

The possibility is attractive because it clarifies the idea that conflicts between capital and labor have not been cultural in America. For if American society has been based on ideology, conflict would be cultural only with the presence of opposing ideologies. And it is true, among industrial societies, that only in America has the working class failed to adopt, in large measure, a socialist or a communist ideology. Only in America have the majority of workers accepted the liberalism of their employers. If political ideology has been the power that shaped American culture, then the circumstance of a shared liberalism would explain how the classes have shared a single way of life.

Attractive as this is, it must be admitted that Trilling, once again, contradicted the drift of his thought. To sever culture from class and to attach it to ideology assumes, as we have seen, an ideological society. If, in the nineteenth century, Americans drew their culture from an ideological well, then theirs was an ideological society and *not* a society based upon class. For a society based upon class—bourgeois society—and ideological society are mutually exclusive. In bourgeois society classes are primary and ideology secondary; in ideological society the reverse is true. Yet when Trilling said that money and class no longer existed as "in the nineteenth century or even in our own youth," he was clearly including the United States in his reflections. So America was, after all, in the nineteenth century, and even in Trilling's youth (he was born in 1905), a society based upon class. Moreover, in the very passage that extolled the fictional potential of ideological society, he concluded that "we have never had in this country a sufficiently complex ideological situation to support this potential in our own practice of the novel. We have it now."[12]

Again, in the United States, ideological society is new. Finally, in an essay entitled "The Meaning of a Literary Idea," Trilling argued that "the root of [the] difference between European and American Literature" is that, unlike American literature, European literature derives its power "from its commerce, according to its own rules, with systematic ideas." Europe, not the United States, by this account, has brought off the literature of ideas; and all these examples bring us back to our first question: if the United States was, in the nineteenth century (as Trilling in the end, agreeing here with Parrington, came to say), a society based upon class, how is it possible that its conflicts of class should not, by their nature, have entailed cultural tensions? From this question follows a second: if the concern of literature is the "question of reality," and the classic American novel had turned away from the essential reality of its world—"the reality of class"—was it not an evasive failure? This, it seems to me, is what Trilling should have said, following from his observation of "abstractness"; and he came close to saying it when he claimed that Howells had failed because, "although he saw the social subject clearly, he did not take it with full seriousness"[13]—

which can only mean that the real basis of the novel had been available in the United States after all, but that Howells had not used it as well as he might have. But in the end Trilling's emphasis was different.

I have reached, then, a hiatus in my discussion. We have seen that Trilling accepted the traditional view that the basis of the novel in its classic intention was the cultural struggle or tension between classes in bourgeois society, and that the enlightening purpose of the novel was realized through the study of society through manners, which cultural tensions brought into observable relief. In addition, by accepting the consensus view that America has lacked such tensions, Trilling argued that the novel of manners had never been established in America. Finally, Trilling suggested the form of the American novel (as he conceived it) when he stated that the characters of American fiction are mythic, abstract, and represent ideas—so that "Hawthorne was acute when he insisted that he did not write novels but romances."[14] It was this clue, rather than the one in the accompanying comment about Howells, that would be taken up by later critics. These ideas rhymed with the efforts of the consensus historians to draw a sharp distinction between America and Europe. They were Trilling's legacy to the theory of the American romance.

At the same time, Trilling failed to make a theory that would have made his discussion plausible. His confusion over the relations of manners, culture, and class in America subverted his explanation of why American class conflict has not been cultural. Even when, in the interest of the coherence of his account, and in a certain context, culture is allowed to be determined by political ideology instead of by class, we have seen how Trilling short-circuited the possible solution to his difficulty by denying that this had been the case in the United States until the contemporary era.

Trilling was a great critic, and his affirmation of the insight of literature, of the value of "the gratuitous manifestations of feeling, of thought, and of art" against the "dull, repressive tendency of opinion"[15] fostered by Stalinism and its fellow-travelers was admirable in principle, and deserves to be reread for the light it can throw on postmodernist criticism of a like dull tendency, if of a different repressiveness. Yet, in his very affirmation, the reaction against repressive radicalism—associating Europe, Stalinism, and native radicals such as Parrington—led him (like Daniel J. Boorstin among consensus historians), too far in his affirmation of American difference, and into inconsistencies he did not resolve.

That the inconsistencies went largely unremarked, or in any case did not compromise the influence of his argument, is a testimony to the importance of *zeitgeist* in the acceptance of opinion. Although Trilling did not intend to overpraise the American novel (nor, for that matter, did Bewley, among romance critics)[16] and aspired to cosmopolitanism in the best sense, a snowball began to roll: the effect of his ideas was to counter the dissatisfaction that insubstantiality in the classic American novel had always generated, a dissatisfaction still felt through the influence of Parrington's *Main Currents in American Thought,* where, for example, approval of Dreiser was mingled with regret that Hawthorne had underused his New England background. It is true that there was naiveté and crudeness in Parrington's attitude. As an economic determinist and populist reformer, he sometimes valued too highly painstaking verisimilitude: this, he believed, would of necessity have a reforming purpose because it would expose injustices and affirm the life of "the people." This was, no doubt, one reason why the kind of fiction he and other Progressives preferred was preeminently that which possessed the quality of substantiality, which is to say, the conscious realization of class, and were dissatisfied with the American novel's relative insubstantiality, conceiving that American novelists had refused, for one reason or another—gentility was the most commonly mentioned—the burden of social observation, hence the burden of the novel. As a consequence, Trilling's objection to Parrington, that his limited idea of reality demanded of literature only a simple reflection of actuality, and denied the autonomy of ideas, was largely justified, as were his attacks on Dreiser and his defense of James against the populist strictures of Parrington's fellow Progressive, Charles Beard. Trilling was also right when he defended artistic variety in subject, method, and interest against the exploitation of literature by partisan politics. But there was more to the Progressive position than naive and crude populism, and more to Trilling's that the rejection of it. For a number of reasons, Trilling's criticism of the Progressive tradition should have been perceived to have been unsatisfactory. For Trilling granted that even Parrington had a "lively sense of the practical, workaday world, of the welter of ordinary undistinguished things and people, of the tangible, quirky, unrefined elements of life," but he did not stop to consider that this might also have informed the Progressive literary preferences he deplored. Moreover, Trilling's willingness to praise abstraction and his attack upon Parrington rhymed with the new nationalist tendency—no longer new, but firm in the fifties—to praise things especially "American." (That Dreiser was also an American is not the point; Dreiser had been a communist.) And when Trilling moved from the Progressives' notion of economic determinism, to imply a similarity between the Progressives' emphasis on verisimilitude and the "socialist realism" that the Stalinists had been promoting, he simplified a complicated issue: it is not only possible to reject the insubstantiality of the American novel without subscribing to Parrington's notions about reality (let alone those of Stalinism), it is also true that in this matter Parrington and the other progressives were simply seconding the opinion of earlier American critics whose vision, in important respects, had little in common with theirs. In short, Trilling's focus on Parrington obscured the extent to which his attack marked a break with the criticism of the past, and not only with

Progressive criticism—as can be immediately seen in his defense of Hawthorne, when he claimed that "Hawthorne was dealing beautifully with realities,"[17] and that Parrington's impatience with Hawthorne was of a piece with the Progressives' impatience with Henry James. But James himself, with the genteel W. C. Brownell and the young Van Wyck Brooks (who were, in other matters, critical enemies), had also questioned Hawthorne's attention to reality—James, indeed, was quite possibly the inspirer of Parrington's complaint—although none had doubted Hawthorne's genius.[18] None of these men had the Progressives' limitations; each in his way believed in and exemplified the kind of mind Trilling was defending. What they did stand for, however, was a cosmopolitan idea of Western civilization, with America as a part of it. They expected America itself to be judged by civilized, not national, standards, and they judged American literature accordingly. This older attitude could be ignored if it could be shown that Hawthorne, with the other classic novelists, had been treating realities different from those that engaged European novelists, owing to America's unique consensus, which had given both American literature and American life a civilization of its own, with its own exceptional standards. Ironically, although Trilling attacked Parrington's image of culture as a "current" (although, in fact, Parrington had used the plural "currents"), in the name of an idea of culture as a dialectic,[19] the effect of his attack was to break the dialectic between cultural nationalism and cosmopolitanism, of which the Progressives had been only a part, leaving the way open for the triumph of an exceptionalism to which he himself might have possibly taken exception.

It was this possibility, rather than Trilling's inconsistencies (or his knowledge that America had once been a class society), that later critics were to take up. Like Trilling, these critics hitched their theoretical wagon to the rising star of consensus history, and their interpretations took two directions corresponding to those the consensus historians had taken before them. Here, too, they had been anticipated, inconsistently, by Trilling.

The directions appeared when consensus historians attempted to weigh the role of ideology in the formation of the American consensus. For Robert Dahl and Louis Hartz, the American consensus was established because, as Dahl put it, "Americans are a highly ideological people . . . agreed on the same ideology." Here we come very close to Trilling's idea of "ideological society," in which ideology is the basis of culture. As Louis Hartz argued, the United States had missed an aristocratic and feudal stage of history: conservatism had never taken root, and intellectual life had been monopolized by liberalism. Within liberalism, of course, there have been disagreements, but none had initiated enduring departures. Like Trilling, Hartz allowed that America had been the scene of conflict, but also like Trilling, he denied that there had been cultural tension between classes. For all Americans, whatever their class, have shared "the American Way of Life, a nationalist articulation of Locke which usually does not know Locke himself is involved."[20]

This was, in my opinion, the most defensible idea of American consensus, but there was a distinguished alternative offered by Daniel J. Boorstin in *The Genius of American Politics*. There conformity was understood "as the consequence of the . . . absence of ideology." Unlike Hartz, who thought American character, having escaped European ideological conflicts, "uni-ideological," Boorstin thought it "non-ideological," reflecting a "pragmatic adaption to life on the American continent."[21] Boorstin's position, as Bernard Sternsher pointed out, was ambiguous, for Boorstin did concede at times the importance of ideology, but the heart of Boorstin's argument was a geographical determinism, expressed in his concept of "givenness"—"the belief that values in America are in some way automatically defined: *given* by certain facts of geography or peculiar to us."[22]

The contrast between these interpretations could hardly be more striking, yet we must not lose sight of their shared perceptions. Both asserted that American history had not been shaped by conservative traditions; both denied that ideological struggle had been important in American history; and both contrasted these alleged facts to the European case—where feudal society had been of obvious cultural importance, and where ideological struggle was presumed to have been a determining factor in European cultural life.

When we turn to the literary critics who were, upon Trilling's ambiguous foundations, developing the theory of the American romance, it is no surprise to discover that they duplicated, in their interpretations, the split that had occurred between the consensus historians

Marius Bewley's *The Eccentric Design*—which remains, in my opinion (although I reject its central argument), an illuminating study—had clear affinities with Dahl and Hartz. This is so although Bewley claimed to discover, in the novels of Cooper, Hawthorne, Melville, and James, "a fundamental conflict or tension that grows out of [their] sense of American society and history," which each novelist tried to resolve. The tension arose from "a struggle to close the split in American experience, to discover a unity that almost sensibly was not there."[23]

The lack of unity in American experience was caused by the absence of a traditional society. As a result. there was "the absence of a rich texture of manners in American life." As a further consequence, the classic American novelists "did not draw on social observation to achieve their profoundest effects." But if this was true, what *did* they draw upon? To answer this Bewley leaned heavily upon Trilling, and identified "the American ethos which gave a primacy to ideas, which made them the proper subject matter of the novelists' art, while . . . the novelist was deprived of that richness and nuance of tone which a traditional society alone can provide."[24]

The classic American novel, instead of dramatizing conflicts in manners (which illustrate cultural tensions between classes), dramatized ideas. We can understand these ideas, whose purpose was to close the split in American experience and to resolve the tension that animated the American novel, when we understand the tension they are meant to overcome. About this Bewley was explicit. Although the split in American experience was partly determined "by those deprivations in American society"—by which he meant the absence of conservative traditions—there was in addition "an opposition between tradition and progress, between democratic faith and disillusion, between past and present and future; between Europe and America, liberalism and conservatism, aggressive acquisitive economics and benevolent wealth." Bewley admitted that the same existed in Europe, but "there they were ballasted by a denser social medium, a richer sense of the past, a more inhibited sense of material possibilities."[25] Because of this, the tension that informed the classic American novel had not been important to Europeans. What was this tension?

"At bottom," Bewley claimed, "the tension is political in character." As a result, the ideas that informed the classic American novels were political as well. These ideas can be found in the writings of three men who helped create "the intellectual and moral climate on which the novelists drew," and who "are the germinal sources of three great conflicting attitudes that run through the best American fiction of the nineteenth century up to James": John Adams, Thomas Jefferson, and Alexander Hamilton. By this account, the classic American novel explored the tensions between the political views of three founding fathers. However, as it turns out, Hamilton's contribution was slight. As "the very embodiment of the acquisitive spirit in the American tradition," Hamilton pursued financial policies that created a rapacious mercantile and industrial class linked by trade to English capital. As a result "it was, or should have been, clear that Hamiltonianism would encourage [in literature] a fatal imitativeness of English models." Indeed, as Bewley argued, the literature that issued from Hamiltonian ideals was that of the deplorable "genteel tradition."[26] It was only from the ideals of Adams and Jefferson that American novelists of genius were able to draw positive inspiration.

About Adams and Jefferson, however, Bewley argued, we notice something peculiar: their political differences were not profound. It is true that Jefferson was the more egalitarian, so that, for example, he approved of the French Revolution. And it is equally true that Adams, temperamentally aristocratic, was the champion of British traditions. Yet the egalitarianism of Jefferson, although genuine, was moderate. Although suspicious of acquisitiveness and of concentrations of wealth, he was no enemy of private property; he believed in an aristocracy of talent and his social vision was of an agrarian, petit-bourgeois republic. This, of course, only says what everyone has known: Jefferson's political philosophy was quintessentially liberal. Yet the politics of Adams, Bewley assured us, were not fundamentally different. Despite the conservative bias, Adams was not a genuine conservative. For all of his regal tastes, Adams' philosophy was, as Bewley reminded us, "a regal republicanism." And of course, at the beginning of the nineteenth century to be a republican at all, even though a regal one, was to be a liberal. The point is reinforced by Adam's attitude toward property, which was much closer to Jefferson's than to Hamilton's. His "High Tory ideal [of a landed class] alive to its traditional responsibilities in society . . . tended to sink its differences with Jefferson's conception of an agrarian republic." Adams himself was aware of this, as Bewley pointed out, when, as an old man he wrote: "I know of no difference between [Jefferson] and myself relative to the Constitution, or to forms of government in general." As a result, Bewley concluded that "the antagonism between Jefferson and Adams is more apparent than real; but both are equally enemies of Hamilton."[27]

Bewley's account of the genesis of the classic American novel developed Trilling's suggestion that the United States was, in the nineteenth century, an ideological society from which a literature of ideas arose. His perspective was nearly identical with that of Dahl and Hartz. Because the United States lacked the heritage of a traditional society, its culture—of which the novel is one example—was determined by the vagaries of a single political ideology. This ideology, although Bewley did not name it, was liberalism. The classic American novel, in short, was the product of a uni-ideological society. It dramatized not manners, but political ideas. The tensions within the liberal political tradition were the tensions dramatized by the classic American novelists.

When we turn from Bewley to Richard Chase and *The American Novel and Its Tradition,* we find a perspective similar to Boorstin's. He rejected Bewley's contentions that the classic American novelists used political ideas "to close the split in American experience" and that political tension is at the heart of the classic American novel:

> The kind of art that stems from . . . the impulse toward aesthetic and cultural unities and thus "struggles to close the split in American experience" . . . this kind of art is practiced often, though not always, by Henry James, but less often by Hawthorne and Cooper, and much less often by Faulkner, Melville, and Mark Twain. . . . Many of the best American novels achieve their very being, their energy and their form, from the perception and acceptance not of unities but of radical disunities.[28]

Since political ideas aim to overcome the radical disunities in a culture, by Chase's account the classic American novelists must not have been interested in political ideas at all. Charging Bewley with "a faulty historical view, as well as an overplus of moralism," Chase asserted that Cooper, for example, "is not at his best in a novel like *Satanstoe,* which is a 'culture-making' novel and in which his mind is moved by an image of aesthetic and political harmony."[29] Instead of *Satanstoe* Chase recommended *The Prairie:*

> In this book Cooper is not inspired by an impulse to resolve cultural contradictions half so much as by the sheer romantic exhilaration of *escape from culture itself,* into a world where nature is dire, terrible, and beautiful, where human values are personal, alien, and renunciatory, and where contradictions are to be resolved only by death, the ceaseless brooding presence of which endows with an unspeakable beauty every irreconcilable of experience and all the irrationalities of life.[30]

If we translate this passage into prose we can see the analogies between Chase and Boorstin. Boorstin, in his effort to advance the idea "that American democracy is unique" had severed all links between American culture and its European antecedents. (We have seen that he went so far as to deny that the European enlightenment had influenced the ideas of the founding fathers.) Free from foreign influence "life in America had been . . . 'The American Experiment.' "[31]

Among the consensus historians Boorstin was the most radical in his understanding of American exceptionalism. Where Hartz had argued that American culture was unique because untouched by *certain* European traditions—feudal relations and political conservatism—Boorstin argued that the culture was untouched by *any* European traditions. In political thought Americans had lacked not simply a conservative ideology, but ideology altogether. American culture, accordingly, has been determined by its givenness—the "pragmatic adaptation" of a people stripped of its European heritage to the demands of a new continent. This view found its literary counterpart in Chase's view that the classic American novel depicts the "escape from culture itself," that it is not concerned with politics, and that it presents us with the confrontation between human beings whose values reflect no common heritage but are purely "personal, alien, and renunciatory," and the irrational forces of an unsettled continent "where nature is dire, terrible, and beautiful." Let us pass over the unanswerable objection to this—that the continent was not at all unsettled, and that when Americans of European descent went West they encountered not only nature, but the Indians. (Cooper never forgot this; Chase did.) For the present the point is how close Chase came to Boorstin—especially in the notion that America is an "experiment" without antecedents. American culture was held to issue from an escape from culture itself, which can only mean, historically, an escape from European culture.

The closeness of Chase and Boorstin is confirmed by Chase's enumeration "of the contradictions that have vivified and excited the American imagination."

These are three, but pride of place goes to "the solitary position man has been placed in in this country." The other two are "the Manichaean quality of New England Puritanism" and "the dual allegiance of the American, who in his intellectual culture belongs both to the Old World and the New." The similarity between Chase's first contradiction and Boorstin's view calls for no elaborate comment. Both men emphasized the primitive content of American experience, a primitivism that Boorstin thought had prevented any political ideology from developing beyond a rudimentary stage. As for Puritanism, both Chase and Boorstin believed that its influence has been felt less in doctrine than in "its metaphors of election and damnation, its opposition of the kingdom of light and the kingdom of darkness, its eternal and autonomous contraries of good and evil," which made "the American imagination . . . seems less interested in redemption than in the eternal melodrama of good and evil, less interested in incarnation and reconciliation than in alienation and disorder."[32]

"Alienation and disorder" we do not associate with Boorstin's optimistic view, but when allowance is made for difference in tone, Chase and Boorstin, even here, were not far apart. Chase's statement that Americans, following their Puritan ancestors, are "less interested in redemption than in the . . . struggle of good and evil" itself, is consonant with Boorstin's belief that, because the Puritans failed in their "beautifully put-together theory of society," yet "succeeded in building Zion in the wilderness . . . the Puritan experience symbolizes the American approach to values." This native approach to values has been simply the practical struggle for existence. Ideologies—even one so beautiful as the Puritan—have been eroded by the demands of subduing a new continent, which have led Americans "away from dogmatism [and] from the attempt to plan and control the *social* environment."[33] And if, as Boorstin said, Americans do not want to "attempt to plan and control the social environment," did not this imply the opinion of Chase—that Americans "are less interested in . . . reconciliation than in . . . disorder?"

Chase's third "contradiction"—that "dual allegiance" of the American to both the Old World and the New—had been anticipated by Boorstin in his discussion of "our cultural hypochondria":[34] the willingness of some Americans to judge America by European standards. Chase seemed especially to have in mind the international character of so many of the American classics. Boorstin, as a historian, naturally did not treat literature at length, but he too allowed that a dual allegiance to the Old World and New has been held by some Americans— although, as we shall see, as a triumphalist of consensus, he did not like the fact and sought to minimize its importance. The idea of a dual allegiance, however, could be squared with the argument that Americans have usually been free from European influence. First, the Americans who have had this dual allegiance, as both Chase and Boorstin implied, have been exceptional—such as the classic American novelists. Second, these people, if loyal to both allegiances, were the people best placed to reveal the uniqueness of the American side of their culture. In the case of the classic American novelists this testimony, Chase claimed, took the form of a genre appropriate to the novelists' unique national character: the American romance.

Although the work of Bewley and Chase paralleled the work of Hartz and Boorstin, I am not claiming direct influence—although Bewley and Chase were certainly familiar with consensus history. Both critics, I believe, took their cues from Trilling, whose influence both acknowledged. The substance of Chase is implicit in Trilling's discussion of the difference between European and American literature: that European literature, unlike American, owes its power to its "commerce . . . with systematic ideas." This remark was quoted earlier to show that Trilling did not believe that the United States had developed a politicized literature of ideas. It is, however, amenable to a further interpretation. It might mean, or be taken to mean, that American literature, unlike European, has not been informed by ideology at all. From this one could draw several inferences: that in Europe, the cultural struggle between classes included conflicts in ideology; that without ideological conflict no class conflict *can* become cultural; and that American class conflict has never been cultural—from American culture's lack of ideology. Hence the United States has never had the social basis for the novel. I believe that Chase derived his argument in *The American Novel and Its Tradition* from some such reading of Trilling. Like Bewley, Chase relied upon Trilling, but rejected Bewley's idea that American culture was the product of liberal ideology. Instead, from one of Trilling's remarks that ideas had not had much "weight or force" in American literature, Chase arrived at a notion of the American novel that rhymed with Boorstin's notion of American culture. Implicit was a consensus perspective, different from Bewley's, that enabled him to distinguish the classic American novel from the European.

Trilling's understanding of American culture, as I have argued, was inconsistent. *The Liberal Imagination,* in seeking to explain the secret of American exceptionalism, pointed in two directions at once. One lead to the uni-ideological interpretation of historians such as Hartz and critics such as Bewley; the other lead to the non-ideological interpretation of historians such as Boorstin, and critics such as Chase. This helps to explain how Trilling could have been such a protean influence on the critics who followed him.

It would seem that the critics who followed Trilling were destined to go in different directions. It is of course true that Bewley and Chase both built upon Trilling: they agreed that the difference between the classic American novel and its European counterpart was the result of consensus. They also agreed that American society was less substantial than European society because of the absence of cultural tensions rooted in social conflict. Finally, both would have certainly agreed that ideological conflict—an integral part of European culture—had been absent from American history and American literature. Yet in

Bewley's view, the lack of traditional society had led American novelists to reflect upon the tensions of a single ideology. While in Chase's view the absence of European traditions had led Americans away from ideology altogether to a consideration of man's primary relations with nature—with his own and that of an uninhabited environment.

The differences, then, between Bewley and Chase were apparently irreconcilable. Yet, oddly, their views of the American novel, in outline and emphasis, were to be remarkably alike.

4

Ideology, Class, and Culture
in the Theory of the American Romance

In its classic phase, the theory of the American romance, despite the different views that informed it, was to have a remarkable consistency. There were three reasons for this. The first arose from an ambiguity in Trilling's use of "liberalism" in relation to "ideology." His attitude to ideology alone, however, was unequivocal. Speaking of the contemporary danger of being "brutalized by [one of] the intellect's . . . surrogates," he declared (quite rightly) that "a spectre haunts our culture—it is that people will eventually be unable to say, 'They fell in love and married' . . . but will as a matter of course say, 'Their libidinal impulses being reciprocal, they activated their individual erotic desires and integrated them within the same frame of reference.'" The activity Trilling condemned was not systematic thought as such, for the "conscious commerce between the poet and the philosopher" should be defended. This "language of non-thought," rather, was the product of ideology: "the habit or the ritual of showing respect for certain formulas to which, for . . . reasons [of] emotional safety, we have very strong ties of whose meaning and consequences in actuality we have no clear understanding."[1]

Ideology, then, as distinct from ideas, is an enemy of reason. It is also a danger in politics, "for in the modern situation it is just when a movement despairs of having ideas that it turns to force, which it masks in ideology." Now liberalism, as a first reading of Trilling suggests, is to be understood as an ideology. It is certainly not a philosophy. For Trilling agreed with Goethe that "there is no such thing as a liberal idea . . . there are only liberal sentiments." It is true that Trilling did qualify this, for "certain sentiments consort only with certain ideas and not with others. What is more, sentiments become ideas by a natural and imperceptible process."[2] Yet, the distinction having been made between the sentiments of liberalism and ideas as such, liberalism, as an ensemble of sentiments that consort with certain ideas, conforms to the description of ideology given above. We might, then, expect that Trilling would have condemned liberalism as he condemned ideology in general.

This he did not do, although he did declare his intention to criticize the liberal imagination in America. Yet his critical purpose was limited to making liberalism "aware of the weak and wrong expressions of itself [as] an advantage to the tendency as a whole"; he wished to criticize liberalism not to decrease its influence, but to increase its relevance. Surprisingly, he did not propose philosophical rigor. Rather, he wished to open up liberalism still more to the influence of the emotions, which it "somehow tends to deny . . . in their full possibility." Adducing Mill's admiration of Coleridge, he hoped that emotion "might modify liberalism's tendency to envisage the world in what [Mill] called a 'prosaic' way and recall liberals to a sense of variousness and possibility."[3]

But if liberalism was to be even more generous in its acceptance of emotion, if it was to learn from irrationalism—here, the conservative romanticism of Coleridge—a sense of variousness and possibility, was not liberalism to be confirmed as an ideology? For Trilling rejected ideology as hostile to ideas and in bondage to the emotions. Of course, in one sense, there is no difficulty: Trilling wanted, and rightly, liberality of spirit. But emotions are rarely innocent, especially from a heart like Coleridge's. As has been often observed, "at the close of the Napoleonic Wars, Romanticism was perceived to encourage indifference to contemporary politics, or to offer outright aid to illiberal governments." It has been suggested that the renewed interest in the romantics in the nineteen-fifties was part of a similar tendency.[4] How could a romanticism conservatively charged not have an ideological effect on liberal politics in a sense much different from liberality of spirit? And if ideology is deplorable, what good influence could liberalism then have? These questions become the more puzzling when we read that "the job of criticism would seem to be, then, to recall liberalism to its first essential imagination of variousness and possibility, which implies the awareness of complexity and difficulty."[5]

Let us pass over Trilling's suggestion that liberalism's sense of variousness and possibility came not from its "first essential imagination," but from its assimilation of conservative and romantic elements. The paradox remains: Trilling disapproved of ideology, yet put himself forward as a partisan of a liberalism he defined as an ideology. The paradox could be resolved—but only if some liberalism were not ideological. A second reading of Trilling, I believe, suggests that this belief was half-formed in his mind.

We recall that modern society received the epithet "ideological." Indeed, according to Trilling, only in modern times has ideology actually organized society. And in "Reality in America" Trilling had argued that modern liberalism—the liberalism of the progressive tradition—did indeed bear the stigmata of the age. Speaking of Parrington, whose "influence on our conception of American culture [has not been] equalled by that of any other writer of the last two decades," Trilling claimed that "in the liberalism which descends from

Parrington ideals . . . urge us to deal impatiently with ideas—a 'cherished goal' forbids that we . . . consider how we reach it."[6]

But what of liberalism in its first imagination of variousness and possibility? That Trilling recalled it suggests he believed that *this* kind of liberalism— the liberalism of the nineteenth century, of John Stuart Mill—was better than its dissolute heir. That, according to Trilling, in the nineteenth century liberalism was the dominant ideology, yet society was not ideological, reinforces the point. And Trilling's account of the liberalism he admired differentiated it from ideology, which always confines and warps the sensibility. Trilling claimed that the modern liberalism of Parrington had "a limited and essentially arrogant conception of reality."[7] But if this was true, then a liberalism of variousness and possibility, and aware of complexity and difficulty, would be the antithesis of ideology.

There was, then, in Trilling (as Delmore Schwartz, his first critic, had almost grasped), a suggestion that in one of its forms—its old bourgeois form— liberalism was not an ideology at all. In a sense, this would reconcile the view that the United States has had a non-ideological culture with the view that its culture has been uni-ideological—so long as the "ideology" in the latter case were not modern, progressive liberalism. The reconciliation would rest, of course, upon an ambiguous conception of the terms. But ambiguity (even when confused) has been influential, especially in ideological cultures. I believe that the consensus historians and the theorists of the American romance often had an ambiguous and confused conception of liberalism's status as an ideology. Trilling suggested that the liberalism he admired was opposed to ideology—by virtue of its imagination of variousness and possibility. At the same time, his description of this liberalism—as an ensemble of sentiments that consorts with ideas instead of as a body of rational thought—fit his definition of ideology. It was moreover, a "political position."[8] The inconsistency was striking, but it has not been uncommon. It has entered history books as the triple assertion that, in their politics, Americans are liberal, that their liberalism is a matter of tradition—of habit, ritual, formulas, emotion, and pragmatic adaptation—instead of rational thought, yet that Americans are not an ideological people.

Regarding the theory of the American romance, I believe that Bewley and Chase shared the same subconscious assumption—that liberalism both is and is *not* an ideology; hence they were closer than they appear. If so, this helps explain the second reason why, in their view of the American novel, they were similar. Bewley, who began *The Eccentric Design* with a political discussion, moved very easily into Chase's concern—the "new" man confronting the unsettled continent. For his part, Chase, although denying the centrality of politics, would speak of the political relevance of the romance.

This is best clarified by a discussion of the intention and characteristics of the classic American novel. Here again, we begin with Trilling. Literature, we recall, is concerned with reality; when valuable, it distinguishes what is from what seems. The reality of the novel is class society, and the truths it tells are about society. But if the business of literature is reality, and if the classic American novelists, owing to consensus, could not examine their social reality, what reality *did* they examine? Although he did not develop the thought (and, as we have seen, contradicted it), Trilling pointed the way that other critics would take when he said that American characters represented ideas. With social reality closed to them, the classic American novelists dramatized ideas—ideas beyond social experience. For if art reveals reality, ideas, in order to serve art, must reveal a reality different from the social when society is unavailable. In the case of the classic American novelists, the reality of their ideas was "mythic." Although Trilling did not define myth, he was certain that its reality, because free from class, was not social.

This returns us to an earlier theme. For the reality Trilling implied must be that of the human condition—which, provided it exists, transcends society and, more profoundly than society (at the level of being), defines men's lives. At any rate, this is what most of the critics who followed, Bewley and Chase included, believed. Seen in this light, a passage of Chase's, quoted earlier, has a new look. When Chase spoke of *The Prairie*'s "escape from culture, into a world where nature is dire," did not this escape imply confrontation—existential confrontation—with existence as such? And when, following Trilling, Chase would claim that the reality of the classic American novel is defined not by social relations, but by the preternatural patterns of "mythic, allegorical, and symbolistic forms,"[9] it was evident he believed that the classic American novel took the human condition as its domain.

To treat this reality, a genre different from the novel, with its concern with manners and its satiric ambivalence, was needed. When Trilling said that Hawthorne was acute to insist that he wrote romances, he directed the efforts of critics for the following decade-and-a-half. The romance of American novelists is not that of feudal civilization, but the American romance shares with it and the epic a signal characteristic. Like them, it deals with a reality not social and historical, but transcendental. As a result, its significance differs from that of the mundane novel.

Bewley and Chase took up Trilling's suggestions systematically. Although Bewley did not often use the term "romance," his distinction between the American and the European novel was, as he frankly acknowledged, based on Trilling's.[10] The American novel, as Bewley described it, has an eccentric design that has "sheered towards abstraction." Since "the matrix of form for the American novel is not manners or society," but the tensions within a political ideology, "the American tradition has provided its artists with abstractions and ideas rather than with manners." As a result "we have no great characters, but great symbolic personifications and mythic embodiments that go under the names of Natty Bumppo, Jay Gatsby, Huckleberry Finn, Ahab, Ishmael."[11] This concern with abstractions, ideas, symbols, and myth led American novelists away from the criticism of social reality, despite their political intention: "As artists [the classic American novelists] are thinkers and a species of metaphysician. . . . They analyze endlessly—not, indeed, the human psyche, but the impersonal moral problems of men, and they analyze them towards abstract ends."[12] Beyond a doubt, the human condition is implied. For only in a reality that transcends the social world could we speak of artists who are metaphysicians, and of moral problems that are "impersonal" and "abstract."

Bewley was echoed by Chase, despite their differences. Indeed, it was Chase who popularized the term "romance." Following Bewley, Chase argued that the American romance, in contrast to the novel, had an abstract and metaphysical quality imparted to it by its cosmic themes (in Puritanism's grand metaphors), and the simplicity and violence of its actions.

> The romance . . . render[s] reality in less volume and detail [preferring] action to character, and action will be freer . . . encountering . . . less resistance from reality. . . . The characters, probably rather two-dimensional types, will not be complexly related to each other or to society or to the past . . . [but] will be shown in ideal relation—that is they will share emotions only after these have become abstract or symbolic. . . . In American romances *it will not matter what class people come from* and where the novelist would arouse our interest in a character by exploring his origin, the romancer will probably do so by enveloping it in mystery. Character itself becomes, then, somewhat abstract and ideal. . . . Astonishing events may occur and these are likely to have a symbolic or ideological rather than a realistic, plausibility.[13]

Although Chase's terms differed slightly from Trilling's and Bewley's, his message was the same. When he said that the romance encounters "less resistance from reality" he did not mean that the romance tells lies. The reality referred to is social. When he spoke of human beings, whose class does not matter, "in ideal relation," he opposed ideal to social relations. As we shall see in a moment, Chase argued that the novel enlightens our social relations, while the romance reports on the human condition, which exists apart from social life. Because the reality of the novel is social, the truths the novel tells us are always limited by the historical nature of social forms. The truths of the romance, however, transcend history—because the reality of the romance transcends society. Its truths are archetypal, universal, and timeless. Indeed, as we realize, Chase not only described the romance; he endorsed it. Nor did the endorsement stop here. We might expect, as the price for abandoning social observation, that the social wisdom of the American novelists would have diminished in inverse proportion to their metaphysical preoccupations. But this, we are told, was not the case. For the world of myth, which refers to the human condition, and the world of society, which refers to history, do not define separate but equal domains. On the contrary, the former contains the latter. As a result, while the insights of the novel are bound by its class-bound civilization, insights into the human condition allow general statements about society. Thus, though the American novelists were not, in the narrow (European) sense, social critics, their ideas have a social application. Precisely because they by-passed contingent observation, their vision, unlike the European, was not historically conditioned and limited. Chase was emphatic about this. Taking up Trilling's claim that the novel had the right to deal with ideas without objective correlatives, Chase made for the romance a very large claim indeed:

> It is not necessarily true that in so far as a novel departs from realism it is obscurantist and disqualified to make moral comments on the [social] world. . . . *The very abstractness and profundity of romance allow it to formulate truths of universal validity.* . . . One may point to the power of romance to express dark and complex truths unavailable to realism. The inner facts of political life have been better grasped by romance—melodrama, as they may be called . . . than by strictly realistic fiction.[14]

While the American romance is sometimes "narrower and more arbitrary" than the European novel—because it deals with abstractions—it is also "more profound and clairvoyant."[15]

A final passage by Bewley shows how he and Chase converged here. The tension that informed the classic American novel, we recall, he thought was political. But while the classic American novelists began with politics, they did not end there. For "they sometimes encountered problems that seemed insoluble, and which deflected them towards despair, and . . . nihilistic glooms." To solve these they sought "a reality beyond the very speculativeness of their intellectual and historical heritage which endowed them with ideas, but no tangible vesture of manners, traditions, institutions, and earthbound history by which their abstractions might live with significant and personal meaning."[16]

For Bewley the novelists' political concern led them to problems whose reality lay beyond not only political ideas, but "manners, traditions, institutions, and earthbound history." As for Chase, he agreed with Bewley that the novelists had a streak of romantic nihilism, from their insight into the human condition, which led them, instead of traditional novelists, to discover "the inner facts of political life." In short, each critic included the other's perspective. The romance explores the human condition. Its gloomy insights have political implications. Some of the problems of the human condition—What is the nature of being? What is the proper relation of the individual to the world?—are themselves political if we follow Trilling and think of politics widely as the "politics of culture," of "the modification of the sentiments," of "the quality of human life."

We now come to the third reason why Bewley and Chase are similar: their disagreement over the nature of consensus was, regarding the novel, superfluous. This is because they agreed that, in form, the American novel was determined not by existing social characteristics but by the absence in America of characteristics of European society. Regarding these, neither Bewley nor Chase added to Trilling's ideas: "substantiality," "the reality of class," and most important, "cultural struggle." Their explanations of America's lucky deficiency, although different, had a common denominator: neither acknowledged sharp ideological conflict in the United States as a basis for the novel, although Bewley, in his reading of Cooper especially, was often at odds with this supposition. As a result, I infer, each believed that the absence of ideological strife had robbed American class conflict of cultural impact.[17] If this were not so, it is difficult to see why ideology—or its absence—should have the importance it had for them. And the failure of each to consider class conflicts and tensions as the possible basis of the American novel would be inexplicable. Only if these had been unimportant could class be safely neglected. It follows, then, they would have also agreed as to why conflict in Europe had been cultural: the conflict had been ideological. But to affirm this leads to a further conclusion. If class conflict becomes cultural only through ideological strife, then ideology, not class, has always been the basis of culture, not only in America, but in the Europe of the novel as well. This conclusion is implied by the uni-ideological interpretation. If a single ideology has been decisive in American culture and European culture differs as a consequence, then the presence of several ideologies in Europe was decisive there—instead of class and class conflict.

In the non-ideological interpretation the same point was made. *The Genius of American Politics* held that the United States was a country of tradition. Its history, "in sharp contrast" to Europe's had an "amazing . . . unique . . . continuity." This came from an "an unspoken assumption, an axiom . . . that institutions are not and should not be the grand creations of men towards large ends and outspoken values."[18] As for the discontinuity of European history:

> Europe has become the noisy champion of man's power to make over his culture at will. Communism is, in one sense, the extravagances of the French Revolution rewritten on the Gargantuan scale, and acting with the terrifying efficiency of the twentieth century. People all over Europe have been accustomed, since the eighteenth century, to the notion that man can better his condition by trying to remake his institutions in some colossal image. Fascism and naziism proposed this; and so does communism. Europe has not yet realized that the remedy it seeks is itself the disease.[19]

As the mention of the French Revolution, communism, fascism, and naziism makes plain, the discontinuity of European history was attributed to the intrusion of ideological conflict. I believe Chase shared this view. For the presence of ideology could not distinguish Europe from America unless it had been determining. Because the European novel, which studies society, arose at the moment—the eighteenth century—when society was split by ideological struggle, Chase, like Bewley, probably inferred that its form had been determined by this struggle. Later we shall see how this inference subverted their traditional understanding of the novel. Here, however, I wish only to note the agreement between their views.

If the concern of the romance transcends social reality, a question of technique must be solved. If society is not a concern, satirically ambivalent observation of manners is pointless. Chase believed that the American romance used mythic, allegorical, and symbolic forms. Bewley's remarks on the subject were in the same spirit, but more precise. The American novelist, with manners closed to him, "discovered his great alternative in symbolism . . . symbol *in art* stands in relation to idea as character in fiction stands in relation to the values represented by traditional social patterns." The symbols used by the American novelists move "inward and downward towards primordial depths of consciousness. Their meanings are not limited by the boundaries of the material world."[20] Their meanings reflect the reality of the human condition.

But if the American romance is symbolist, there is a further consequence. According to Trilling, Bewley, and Chase the novel, as distinguished from the romance, is the novel of manners—the kind of novel that flourished throughout the nineteenth century, some of whose major authors were Stendhal, Balzac, Dickens, George Eliot, Flaubert, and Tolstoy. The American romance, although it flourished at the same time, was more akin to the ancient forms of the medieval romance or the epic. However, both Bewley and Chase hinted that the American romance was not only backward looking, but Janus-faced. The hint is given by "symbolism." For we think of symbolism as a modern technique, at the center of the early modernist movement. As a result, the American romance, if symbolist, was the precursor to the modernist novel of the twentieth century. This idea, generalized to include not only fiction, but poetry and the essay as well, was the thesis of Charles Feidelson's interesting book, *Symbolism and American Literature*. Feidelson, who, like Bewley and Chase, acknowledged the influence of Trilling, argued that classic American literature, owing to its symbolism, had "a new subtlety of achievement. Modern literature becomes . . . less unaccountable . . . naturalized in a long, rather covert historical movement of which American writing is a major phase."[21]

Technique, of course, does not exist in the finest literature as an end in itself. Similarities in technique usually imply similarities in outlook, and this too was part of Feidelson's argument. To see how closely the American novel, as described by the theorists of the American romance, resembled modernist fiction in intention and technique, let us turn to a summary of modernism by the historian George Lichtheim, writing independently of our concern.

The principle change in literature [at the advent of the modern age] is the decline of the novel as social portraiture, and the rise of a type of fiction whose hero, or anti-hero, broods on the human predicament. . . .

. . . The basic experience of the specifically modern artist and writer is the discovery of what has been termed a "second reality," fused with ordinary experience but nonetheless significantly different from it. The dream becomes the stylistic ideal of the artist because it makes possible that peculiar intertwining of reality and unreality which corresponds to the feeling that we live simultaneously on different levels of existence . . . the sewing machine and the umbrella on the dissecting table, the donkey's corpse on the piano, the naked woman's body which opens like a chest of drawers, are symbols of a reality which has invaded everyone's existence.[22]

Lichtheim's terms—"the human predicament" and "second reality"—are equivalent to "the human condition" and those "primordial depths of consciousness" which the classic American novelists were supposed to have probed. His account of modernism might well be an abstract of the characteristics attributed by the romance theory to the American novel.

Now one might argue, as did George Lukacs very late in his career, that a direct concern with the human condition is just what is wrong with modernism. All literature, in some sense, treats the human condition, but in Lukacs' opinion there is no human condition apart from social reality. Those who seek a "second reality" are pursuing a mirage. As a result, modernist fiction can never match the fiction of "critical realism" (the novel of manners) in insight, which is always historically specific.[23] I pass on the dispute (to return to it later) but think it safe to say that such reservations were not on the minds of either Trilling or Harry Levin when each suggested that Hawthorne had anticipated Kafka.[24] Rather, these critics were thinking in glamorous terms of an American avant garde. They took the modernist achievement for granted.

I can now recapitulate the theory of the American romance in its classic phase, as consolidated in the fifties. The social basis of the (European) novel was the constituent element of bourgeois society: cultural struggle or tension between classes. Originally this had been between the conservative aristocracy and the liberal bourgeoisie; later (and more briefly) between the bourgeoisie and the more radical working class. In the end, the dissolution of bourgeois society and the simultaneous rise of modern society eliminated the traditional basis of the novel. Until then, cultural tension brought manners into observable relief and generated satiric ambivalence, hence the elements that distinguished the novel from the epic and the romance. The essence of cultural struggle or tension between classes—what rendered this fully cultural—was ideological conflict. Because of its several ideologies and many traditions of manners, the society that produced the novel can be said to have been substantial. Its substantiality, however, was too thickly textured for a form that could look beyond society and examine the human condition. In contrast to the novel, the American romance was the product of a society unique among those with a flourishing bourgeoisie: homogenous in its culture, united in either its liberalism or its lack of ideology, and (in either case) devoid of class conflict with a cultural dimension. For this reason American society lacked the ideas, the problems, and the variety of manners of Europe: it lacked substantiality. Its artists did not, because they could not, focus upon society. American novelists, with little to observe and no cultural conflicts to criticize, turned to the metaphysical problems of the human condition and produced the romance. The romance, like American culture itself, expressed American society's one-dimensionality—its seamlessness. Because of this, it looked beyond society and, more firmly than the novel, grasped the facts of human nature. In brief, the novel was a form appropriate to the critical culture of Europe, while the romance was a form appropriate to the uncritical culture of America: a culture that could dispense with social criticism because the social problems of Europe had been solved in the United States.

The American romance, unlike the novel, was abstract in characterization, melodramatic in plot, symbolic in technique, and metaphysical in meaning. Its concern was not social criticism but the exploration of the human condition as exemplified by mythic archetypes. The human condition is a reality different from and more profound than the social, although its ambience is more rarified. The novel, in contrast, was concrete in its attention to journalistic detail and relied upon verisimilitude in both its characterization and its plot. It avoided symbolism to study manners in situations of class and ideological conflict, and its meanings could usually be reduced to prescriptions for social reform. Its concern was not the eternal human condition, but social history and social criticism. This made it at once more ample in scope, but less profound, than the romance, for unlike the truths of the romance its truths were always provisional, society (unlike human nature) being subject to change.

Finally, the American romance had affinities with both pre-bourgeois and post-bourgeois forms: it followed distantly the romance of the middle ages, yet was a precursor to the modernist novel. Both of these affinities existed because American society had always had affinities with both pre-bourgeois and post-bourgeois societies. Like them, it had not been shaped by cultural struggle because it possessed, through consensus, a culture that transcended class divisions. American society, then, had been the only heir to the cultural integration of pre-bourgeois society. It was also the precursor to contemporary—ideological—society. (This perspective was adapted to either the uni-ideological or the non-ideological interpretation. For just as the American consensus has been defined in alternative ways, so has that of contemporary society. Trilling, for example, referred to modern society as "ideological society," while Daniel Bell spoke of it as representing "the end of ideology" in social life.) Like both pre-bourgeois and post-bourgeois societies, American society, at least during the era of the classic American novel, was an "integrated civilization."

This last term returns us to earlier themes. I have mentioned how American intellectuals during the Cold War had argued for an American exceptionalism so complete that the United States was understood as a unique civilization, very different from the European. This was owing to its consensus, which entailed that cultural forms did not develop a critical relation to American society. American civilization during the era of the classic American novel was held to be at once conservative and avant garde: conservative, because unlike bourgeois society, it had retained the cultural integration of earlier civilizations; avant garde, because it foreshadowed the cultural integration of contemporary society. By the same token, European bourgeois society, although misunderstood by misguided Europhiles as a logical stage in the development of the West, could now be understood as the historical aberration it was. Cultural tension between classes, the artistic forms it had engendered, and uncomfortable doctrines and political movements such as socialism, communism, and fascism, could all be regarded as of only local (European) interest, with little relevance to an understanding either of the American past or the future of the West—now that Europe too had passed beyond the bourgeois era.

The theory of the American romance was part of this intellectual movement. American civilization, despite its insubstantiality, was superior to European bourgeois society because it had avoided, thanks to consensus, the horrors of cultural struggle between classes. And the classic American novel, despite its abstractness and lack of verisimilitude, was superior to its European counterpart. Because its concerns were profound and its truths had universal validity, the classic American novel had a continuing relevance denied to the historically limited subject and insights of the European novel. It demonstrated that American cultural superiority that the consensus interpretation had tacitly—sometimes explicitly—advanced. For American society had not been the object of criticism by the major genre it produced, yet the uncritical nature of the genre—the American romance—was a part of its superiority to the European novel. Since the American romance, superior as it was, had not practiced social criticism, had it not endorsed American society? In the end, one might wonder why the uniqueness of American culture, to say nothing of its superiority, had gone unrecognized for so long. The blame would have to fall upon those native intellectuals, seduced by the mundane charms of Europe, who had proven unable to appreciate that rarer, metaphysical ambience in which America had been refined. This condemnation, implicit in some consensus history, was explicit in the work of Daniel J. Boorstin.

There is no denying that our intellectuals, and most of all, our academics, being the most cosmopolitan part of our culture, have been especially susceptible to the well-meaning advice of our sick friends in Europe. Like many sick friends, they are none too sorry to be able to tell us that *we* are not in the very best health. We have, in a word, been too easily led to deny our peculiarly American virtues, in order to have the peculiarly European vices.[25]

As we should now expect it was Richard Chase, among the theorists of American romance, who came closest to the spirit of Boorstin's remarks, resorting, indeed, to some of the same imagery. With special reference to D. H. Lawrence, he criticized those who took the European novel as the norm:

Like [many] observers of American literature . . . Lawrence was trying to find out what was wrong with it. . . . He thinks that the American novel is sick . . . perhaps it is sick—but a too exclusive preoccupation with the wrongness of the American novel has in some ways disqualified him for seeing what, right or wrong, it *is*.[26]

This was disingenuous. For Chase, as we have seen, did not think for a minute that there was anything "sick" about the classic American novel. He went on to criticize the Europhile spirit of Henry James and other observers of American culture and literature.

Much of the best American fiction . . . has not made the circuit James requires of the "largest responding imagination." And the closer it has stuck to the assumptions of romance the more capital it has made. . . . James does not acknowledge or know [this] . . . hence his own hostility, and that of many of his followers to the more extreme forms of American fiction.[27]

Whatever the truth of American culture, both the theory of the American romance and the consensus interpretation, in their triumphalist manifestations, were rooted in the nationalism of the times—as the praise for "extreme" American forms, the tone struck by words such as "sick," and the attack on cosmopolitanism reveal.

At a distance of over thirty years, what is now most striking about the claims, even when stripped of nationalist rhetoric, is how sweeping they were. This should have been obvious even then, in the idea that the American novel had been avant garde. This is not to deny American precursors to the modernist novel. They existed, but most of them were not very interesting. (I confess to having been defeated by *The Confidence Man.*) Premodernism in the novel had as hard a time in the nineteenth century as the realist tradition in the twentieth. The reason was the same: the technique was more appropriate to the experience and the social conditions of another age. Moreover, the few premodernist triumphs (such as *Caleb Williams*) were more likely to have been European than American.

Most obviously, the novel, as a popular genre, has been usually conservative, rarely innovative. Innovations in the novel have usually been preceded by innovations in other, often less marketable, genres. The eighteenth-century novel, at least in England, owed more to *The Spectator* than it did to *The Pilgrim's Progress*. It was Rousseau's *Confessions* and works of the romantic poets, such as *The Prelude* and *Eugene Onegin,* that more certainly prefigured *The Red and the Black, David Copperfield,* and *Anna Karenina* than either the picaresque or the epistolary traditions of eighteenth-century fiction.[28] It would have been strange indeed if the modernist novel, in its genesis, had departed from this pattern.

In fact, with some exceptions, the successful precursors to modernism in the novel were the French symbolist poets. Baudelaire in "Les Sept Vieillards" has more in common with Kafka than Hawthorne does in his novels. In poems such as this, in which a lonely inhabitant of the metropolis (*"fourmillante cité, cité plein de rêres / Ou le spectre en plein jour raccroche le passant"* ["antlike city, full of dreams / where the spectre in broad day accosts the passerby"]), seeking relief from his alienation, quits his apartment only to be caught in repeated encounters with a phantasmagorical image of evil, Baudelaire touched the paranoid theme that has haunted the imagination of modern literature. While in other poems his insight into the nature of sexual desire and fantasy, his search for a *"paradis artificiel"* transcending the dull chaos of modern urban life, and his nostalgia for an innocent sensuality—*"la vie antérieure"*—have all been incorporated into the folklore of contemporary culture. Something similar may be said of Rimbaud, whose carefully cultivated yet passionately felt *"dérégle- ment de tous les sens"* prefigured the use of stream-of-consciousness to portray the dissolution of consciousness itself. These *poètes voyants,* and to a lesser extent figures such as Mallarmé and Laforgue, led to innovators in fiction such as Joyce and Proust, as well as contemporary "magic realists" such as Garcia Marquez, Calvino, and Borges. The classic American novelists, whose styles, though varied and often effective, were traditional, whose techniques were usually conservative, and whose prudishness was at once universal and invinci- ble, had little in common with either the great poetic revolutionaries of the nineteenth century or their twentieth-century heirs in the novel.[29]

These general remarks are sufficient to indicate my position. In the United States as in Europe the major tradition in the novel throughout the nineteenth century was the same: that of the novel in its classic intention. This was because American society and the societies of Europe were not radically different: all were part of a civilization whose motor force, at this time, was cultural struggle or tension between classes. All were, or were on the way to becoming, bour- geois societies. I do not deny that the American novel had national characteris- tics. Of course it did, because the Americans were a nation. But the novel in England, France, Germany, and Russia also had national characteristics, and for the same reason. American society *was* different from English, French, German, and Russian society, but no more than these societies were from each other. We cannot set the classic American novel on one side of a cultural divide and the European novel on the other, because the alleged distinction between an American civilization and a European civilization was mistaken. The following chapters will advance, in greater detail, reasons for the truth of these assertions.

5

Ideology, Class, Culture, and the Novel: A Critique of the Classic Theory of the American Romance

The closing remarks of the last chapter may have left a misleading impression: that I believe that the theory of the American romance was an intellectual sham. In fact, although I reject the theory, I find both it and consensus history impressive in range and synthesizing power. Its impulse and its success, I believe, were owing to the times; even so it deserved a serious hearing. Yet I believe it failed, very nearly completely, to give a satisfactory account of either the social origins or the form of the classic American novel.

This was largely because the theory was grafted onto the consensus interpretation. As the consensus interpretation has come under attack, doubts about its validity extend to the theory itself. To an extent I assume that the converse is true: to criticize the theory is to criticize the idea of consensus. Yet at this very point a caution must be introduced. For the theory was and remains far more vulnerable than the consensus interpretation itself. A modified version of consensus might be held even if the theory were rejected out of hand.

This is evident when we consider the idea of cultural struggle or tension. The link between the theory and the consensus view is the belief that this has been absent from American history, with the result that American culture has been exceptional. The validity of both hangs on the truth of this. A distinction, however, exists between them. The consensus interpretation could survive in a modified form—even had there been in American history moments when consensus broke down—so long as these had been brief and consensus repaired. The same is not true, however, for the theory of the American romance.

When Trilling declared that the basis of the novel had *never* existed in America, the "never" was not fortuitous: the cogency of his idea could admit no exceptions. For if history cannot be made from exceptions, novels certainly can. Given exceptional cultural tensions, one could claim that the American novelists had drawn their inspiration from these. One could easily allow that periods of consensus had dominated—and had not inspired good novels at all. As a result, one could still believe that American society had been largely consensual, but that the social basis of the American and European novel had been the same.

The hypothesis is attractive for two reasons. First, it allows us to dismiss the theory while retaining a modified belief in consensus. Second, it suggests an explanation for two characteristics often ascribed to good American literature in the nineteenth century: (1) its sporadic production, clustered, as it is, about the American Renaissance and the upsurge of naturalism; and (2) the circumstance, as Bewley put it, "that America produced several of the greatest novels . . . but no minor novels tnat we can take seriously."[1] While I think Bewley's point demands qualification (*Modern Chivalry, Swallow Barn, Democracy, The Awakening,* etc.), we could nevertheless attempt to link moments when very good novels were written to moments in American history when consensus did not prevail. The prelude to the Civil War and the Progressive and Populist era would be candidates for this. At the same time, the absence of cultural tension at other times could account for the unevenness of periods of good writing and the failure of minor talent to develop.

While I think the idea has merit and will return briefly to it in other chapters, an extended attempt will not be made here, for reasons already advanced. That is, while I believe that the basis of the American novel was cultural tensions, the importance of these implies more than a few interruptions in an otherwise harmonious consensus. Their importance, I believe, discredits the consensus interpretation, in culture, for the nineteenth century as a whole.

Yet I must admit that I cannot refute consensus history in these pages. Literature itself (let alone the novel) offers only one of the ways to understand a society and its culture, even if it is the best way. It may be that consensus history is right about things that did not affect the American novel. As a result, my purpose must be relatively modest: to argue against it for the novel alone. Only so far as the rejection of the theory of the American romance changes our understanding of American history—only so far will consensus history be discredited by the theory's demise.

I believe the extent to be substantial, for art is an essential element of its larger culture. That this was especially true for the novel is a point Raymond Williams made in *The English Novel from Dickens to Lawrence.* After speaking of a "crisis of society" brought about by "the Industrial Revolution, the struggle for democracy, [and] the growth of cities and towns," he wrote that "these were not simple moulds out of which new forms came." The "crisis of experience," once embodied in the great English novels, helped to define the society—through its effect on the imagination and on opinion—"rather than merely reflecting it."[2] If literature has (or once had) this importance, and I think in the nineteenth century it did—in the United States as well—then our understanding of a society and its culture is inseparable from its literature.[3] If the European and the American novel had the same form, then consensus history has a difficulty. It will have to admit that the novel is an exception to its understanding of American culture. Yet an interpretation of a culture cannot claim complete success if one of the essential elements of the culture escapes its argument.

It is time to turn to the weaknesses of the theory of the American romance. In speaking of them I shall be speaking as if the theory were still current, and owing to its partial revival, to which I shall come, in a very real sense it is. The weaknesses are four. First, the theory's account of society and culture in Europe and America was contradictory. It gave too much importance to political ideology and to ideological conflict. Second, it was naive about the nationalism of the major American novelists, and took their claims to singularity too much at face value. Third, and connected to this, the theory suffered from a fatal provinciality, which is, I believe, one of the few American characteristics that date from the earliest settlements. This provinciality, especially marked in Chase and in A. N. Kaul (a later critic, whose work we have yet to examine), led the theorists of the American romance to blunder when they adopted a comparative approach. As we shall see, they were often right about the relation of American society to its novel, but because they failed to realize that the same relation existed in Europe, they went on to claim an American exceptionalism where none in fact existed. Finally, from all of these weaknesses, the theory suffered from faulty history. It did not realize that there were cultural tensions in America like those in Europe, and that they were the basis for the classic American novel. And yet, to the candid eye, the tensions and their relation to the novel are, if not obvious, at least not hidden away. In sum, the theory has been a distorting lens; the result has been, in critical study, an optical illusion.

Let me turn to my first criticism. The theorists of the American romance, in their distinction between the European and American novel, gave great importance to political ideology (or its absence) as the basis of the cultures of these forms. The common denominator for Bewley and Chase, we recall, was the belief that conflict between ideologies had not been important in the United States. The same is true for Trilling, whose understanding of ideology was the firmest of the group. It was Trilling who first suggested (inconsistently) that class conflict was cultural only when infused with ideological conflict, when he denied that conflicts between capital and labor in the United States have been cultural because the classes have shared a single life—a common culture partaking of a "liberal imagination." Implied was a contrast to Europe, where conflict had been cultural by virtue of ideological strife. From this it followed that in the societies that made the novel, American and European alike, political ideology had been more important than class. Were the reverse the case one could not speak as Trilling did. Were class the basis of culture—different classes having different cultures—class tension would be cultural tension with or without ideological conflict. Indeed, class tension and cultural tension between classes would be identical. This further assumption, that ideology (or its absence) rather than class was the basis of culture in the nineteenth century, is present in all the theorists of the American romance, and leads them to striking judgments, among them Chase's belief that in the classic American novel "it does not matter which class people come from"—an opinion that makes sense only if class has had little cultural significance in the history of the United States.

Now it is certainly true that there have been societies in which class has not been the basis of culture. Integrated civilizations are examples of these. There are also societies in which political ideology, more than anything else, shapes culture, most obviously the totalitarian societies of our own century. Moreover, following Trilling, we can extend the term "ideological society" to most of the advanced industrial world, including contemporary America. Indeed, the idea that bourgeois society—"a society based upon class" as Trilling put it—has yielded to ideological societies, with major consequences for the novel, is an important theme of *The Liberal Imagination,* and one that Trilling discussed impressively.

Yet how far can this idea be extended to the society that produced the traditional novel? We do well to remember the alleged distinction made between the social origins of the European novel and those of its American counterpart: the distinction between a society whose class conflicts were cultural, owing to ideological strife, and a society whose similar conflicts were not, because ideological strife had not occurred. If this is held, the case for American exceptionalism rests upon the idea that, in the age of the novel, political ideology, not class, was the basis of culture. Only if this were so could the theory of the American romance be true.

And yet it would be false. For here the understanding that supports the distinctions reveals its incoherence. In brief, the theory of the American romance made use of two different accounts of the relation of the novel to bourgeois society. It used one when it drew the distinctions just mentioned, and the other whenever it discussed the traditional novel in isolation. And each is hopelessly at odds with the other. The contradiction is not obvious, however; to explain it requires retracing familiar ground.

The novel is distinguished, according to Trilling, by its satiric ambivalence and its single-minded study of manners. Both characteristics arose with the collapse of the integrated feudal civilization and its replacement by bourgeois society, with its class-based cultural pluralism. Satiric ambivalence arose because the disappearance of a common culture and an integrative ideology removed the familiar supports that had previously steadied belief and behavior. The increasing interest taken in manners also followed from this. Without a common culture and an integrative ideology, culture increasingly became a function of class. Manners, as expressions of class, became the key to men's lives: they indicated the direction of men's souls. This is only possible when class, and class alone, is the basis of society and culture. Were this not so, the observation of manners could not have yielded the profound insights it did. For manners, as Trilling observed, are class traits, and cannot yield insights into areas of life that class does not govern. (For this reason, the novel cannot treat religious themes with the success of premodern forms.) When something other than class begins to shape culture, the observation of manners cannot illuminate the aspects of life it shapes. The novel of manners could come into its own only when class animated most experience. Then and only then could one infer from manners not only class, but the direction of a soul. Only then—when ideology was a function of class interest—could manners be "the living representation of ideals and the living comment on ideas." The form of the novel, then, was derived from the singular nature of bourgeois society, whose very essence was class.

So much for the novel and the social basis that distinguished it from the epic and the romance. What of the difference between the traditional novel and the modernist fiction of ideological society? That society is no longer based upon class alone is also, we have seen, a theme of *The Liberal Imagination*. Trilling was certain that this social change would have—indeed was having—practical consequences for the novel, and he attempted, in a speculative way, to outline these. Although he did not elaborate their theoretical implications, the direction of his thought can be inferred.

In a society based upon class, observation of manners allows us to infer both a person's class and the direction of his soul because class determines both. In an ideological society, however, the inference of class *and* culture—the direction of our souls—from manners is no longer possible: the rise of political ideology as a basis of culture has driven a wedge between culture on the one hand and class and manners on the other. Manners continue to be, for the most part, class traits, but culture is increasingly shaped by ideology, which extends its influence through the vastly expanded state and technical means of communication. As a result, in ideological society we encounter two phenomena rare in a society based upon class: first, groups from different classes, with differing manners, who yet share a culture because they share an ideology; and second, cultural tension where class and manners are the same but ideology differs. The effect of this on the novel is that realism is often less profound than it was. The observation of manners, which refers to the reality of class, no longer tells us enough, for class is no longer the only basis of our lives. Class and manners remain (it should be emphatically noted), but, as Rimbaud claimed, increasingly "life is elsewhere." Modernist writers have turned to that "second reality" which, with the rise of ideological society, has either grown up or been revealed to exist behind the reality of class. Hence the turn to symbolism in order to communicate what manners cannot reveal. Serious critical realism is now usually confined to situations so extreme that manners acquire a transparent significance they no longer ordinarily have. War (*Red Cavalry, In Our Time, Fires on the Plain*), revolution and counter-revolution (*The Silent Don, Man's Fate, Dr. Zhivago*), concentration camps (the Auschwitz stories of Tadeusz Borowski, *One Day in the Life of Ivan Denisovitch*) and other hermetically sealed environments (*The Magic Mountain, Cancer Ward*) provide most of the subjects that realism can exploit in societies that have passed beyond the bourgeois era—although even here, as the examples indicate, the observation of manners is likely to be reinforced by symbolist techniques.

These situations aside, cultural conditions in contemporary society are often unsuited for the traditional novel of manners. In rich countries, the vestiges of a cultural pluralism based upon class jostle uncomfortably with an emerging mass culture based upon an ideology formed by the merger of consumerism with a single politics—an ideology whose coherence was never more evident than at that very moment when the end of ideology was being announced. Realism in the novel now often generates a nostalgia at odds with the novel's critical intention in the nineteenth century. In the twentieth century, when unparalleled barbarism and unparalleled prosperity have existed side by side and have sometimes engaged in a fantastic dialectic, the culture of bourgeois society, of which the novel was one example, now provides entry into a simpler, more coherent world, whose certitudes, although tenuously achieved, possess an enviable solidity. As Trilling remarked, we know what the writers of that society did not often, to their credit, know (although some of the people who left no literature behind them probably knew it)—that "Thackeray was wrong; Swift right . . . the simple eye of the camera shows us, at Belsen and Buchenwald, horrors that quite surpass Swift's powers."[4]

So much for one aspect of ideological society. Yet, however sympathetically we read Trilling at this point, we are obliged to qualify his further remark that "the great psychological fact of our time is . . . that there is no possible way of responding to Belsen and Buchenwald. The activity of mind fails before the incommunicability of man's suffering."[5] As shown by books yet unwritten or unavailable to Trilling—in particular, Tadeusz Borowski's stories and Solzhenitsyn's fiction and autobiographical works—suffering, however intense, remains to some degree communicable. The irony here is that explicit modern horrors have been in fact communicated best by writers of traditional technique, for realism remains the most effective means of portraying violence. And yet Trilling's point survives: twentieth-century life—whether in the advanced industrial world or in post-colonial societies, with their hallucinatory cultural deformations—often requires untraditional forms. As Trilling observed, "in the [traditional] novel manners make men."[6] And class makes manners. So far as ideological society has replaced bourgeois society the novel of manners has seen its relevance limited.

According to Trilling and the critics who followed him the fate of the novel was linked to the rise and fall of bourgeois society—in which ideology led a dependent life. The reason for this was the dissolution of feudal civilization and the collapse of its integrative ideology. To explain the decline of ideology as a cultural force a further circumstance may be cited: the destruction of absolutism by the conquering bourgeoisie led to a drastic reduction in the power of the state. Since the importance of political ideology is largely determined by the power invested in political institutions, the power of political ideology shrank with the state, and politics touched upon life only in limited ways. Wherever bourgeois society had triumphed the citizen was likely to have a lively interest only in foreign policy and the question of free trade and protectionism. So long as he perceived that sound policy prevailed and that the workers were quiet he did not take politics seriously, nor did he play an active political role. Hence the bourgeoisie was content to allow the aristocracy to furnish the political leadership, even in countries such as England and France, where the aristocracy's power had been broken. This symbiotic relationship was remarked by contemporary observers. As Joseph Schumpeter put it as late as 1919:

> Whoever seeks to understand Europe must not overlook that even today its life, its ideology, its politics are greatly under the influence of the feudal "substance," that while the bourgeoisie can assert its interests everywhere, it "rules" only in exceptional circumstances, and then only briefly. The bourgeois outside his office and the professional man of capitalism outside his profession cut a very sorry figure.[7]

It need hardly be said that this was possible only because political ideology was not the paramount force for either major class. (The same was true for the United States in the early republic: the economically dependent South furnished most of the nation's presidents. The Northern bourgeoisie was quite complacent until the South ceased to produce Jeffersonian aristocrats with liberal ideals and began to equip itself for its own war of independence.) As for the proletarians, the incredibly arduous working day, their poverty, and their disenfranchisement ensured that political ideology entered their lives only when changes in material conditions led them to collective action. Life was structured by a class system rooted in capitalism and the market instead of, as formerly, by the decrees of an absolute monarch, an aristocracy, or a church. In this context Marx's celebrated remark—"it is not the consciousness of men that determines their existence, but on the contrary, their social existence determines their consciousness"—was no more than common sense. With class the basis of experience and ideology pushed to a corner, consciousness in bourgeois society, with culture itself, was indeed for most a function of class. Unquestionably, this was Trilling's understanding as well. For Trilling's notion of class in bourgeois society was substantially the same as Marx's, for all that he had broken with the dogmatic Marxism of his youth. One of the graceful ironies of *The Liberal Imagination* was its use of Marxian categories in order to underwrite a politics much different from that of the "Marxism" of the time. And indeed the similarity between Trilling's view of bourgeois society and its relation to the novel and that of Marxist critics such as Lukacs has been remarked upon by several writers.[8]

However, this returns us to the idea that in bourgeois society class conflict and cultural tension between classes are identical. It could not be otherwise if class were the basis of culture. This was true even for that simplest form of class conflict, the struggle over money, for money touched upon the constitution of class and upon the foundation of culture. Hence Trilling was right to speak of the very rich and the very poor as different from us. Because class conflict—indeed, the very notion of class—in bourgeois society entailed cultural tension; the absence of ideological conflict when classes opposed one another did not remove the cultural dimension from their opposition. Even were it true that European class tensions, in contrast to American, had been accompanied by ideological conflict, one could not claim from this alone that European class tensions had been cultural tensions while American class tensions had not. Because of ideology's minor role, the presence or absence of ideological conflict within a bourgeois society is no proof of that society's cultural singularity.

Here, then, is the contradiction. When Trilling spoke only of society in general and its relation to the traditional novel, he argued that class had shaped culture and that ideology had not. But when he (with Bewley and Chase) distinguished European class tensions from American, ideology was given an importance that in effect had been denied—as if ideology had been responsible for the cultural dimension of European class tensions, as if it, not class, had shaped European culture.

Neither variant of the consensus interpretation offers a way out of this dilemma. If it is claimed that the United States was uni-ideological, and different from Europe because it was also an ideological society—the world's first, presumably—one is faced with a critical description by Trilling of the ideological nature of contemporary liberalism. Acknowledging the necessity of liberal organization, he declared "that organization means delegation, and agencies, and bureaux, and technicians, and that the ideas that can survive delegation, that can be passed on to agencies and bureaus and technicians, incline to be ideas of a certain kind and of a certain simplicity."[9] This was one way of saying that liberalism has adapted itself to history: the revival of the state, the rise of other forms of corporate, and often monopolistic, power, and the decline of both the market and its entrepreneurial spirit and activity. Now organization, delegation, agencies, bureaus, and technicians are both cause and consequence of that decline of competitive, possessive individualism without which no ideological society has ever come into being. And it is a matter of fact that they were not present in the America that produced the classic American novel. Indeed, as one distinguished historian has observed, there was an "absence of effective institutions, of government and law . . . and the scope for the powerful and unscrupulous rich was virtually unlimited. . . . The United States, alone among the states of the bourgeois world, was a country of private justice and private armed forces, and never more so than in our period [1848–75]."[10] This just description is of a society that does not remotely resemble an ideological one.

However, the idea that America's singularity was owing to its lack of ideology fares no better. We have observed that one characteristics of European society was the reduced significance of the state and hence of political ideology. If the United States had carried this process further, and had eliminated political ideology altogether, this would mean that the United States, far from being exceptional, was simply the bourgeois society *par excellence*. If ideology played *no* role in shaping American culture, then what *did* shape it? In the light of Mr. Hobsbawm's remarks (whose import is by no means novel) the answer leaps to the eye: money and class. But since money and class are just what, by Trilling's account, lay at the heart of society that produced the novel, this answer is also fatal to the theory of the American romance. In short, the idea that American society was too little based upon class for the novel to develop has never been demonstrated.

As a result, the idea that European society and culture were different, because shaped by ideological conflict, seems attractive. We could then maintain that class conflict in Europe, because it was also ideological, was different in kind from class conflict in America, where ideological conflict had been absent. In fact, as we shall see, the idea that America has been without ideological conflict is false; but let us, for the moment, assume it is true. The theory of the American romance still faces insuperable difficulties. First, it now must argue that, in the society that produced the novel, class conflict became cultural only through the addition of ideological conflict. We must abandon, therefore, the traditional view that European society was based upon class—while ideology played a minor role. This calls into question the very idea of a class society and makes hash of Trilling's careful (and convincing) distinction between class and ideological society. If nineteenth-century Europe was not based upon class when may it be said that a society based upon class has ever existed? And how was that society different from contemporary society if political ideology played so important a role?

More to the point is the damage done to the traditional conception of the novel accepted by all the romance theorists. If class had not been the basis of culture, where is the profundity of the novel of manners? For, as we have seen, Trilling's account of this assumed that its profundity was rooted in class society. Under other circumstances, such as those of ideological society, class traits such as manners do not indicate the direction of men's souls. But if we try to salvage the reputation of the novel by claiming that it was not after all a novel of manners, we have departed from that very understanding which the theorists of the American romance all accepted. If the European novel was not a novel of manners, by what standard may the singularity of the classical American novel be measured—since the American novel is not supposed to have been a novel of manners either? In other words, if we argue that the novel developed in Europe because of ideological conflict we have rejected both the traditional conception of the novel of manners and the society that produced it. Yet the theory of the American romance manifestly did not do this.

Nor could it have. If political ideology had been the basis of culture tension (without which the novel could not have been born) we should expect to find much more political ideology and ideological conflict in the European novel than actually exists. We should further expect, since the tension between the aristocracy and the middle-class was the basis of most novels, that a great many novels would take as their subject the moments when ideological conflict had been sharpest: the periods of revolution in England and France, when the stake was the structure of civilization itself. On these occasions the classes espoused, if ever they did, opposing ideologies. But in fact, neither the seventeenth century in England nor the late eighteenth century in France was a good one (*Les Liaisons Dangereuses* aside) for the novel. Revolutionary periods rarely are, because they breed partisanship, and partisanship is not easily compatible with the ambivalence a novelist needs. This is one reason why, when the greatest novelists began to write, the era of ideological conflict was waning. We see this especially in France. Not only did the great realists—Trilling mentioned Balzac and Stendhal—write after the French Revolution, they were also, especially Balzac and Stendhal, quite sharply aware that their heroes belonged to a post-revolutionary society; ideological engagement, among the upper classes at least, was no longer very evident, and was of no great account. Julien Sorel's awareness that the era of heroic political ideals is over provides the motive that sets him upon his checkered career in *The Red and the Black*.

Elsewhere in Europe the situation was comparable. The heyday of the novel everywhere occurred after the aristocracy and the bourgeoisie had begun that resilient symbiosis of which Schumpeter took note: the bourgeoisie took care of business, while the aristocracy administered the state in the interests of both propertied classes. The terms of this mutual dependence varied, of course, from state to state. In Western Europe, where the bourgeois revolutions had largely been successful, the defeated aristocracy had made its peace with liberal capitalism. An actual reactionary return to feudalism was rarely contemplated, and aristocratic conservatism, such as it was, merely added paternalistic touches to a consensus liberal politics, as anyone can testify who has taken a look at either the legislation or the novels of Disraeli (who was not Lord Beaconsfield for nothing). Nowhere in England, for example, were the cardinal points of political liberalism—parliamentary government and capitalism—questioned by the privileged classes. Yet England's fiction was essentially realist. Meanwhile, in Central and Eastern Europe the reverse was true, to the same effect. In Russia, after the fiasco of the Decembrists, and in Germany and the Austrian Empire—especially after 1848—the bourgeoisie abandoned revolutionary pretensions and accepted the conservatism of these imperial regimes. Rarely, in other words, was cultural struggle or tension in the novel or in life touched by political ideology. Far from struggling over political fundamentals, the two classes were tacitly allied in both political ideology and practical policy. And the alliance was more than tacit whenever confronted by the groups demanding fundamental change and possessed of ideologies at odds with the status quo: the workers and the radical intelligentsia. But these are rarely important in the novel until the end of the century when the novel itself was beginning to be transformed. It was no accident that the century's greatest political novelist, Dostoevsky, lived in the country where bourgeois society had made fewest inroads and where the coming of ideological society was closest at hand.

Politics, in the literal sense, were uncongenial to the novel because the novel was chiefly concerned with those classes whose conflicts of political ideology were unimportant. As a result, political ideology could only appear as an intrusion. The greatest novelists knew it, hence Stendhal's famous remark: "politics in a work of literature is like a pistol-shot in the middle of a concert, something loud and vulgar, and yet a thing to which it is not possible to refuse one's attention."[11] In summation, then, because the novel examined the cultural tension between the aristocracy and the bourgeoisie, it follows that in bourgeois society the cultural tensions basic to the novel were not dependent upon ideological conflict. Were this not so, we would be forced, following principles laid down by Trilling, to consider the class conflict between the aristocracy and the bourgeoisie to be merely "a contest for the possessions of a single way of life," out of which no good novels could have been written.

Wherein, then, lay the essence of cultural struggle? The answer is traditional. In bourgeois society it was not ideology, but the way of life that animated the culture of each class. The classes differed in social experience, which was independent of political directives. Hence cultural differences appeared not in political ideas, but in behavior—in manners. These differences led to conflicts in relations, expressed through manners, that were the basis of the novel. The struggle was real and profound: the issue was not simple power, but the possibilities for civilization suggested by the differing lives of the classes.

This interpretation is reinforced when we turn from Europe to America and examine there a distinguished tradition in the novel which, upon Trilling's principles, cannot possibly have existed and was denied to have existed. This was the line of good novels that take as their starting point the conflict of capital and labor—a conflict not supposed to have yielded good results because only "the goods of a single way of life" were in question. Again I mention that Trilling did not mean the absurd idea that factory workers and factory owners in the United States have had the same social experience and manners. He meant that they have shared the same culture because there can be no cultural tension between groups that have "no . . . conflict of ideals, for the excluded group has the same notion of life and the same aspirations as the excluding group."[12] The middleclass and the workers of America have shared the same liberal ideology— or are alike in having had no ideology at all.

Now it is certainly true that, with the collapse of the Socialist Party in the First World War and the triumph of the New Deal, the great political fact that separates America from other democracies is the failure of democratic socialism to develop. It is also true that as the United States has become an ideological society its liberal uniformity has given it a patina of cultural homogeneity. (How deeply that patina reflects the substance is another question: the answer is, I believe, a great deal, the large culture of poverty aside.) But even if we claim that cultural consensus exists now because liberalism is the only ideology, would the claim be justified for an earlier era? The answer must be no, for the reason just given: while conflict or consensus in ideology have decisive importance in an ideological society, neither was important in bourgeois society.

Evidence for this is provided by the naturalist tradition, by writers such as Crane, Dreiser, Norris, Dos Passos, Farrell, Algren, and Wright. Each was concerned in some of his work with the working class and the struggle, or absence of struggle, between capital and labor. These concerns, on Trilling's principles, were misguided, because the situation of American workers—materially at odds with the bourgeoisie but failing to transcend liberalism, with the result, I should add, a brutal and pathetic waste—is supposed to have lowered the struggle between capital and labor below the level of significance. In fact, this situation provided these novelists with their opportunity. Trilling, in a great passage, spoke of the mythic hero of the realist tradition as "the Young Man from the Provinces. He need not come from the provinces in literal fact, his social class may constitute his province. But a provincial birth and rearing suggest the simplicity and the high hopes he begins with—he starts with a great demand upon life and a great wonder about its complexity and promise."[13] Trilling did not see clearly that, as naturalism grew out of realism, there is in *An American Tragedy, U.S.A., Studs Lonigan, Never Come Morning,* and *Native Son* a transformation of "the Young Man from the Provinces."[14] In each of these novels the hero either comes from, or enters, the working class, and his desperate struggle against circumstance forms the substance of the plot. This is true of many European naturalist novels as well, but herein lies a difference. The European working classes, unlike the American, did develop political ideals of their own, either social-democratic or anarchist (communism came late, and was less home-grown), which opposed the political consensus. However one evaluates these, they did provide workers and others socially estranged with an interpretation of society's failures. And when people have an interpretation of society, their efforts to better themselves—collectively or individually, materially or spiritually—are usually informed by understanding and purpose. European naturalism, sometimes obliquely, acknowledged the growing political and social consciousness of the European working class. Working-class characters in European naturalism are usually less baffled than their American counterparts, and their struggles are usually less futile. In *Germinal,* the strike's failure does not cause the hero to despair, although Etienne Lantier has also suffered immensely. In contrast, American naturalist novels have little expectation of social reform and, very often, no social hope.

Behind this lies the circumstance that the American working class has never developed an independent ideology. I do not mean here to deprecate liberalism, but to say that it places peculiar burdens upon its working-class adherents. For in the mind of liberalism is the image of the successful entrepreneur, who may fairly be said to represent its *beau idéal*—an ideal that is bound to cause some frustration for those who believe in it, but do not live up to it. When these are workers with little chance to rise in class, the potential for frustration is great. A European worker who believes in social democracy is not compelled to see his continued residence in the working class as a personal failure. An American whose ideal is the entrepreneur has often some difficulty *not* to see the same circumstance as a reason for self-reproach.

Despite the faults of social democracy and anarchism (and whatever the virtues of liberalism), in nineteenth-century Europe these doctrines did improve the morale of workers as workers. Social democracy even had a civilizing influence. In the United States, there has rarely been a comparable source of moral support. Because of this, and because America seemed to offer unlimited opportunity for the entrepreneur, failure to rise from the working class, or failure to find purpose in work or leisure (when it existed) could be demoralizing. Nor would it be surprising if those who failed should see themselves as victims of an inscrutable destiny—since their belief (at least tacit) in the liberal principles underpinning society precluded a social explanation of failure.

Such failures, in any case, suggest the story that American naturalism tells. In the novels I have mentioned the heroes, either born or made workers, struggle toward an ill-conceived goal of personal success. They do this against circumstances often perceived (by them and by critics of these novels) as the manifestations of an inscrutable destiny, but which in fact are social impositions. Their ignorance is reinforced because, unlike Etienne Lantier, they have no ideology to help them learn that some of their goals are unworthy, and that some of the obstacles, especially class, are nearly insurmountable. Hence their misfortunes rarely lead to understanding or cooperative effort. Their destinies remain isolated, their efforts wholly private. By failing to perceive the social nature of their bondage they remain competitive individuals, thus perversely retaining the entrepreneurial ethos of the society against whose compulsions they are struggling. Since their struggles are uninformed, they usually end in disaster—a disaster to which the characters often respond by adopting a metaphysical pessimism appropriate to those who have no explanation of failure. "I knew I would never get to be twenty-one anyhow." The last sentence of Algren's *Never Come Morning* can serve as an epitaph for most of American naturalism's doomed heroes.

It also indicates American naturalism's frequent bathos. The consensus of readers is right to say that naturalism achieved less than the classic American novel (although naturalism gives us something the classic novel usually does not). This, however, is not evidence that American society lacked subjects. The naturalist novel in Europe was also inferior to the novel that preceded it. The virtues and defects of naturalism on both sides of the Atlantic were much the same—thus suggesting that European and American society were alike. True, the American naturalist, more than the European, had a tendency to subscribe to a metaphysical pessimism resembling his characters,' and thus undercut his own social criticism—if the malign universe is responsible for misery why bother to criticize society? Naturalist novels, which often begin as critical commentaries on purposeless lives, often become purposeless before they end. However, American naturalists often are superior to their European counterparts in evoking the nightmarish experiences of metropolitan life.

For the rest, as most readers allow, naturalism in both Europe and the United States suffered from a simplistic determinism and psychology. Hence naturalism tended to take an external approach to its subject matter (a point Trilling was obviously aware of in his attack on Dreiser). It produced no novelists of obvious genius either in England or in the United States, unless we include Lawrence in his early work. The young Lawrence's status as a naturalist, however, depends on whether we think of naturalism in terms of its subject matter, which he shares, or in terms of its characteristic defects, which he avoids. Paul Morel is as fully a product of his environment and divided family as any of the Rougons and Macquarts. But although his destiny is in some sense determined, neither he nor any other characters in *Sons and Lovers* are merely determined. Lawrence is able, like the realists before him, to do justice to his characters' humanity. In any case, Lawrence's triumphant use of materials that defeated most of the naturalists indicates the source of their weakness. The incalculable factor of genius aside, the problem was sociological.[15] Unlike the realists, who were usually from the same classes as their heroes, the naturalists often were not, and lacked empathy. Lawrence, through his father and childhood environment, had an intimate knowledge of working-class life. This helped him to go further than the naturalists into the psychology of his characters.

Reservations duly noted, we can agree with Henry James about the originality of naturalism—what it brought to the novel beyond what it conserved from its realist antecedent. This was the ability to render both the collective experience and the sheer materiality of industrial life.[16] Never before had the crowd been treated so effectively, and never before, except in the work of Balzac and Dickens, had ordinary objects been endowed with such a palpable life and importance. It might be said that the greatest characters in naturalist fiction are collectivities and the material environment itself, whether these are the miners and the workplace in Zola's *Germinal;* the second-generation Irish and their ghetto in *Studs Lonigan;* or the wandering workers and the vast, shifting, restless industrial nexus that straddles the continent in Dos Passos' *U.S.A.*

Here is the point. First of all, while in many ways naturalism marked the end of the novel in its classic intention, no one, I suppose, has ever argued that the naturalist novel (*U.S.A.* aside) is anything but traditional in form. Trilling, at any rate, did not, writing that *Studs Lonigan* (mentioned in the same breath as *The Iliad* and *The Possessed*) is a work "whose concern with manners is of [its] very essence."[17] Second, despite his dislike of Dreiser (who *is* a contentious subject), Trilling's critical but sympathetic judgments of Dos Passos and Farrell indicate he thought that the naturalists had written some good novels—even though their workers had shared the liberal imagination. The absence of ideological conflict was not a drawback to the naturalist writers, but gave them a theme. Nor is this surprising. For what counts in cultural struggle or tension is not that the parties involved are aware, but that the novelist is. When we add the example of European realism, we can see that neither ideological conflict nor even the fact of political ideology was a prerequisite for the novel in its classic intention. Hence, even if true (it is not) that American society had never known ideological conflict—either because Americans have always been without, or have shared, an ideology—this would not prove that the basis of the novel has never existed in America. We should assume, from the fact of class, that it had.

What is evident now, I believe, is how much the theory in its classic form incorporated the nationalist consensus of the fifties: the desire, already mentioned, to praise things especially "American," and the desire to deny the reality of class in American history. The simplest explanation for the insubstantiality of the American novel, which older critics had sometimes advanced—that the novelists had been given their chance and had written real novels that had partially failed—became nearly unthinkable, although Trilling himself, major critic that he remained, came close to thinking this at times. As the fifties drew to a close, the desire to praise the American novel remained, but a willingness to acknowledge conflict in the present led to a franker appraisal of the past. It began to occur to some critics that if the American novel was exceptional, the explanation could not be found in the incoherent determinism of the theory as it stood. As a consequence the theory was to be reformed, but again unwittingly subverted.

6

A. N. Kaul:
The Theory Revised, Consensus Abandoned

The second and third weaknesses of the theory, its mistaken acceptance of nationalist claims and its poor comparative focus, can best be discussed with the theory's reform by A. N. Kaul. This is because *The American Vision* (1963) was the most consistent statement of the theory, but represented, at the same time, its unintended dissolution. It was consistent because Kaul had a simple but convincing sense of American society. This allowed him to ignore the consensus idea, with its social determinism, and to establish the theory on a plausable basis. The price was a weakening of exceptionalist claims, although Kaul was happy to pay it: the decade had changed and social concern was having a new hearing.

I have said that his sense of society was convincing, but an ambiguity must first be noted. At one point Kaul nearly claimed American exceptionalism, alluding to an American "lack of institutions."[1] Although the idea is perennial, it must be said that it is curious. America had plenty of institutions, including, in slavery, an aristocratic one no longer found in Europe, meanwhile, its bourgeoisie was flourishing as nowhere else. The ambiguity was a vestige of the ideas Kaul was reforming; in the end it was uncongenial and set aside for the view taken here. That is, even if the form of the American novel was the romance, none of the idiosyncracies of American society can account for it. In a very persuasive passage Kaul observed that American society was simply not very exceptional. After describing the English novel as realistic and concerned with social reform, he declared that "the social situation [was not] radically different" between England and America. "In both the 1830's and 40's marked a period of social movement, change, and reform activity. In America . . . moral energy . . . [turned] increasingly from . . . evil within the human being to . . . man's social environment." The result, as in England was, "numerous reform movements, . . . cultistic communities, spiritualism, vegetarianism, hypnotic healing, mesmerism, phrenology, as well as the various forms of socialism." Despite "ridiculous . . . activity" criticized in America by Emerson and in England by Mill, "America lacked as little as England in genuine occasions" for reform. "Slavery and the race question, workingmen's condition[s] and child labor, democratic equality and the widening of suffrage—these were weighty problems, which engaged the novelists' personal convictions." Had a novelist like Charles Dickens turned his attention to these, Kaul affirmed, the result would have been "profoundly moving masterpieces of fiction."[2] In short, there was no reason in principle why the traditional novel could not have taken root in America, and indeed, Kaul did state flatly that the American difference had been exaggerated.

Rejecting the Jamesian idea of a "paucity of raw materials" and (a little too quickly I think) the idea of "technical incompetence," Kaul offered as proof a wide body of fiction.

> American novelists were quite capable of writing in the best manner of European fiction. They have left considerable proof of this ability, as well as of the availability of necessary materials in such portions of their work as the Albany scenes of *Satanstoe*, the Boston scenes of *The Blithedale Romance* (not to mention the Salem of *The Seven Gables*), and the urban descriptions in *Pierre*. As for Twain, leaving aside the masterful evocation of a well-defined regional milieu in *Tom Sawyer*, *Huckleberry Finn*, and *Pudd'nhead Wilson*, we have the whole of *The Gilded Age*—or at least Twain's contribution to it.[3]

In addition there was the possibility of supplanting "their native situations" with foreign travel in "the Jamesian way"[4]—as indeed all the novelists did. Most of them lived in Europe for a time, and all set at least one, and some more than one, of their important novels there.

As should be clear, Kaul tacitly rejected most of the consensus idea, whose point was that American society and American experience have been exceptional. It is a pity, therefore, that Kaul did not comment on American and European class structures (this we shall have to do ourselves). It is because of this lapse that I called his persuasive social understanding simple. (The transparent social concern and absense of social analysis make it tempting to think of *The American Vision* as New Frontier criticism.) Kaul's general account of nineteenth-century society lacked Trilling's analytical sharpness—a weakness, since he was at odds with Trilling over the issue of American exceptionalism. The question of cultural tension between classes did not even arise in *The American Vision*, and it was not answered adequately by the discussion of social reform. This said, there was a very good reason for Kaul's inattention here. Little importance was attached to the organization of American society because—unlike Trilling, Bewley, and Chase —he did not believe that it had determined the form of the classic American novel. Paradoxically, this is because he agreed, after all, that the classic American novel was romance. But, in contrast to social determinism, he sounded a voluntaristic note. The classic American novelists could have written traditional novels had they chosen to;

their society had certainly offered them sufficient possibilities. (On this score, Kaul quite rightly mentioned that James had thought so too.)[5] Instead, a little like Bartelby, the novelists had expressed another preference:

> Unlike James, they did not choose to explore or develop [the] possibilities. James himself recognized this fact in his study of Hawthorne. In commenting upon the absence "of that quality of realism which is so much in fashion," he was careful to say that Hawthorne had "not *proposed* to himself" to utilize the [realistic] themes which he mentions. (italics Kaul's)[6]

An obvious question presented itself: Why not? Kaul's explanation, although again a little ambiguous, was persuasive because simple and faithful to the facts of American intellectual history. Like novelists everywhere, Cooper, Hawthorne, Melville, and Twain were dissatisfied with their society. As novelists, they expessed their dissatisfaction in fiction, and here the great fact is that their ideals were drawn from a peculiarly American cultural tradition—"the great myth of America," which "grew out of a definite sociohistorical moment and was eventually defeated by the historical development of its own paradoxical nature," but which "remained for a long time operative in the American creative sensibility."[7]

Like Bewley, Kaul believed that the essence of the classic American novel was ideological, but, unlike Bewley, he did not believe that the ideology was chiefly political, although politics were a part of it. The ideology was, as suggested by Trilling, mythic, although it did not have the character that Trilling had imagined. The defining feature of the great American myth was, Kaul believed, "the concept of community life . . . an unstated ideal, a measuring rod rather than a blueprint for actuality." An unstated concept proved, of course, a little hard to define; luckily it is not necessary to discuss all of the changes that Kaul rang upon his theme. In its simplest form, the concept was one of the three characteristics of the American sensibility. The other two were "the insistence on the individual as the only proper unit of social calculus; and a definite feeling that what people generally call 'society' is no more than an evil and chimerical invention that one can destroy by simply wishing it away."[8] These were both complemented and qualified by the concept itself.

> It qualifies the concept of individual freedom and prevents it from degenerating into an attitude of selfishness and irresponsibility. It postulates a set of values for relationships between individuals which, in their turn, provide a basis for the criticism of actual society when it seems to become cold and impersonal, or when its very foundations seem to rest on cruelty, greed, and acquisitiveness, to the total disregard of the claims of fellow human beings.[9]

The concept was, essentially, a utopian idea, "not a program but a vision"[10] against which the moral failures of both individuals and society might be measured.

The concept of community life arose, as noted, from a sociohistorical moment. This was the Puritan settlement of New England, when it was sustained by messianism and the abundance of the American continent, which seemed to promise that the material resources to build a good society would never be lacking. Yet even after that moment had passed, the concept continued to develop and to work its spell over succeeding generations. In its final form it incorporated three subsidiary ideals. Adducing the thought of the elder Henry James, Kaul argued that two of these were the ideals of "universal brotherhood and the necessary destruction of selfhood," although neither should be taken as a recommendation for that "squalid conformity" which not only James, Sr., but Emerson and all the classic American novelists attacked. For the third idea of the concept Kaul drew upon Crèvecoeur and Tocqueville, and decided that it was a profound faith in democracy. This had led Americans to sound a "note of conscious superiority of American over European social institutions, or pride in democratic equality and abundance of opportunity, which we hear again and again in the subsequent literature of the country, though with increasingly critical qualifications."[11]

The communitarian ideal, according to Kaul, determined the form of the classic American novel. It was the perspective from which American novelists criticized society, and it provided the difference between the classic American novel and the novel in its classic intention—which, Kaul implied, offered no ideal standard.

It it obvious that, in order to establish the theory of the American romance more firmly, Kaul abandoned the advanced positions staked out by earlier critics. He not only disbelieved that either American society or American experience had been unique, there is a further point, consonant with his argument, that he did not make, that two of the characteristics of the American sensibility were not specifically American either. The belief in the primacy of the individual and the distrust of society came from the evolution of puritan culture into bourgeois romanticism, which, as Harold Bloom pointed out, took place in Europe too.[12] This leaves, as specifically American, only the concept of community life, yet even here we must discriminate. A belief in the "universal brotherhood of man and the necessary destruction of selfhood" is simply Christian. Only by their belief in democracy, then, could Americans claim to be different from Europeans. Even here, however, we cannot press the case of exceptionalism too far. Democracy was on the agenda in Europe, and most Europeans—witness Tocqueville—knew it.

This is important precisely because Kaul, as I have mentioned, rarely took up the issue of American cultural tension between classes. He did, however, when discussing the democratic element, lean heavily on Crèvecoeur and Tocqueville. These observers agreed that democracy, although indeed in the national character, did *not* exempt America from the cultural struggles of

Europe. *Letters from an American Farmer* ends with a lament that the vices of European society, "war, destruction, pillage"[13] among them, had immigrated to the New World, while Tocqueville added this sober note near the end of the first volume of *Democracy in America:*

> Whatever faith I may have in the perfectibility of man, until human nature is altered and men wholly transformed I shall refuse to believe in the duration of a government that is called upon to hold together forty different nations spread over a territory equal to one half of Europe, to avoid all rivalry, ambition, and struggles between them, and to direct their independent activity to the accomplishment of the same designs.[14]

The prediction, of course, was borne out by the Civil War.

The picture that emerged of the novel and society in *The American Vision* was sensibly subdued, and, in a sense, inverted the picture that earlier critics had painted. Trilling, Bewley, and Chase had argued that the novel's form had been shaped by a unique consensus, but Kaul quietly banished consensus, implying that any uniqueness was owing to the novel itself and perhaps to the concept that had shaped it. This last is "perhaps" because Kaul did not make clear how specifically American he thought it had been.

Certainly, none of its elements was especially singular except, in part, the belief in democracy. Moreover, concepts of community life had been important in Europe. Nevertheless, Kaul believed that only in America had such a concept been incorporated in the novel, with the result that the American novel had been given an exceptional form. Apart from the dubious possibility that the concept had been simply more powerful in America, Kaul's only explanation for its American importance was its nationalist, anti-European bias. Kaul alleged that, for American writers, Europe had been the symbol of social corruption. Hence the rejection of Europe was one with the turn to the concept itself: it enabled Americans to kill two birds with one stone. The concept allowed American novelists to criticize their society while maintaining—because corruption was European—the "general feeling that America was the land of social experimentation." America, therefore, despite its faults, was more likely than Europe to approach communitarian ideals. As Kaul observed, "seen in this light, the American hero's . . . right to separate himself from a society which he judges to be corrupt becomes a testament to the vitality of his American heritage."[15] The turn away from the novel of manners can be explained not by American conditions, but by its association with Europe. As a "European" form it was suspect.

Nevertheless, Kaul narrowed the gap between America and Europe in society and the novel. American society was not importantly different; culturally America was different only so far as a concept of community life was more important to it; the classic American novel diverged from the European only so far as it incorporated the concept. Although the classic American novel may indeed be termed romance, Kaul provided little support for the idea that it was a precursor to modernist fiction. For Kaul, the classic American novel was utopian, not existentialist. Like the novel of manners, it examined social relations instead of the human condition. Despite their use of symbolism the American novelists were moralists instead of incipient surrealists, having more in common with Bunyan than with Kafka.

Kaul made, I believe, a contribution to the understanding of the American novel. The idea that its form was shaped by the concept of community life, and that the content of this was social, although utopian, remains persuasive, as does his tacit dismissal of the consensus interpretation. His solution to the problem of insubstantiality was very neat: although socially minded (*pace* Trilling), American novelists intermittently left the social earth for a conceptual heaven, where they laid aside the broad brush for a quill. Yet here Kaul overshot the mark: he confused insubstantiality and abstraction with the use of ideas. In other words, his account was unconvincing just to the extent that he argued for exceptionalism.

To understand why, let us turn to the claim that American novelists did not write traditional novels because of the anti-European bias of their communitarian ideal. In considering this, we should remember that by Kaul's account we cannot separate the choice not to write like Europeans from the choice to write romances. The two were one and the same.

It certainly is true, in nineteenth-century America, that there was a strain of thought that opposed America to Europe. This often became a cultural chauvinism whose belligerence was as ludicrous as it was insistent. In *America's Coming of Age* Van Wyck Brooks tells a story about Whitman (drawn from *Specimen Days*) who once

> solemnly posed as he records it, before a vast canvas, twenty feet by twelve, representing "Custer's Last Rally," the work of one John Mulvany. . . . [He found] its "physiognomy realistic and Western" with an "almost entire absence of the stock traits of European war pictures" and recommen[ded] that it be sent to Paris "to show Messieur Crapeau (sic) that some things can be done in America as well as others."[16]

Such attitudes were common, and Kaul was quite right to say that they were also, in varying degrees, held by some American novelists. He offered Hawthorne as an example of one who had turned from the novel on just these grounds, citing not only James' disapproval of the choice, but a remark of Hawthorne's later years that he wished he could find some part of America "where the cursed shadow of Europe had not fallen."[17] Yet the issue goes beyond the expression of nationalist intentions. What has to be asked is this: Did the classic American novelists, because they rejected the European example, succeed in departing from it? Did they in fact work in a spirit radically different from that of their European contemporaries? And did they succeed in developing a new form? Kaul's answer to these questions was yes, and here, I believe, he went wrong.

This can be seen if we take Hawthorne as our chief example. Hawthorne is important, first of all, because of his influence on Melville and James. Second, it was Hawthorne that Trilling singled out when he first suggested that the American novel was romance. And no wonder, for in Hawthorne's prefaces, especially the preface to *The House of the Seven Gables,* one finds the first attempt by a major writer to give "romance" a precise meaning. Finally, it was this very preface that Richard Chase claimed as a traditional warrant for his argument in *The American Novel and Its Tradition.* Here is the famous opening passage.

> When a writer calls his work a Romance . . . he wishes to claim a certain latitude . . . a Novel [aims] . . . at a very minute fidelity, not merely to the possible, but to the probable and ordinary course of man's experience. The [romance]—while, as a work of art, it must rigidly subject itself to laws, and while it sins unpardonably so far as it may swerve aside from the truth of the human heart—has fairly a right to present that truth under circumstances, to a great extent, of the writer's own choosing or creation. . . . [H]e may so manage his atmospherical medium as to bring out or mellow the lights and deepen and enrich the shadows of the picture. He will be wise, no doubt, to make a very moderate use of the privileges . . . especially, to mingle the Marvellous rather as a slight, delicate, and evanescent flavour, than as any portion of the actual substance of the dish offered to the public.[18]

With this preface, and especially its reference to "the truth of the human heart" Hawthorne, according to Chase, "was in effect announcing the definitive adaptation of romance to America."[19] This was consonant with Kaul. Yet when we turn to Kaul's discussion of *The House of the Seven Gables,* we find a surprising judgment. Kaul compared the book with Cooper's Littlepage trilogy, which he and Chase (with everyone else) believed is in the tradition of the novel. Kaul then argued that *The House of the Seven Gables* is often even more of a novel than Cooper's, for in "Cooper the original wrong . . . [is] done to the Indians; whereas in *The Seven Gables* the wrongfully dispossessed man is the plebeian artisan. . . . Hawthorne, that is to say, deals with class from the out-set."[20]

As may be seen immediately, the subject matter of *The House of the Seven Gables* is, according to Kaul, none other than a cultural struggle between classes. The novel is "a parable of the levelling democracy in America." Kaul went so far to assert that when discussing the difference between European and American fiction we can "leave aside *The House of the Seven Gables* about whose status as a regular novel there is no disagreement."[21] Here then is a poser: was the first major American novel that was styled a romance in fact a romance?

Kaul's answer was no, and here he had been preceded by Chase, for whom *The House of the Seven Gables* was rare because it "approach[ed] the novel of manners."[22] This, if true, leads to the unavoidable conclusion that when Hawthorne called his novel a romance he did not know what he was saying. If so, what can be said about Chase—who used its preface to show that the classic American novel (but not this one) was indeed just that? What can be said about both Chase and Kaul, who did not point out what should have been (for them) the very obvious gap between Hawthorne's intention and the result?

These questions lead me to believe that altogether too much importance has been given the fact that American writers often expressed the desire to write something new, something especially "American." This desire, I believe, was simply a piece of nationalism, which was by no means confined to the United States. It was common in the nineteenth century to see one's national culture as unique and to contrast it to the rest of the world (often seen as an undifferentiated mass). It remained common well into the twentieth century. As late as 1918, Thomas Mann, in *Reflections of an Unpolitical Man,* praised Germany's inward *kultur* at expense of a moralistic Western *civilization.* Barrès had exalted traditional France in *Les Deracinés,* and his friends at *Action Française* were expressing a similar chauvinism. England had produced Kipling, the Georgians, and the cult of "Englishness"; Italy, Marinetti and D'Annunzio; Spain, Unamuno and Azorin; Russia, the Slavophiles. These are but a few late examples; a complete list would go back to the nationalist upheavals triggered by the French Revolution and the Napoleonic Wars. Nor is this surprising. As has been justly noted, before the First World War: "so far as European society possessed something like a common outlook, this community of mind and feeling took the paradoxical form of national exclusiveness. That is to say, what was common to all Europeans was their mutual detestation and their readiness to go to war against one another."[23] That the reference here is to nationalism in politics instead of in culture does not matter: it is precisely a national culture that is the precondition for a nationalist politics. If America had a national culture so did each European nation; if American writers were strident about the virtue of their culture, so were others. It is of course true that extreme self-centeredness was expressed in different ways in different countries: Americans were likely to exalt democracy; the English, liberalism (not the same thing) and empire; the Germans, reactionary romanticism; the French, either Jacobinism or ultramontane conservatism, and so on. The ways nationalist writers defined their traditions were likely to shed light upon national distinctions, but the claims to uniqueness say nothing unique about the nations for which they were made. Nor do they show that if writers thought that they were writing in a new national way, they were actually doing so. Indeed, nationalism was so ubiquitous as to suggest the reverse: at the very least, that Americans and Europeans swam in the same ideological currents. This suggests that they were members of the same civilization. Unless we keep the ubiquity of nationalism in mind, it is easy to exaggerate its effects upon the originality of any national school of writers. This is what Kaul did, as is seen when we return to the prefaces of Hawthorne.

Nowhere did Hawthorne claim an American originality for his romances. The preface to *The Blithedale Romance* shows that Hawthorne thought of the romance as a European form.

> In the old countries, with which fiction has long been conversant a certain conventional privilege seems to be awarded to the romancer; his work is not put exactly side by side with nature and he is allowed a license with regard to everyday probability, in view of the improved effects which he is bound to produce thereby.[24]

It is, moreover, a form to which Europeans have long been habituated. Although in other prefaces—most notably to *The House of the Seven Gables*—Hawthorne did make a distinction between the romance and the novel, it is clear that he did not believe, as did the theorists of the American romance, that the novel of manners is appropriate to Europe while the romance is appropriate to the United States. In the preface to *The Marble Faun* he stated the reverse.

> Italy as the site of his Romance was chiefly valuable to him as affording a sort of poetic or fairy precinct, where actualities would not be so terribly insisted upon as they are, and must needs be, in America. No author, without a trial, can conceive of the difficulty of writing a romance about a country where there is no shadow, no antiquity, no mystery, no picturesque and gloomy wrong, nor anything but a commonplace prosperity, in broad and simple daylight, as is happily the case with my dear native land. It will be very long, I trust before romance-writers may find congenial and easily handled themes, either in the annals of our stalwart republic, or in any characteristic and probable events of our individual lives. Romance and poetry, ivy, lichens, and wall-flowers, need ruin to make them grow.[25]

The passage is unequivocal: it is easier to write romance in Europe than in the United States. It is precisely the weight of an ancient past—one is tempted to say its substantiality—that gives Europe this advantage. Hawthorne's complaint is very like the one that Henry James would later make, but where James spoke of the novel, Hawthorne spoke of the romance, suggesting that for Hawthorne "romance" had no portentious meaning. At the least, the reference to Europe's advantage leads to an inescapable conclusion: the term "romance" did not mean for Hawthorne what it meant for the theorists of the American romance.

Certainly Hawthorne's use of the terms "romance" and "novel" in his prefaces does not support the view, advanced by the early theorists of the American romance, that the romance and the novel treat different realities. As we have just seen, in the preface to *The House of the Seven Gables,* Hawthorne stated that all art—the romance and the novel included—"must submit itself to laws . . . [and] sins unpardonably so far as it may swerve aside from the truth of the human heart." This is not the voice of a protomodernist writer who consigns one reality to the novel of manners and stakes out a "second reality" for the romance. According to Hawthorne, the concerns of the romance and the novel are the same. Because this is consonant with Kaul's reading, it might be thought that Hawthorne's understanding of the romance could still be compatible with his.

This is not the case, however. Hawthorne, it turns out, has several uses of the term "romance" but none supports Kaul's interpretation. The first of these, and the most trivial, is present in all of his prefaces: Hawthorne insists that his characters and plots do not approximate real people or real events. In the preface to *The House of the Seven Gables* Hawthorne warns against "an inflexible and exceedingly dangerous species of criticism," that is, one that would bring "his fancy pictures almost into positive contact with the realities of the moment." He insisted that "the personages . . . are really of the author's own making . . . their virtues can shed no lustre, nor their defects redound, in the remotest degree, to the discredit of the venerable town of which they profess to be inhabitants."[26] In the preface to *The Blithedale Romance* we come upon a similar disclaimer. After acknowledging that he had drawn upon his experiences at Brook Farm, Hawthorne hastened to add "that he has considered the institution itself as not less fairly the subject of fictitious handling than the imaginary personages." As for these, "it would, indeed . . . be a most grievous wrong to his former excellent associates, were the author to allow it to be supposed that he has been sketching any of their likenesses."[27] This disclaimer is particularly revealing since it comes just before the remarks, quoted above, about the conventional privileges of the romancer in Europe. It indicates, as does the quotation from the preface to *The House of the Seven Gables,* that Hawthorne, in this use of the term, meant nothing more than that a romance should not be understood as a *roman à clef.*

Second, Hawthorne spoke of romance in order to indicate that his work departs from that "very minute fidelity . . . to the probable" which he thought was a mark of the novel. The "atmosphere of strange enchantment" and "license with regard to everyday probability" fall within the province of the romance, and serve two purposes. The first is to further characterization. In the absence of a poetic atmosphere, Hawthorne explains in the preface to *The Blithedale Romance:* "the paint and pasteboard" of "the beings of the imagination"—by which he simply meant fictional characters—would be "too painfully discernible."[28] The second is the development of a moral theme, especially brought out in the preface to *The House of the Seven Gables* when he wrote that when romances "teach anything . . . it is usually through a far more subtle process than the ostensible one. The author has considered it hardly worth his while, therefore, relentlessly to impale the story with its moral as with an iron rod."[29]

The romance, as used here, is simply a form that avoids didacticism, despite its moral purpose.

In his second use of the term, Hawthorne was making that familiar romantic claim for poetic license whose classic expression is Shelley's *Defense of Poetry*. The imagination is endowed with vivifying and moral powers. Although the artist may depart from verisimilitude and didactic purpose he creates an art truer to life and more moral than if he stuck to the commonplace and stated his moral plainly. Taken far enough, of course, poetic license could, and did, result in "romance" of an obvious kind: the philosophical fantasy such as *Gulliver's Travels, Rasselas,* and *Frankenstein.* But it is not on American cognates such as *Mardi* that the theory of the American romance rested its case, nor did Hawthorne have anything like this in mind; he mentioned, we recall, "the artist will be wise . . . to make a very moderate use of [his] privileges . . . and to mingle the Marvellous rather as a slight, delicate and evanescent flavor, than as any portion of the actual substance of the dish offered to the public."

Hawthorne's conception of his art, in this instance, is simply in the mainstream of nineteenth-century romanticism. How much did it differ from the conception of his European contemporaries? When we turn to the European novel we find that it is not always faithful to verisimilitude either, nor does it engage in direct moral statement. In other words, the qualities attributed to the American romance were incorporated into it, just as in America. This the theory of the American romance did not sufficiently take into account: the genre distinction it proposed was much too sharp. Only by underestimating the variety of the traditional novel could one possibly believe that verisimilitude, in the narrow sense, characterized it. To "mingle the Marvellous" with the mundane was common practice—especially in the "romantic realism" (as Henry James called it, referring to Balzac)[30] of the early part of the nineteenth century. When Stendhal created an imaginary kingdom for *The Charterhouse of Parma;* when Balzac grounded the entire plot of *The Fatal Skin* in magic and surrounded Vautrin, the most famous character in *La Comédie humaine,* with a supernatural and satanic aura; when Dickens killed a character by spontaneous combustion in *Our Mutual Friend,* and caused the Clennam house to collapse on the villains of *Little Dorrit*—a great deal of poetic license was being exercised by these great "realists." Even though this license declined as the century wore on, it did not die out. Take this scene from that most mundane of classics, *Madame Bovary.* Emma has no money, and she has just encountered Homais. Together, they meet a blind beggar:

> "Delighted to see you!" [Homais] said, offering Emma a hand to help her into the Hirondelle. . . .
> . . . But when the blind beggar made his appearance as usual at the end of the hill, he exclaimed in indignation:

"I cannot understand why the authorities continue to tolerate such dishonest occupations! All these unfortunates should be put away—and put to work! Progress moves at a snail's pace, no doubt about it: we're still wallowing in the midst of barbarism!"

The blind man held out his hat, and it swung to and fro at the window like a loose piece of upholstery.

"That," pronounced the pharmacist, "is a scrofulous disease.". . .

. . . He urged him to take only good wine and good beer, and to eat good roast meat. The blind man kept singing his song: actually, he seemed fairly close to idiocy. Finally Monsieur Homais took out his purse:

"Here—here's a sou: change it for me and and keep half of it for yourself. And don't forget my suggestions—you'll find they help.". . .

. . . "Come now," said Hivert. "Show the gentleman you're grateful by doing your act."

The blind man squatted on his haunches and threw back his head, and rolling his greenish eyes and sticking out his tongue he rubbed his stomach with both hands, meanwhile uttering a kind of muffled howl, like a famished dog. Emma, shuddering with disgust, flung him a five-franc piece over her shoulder. It was all the money she had in the world: there was something grand, she thought, in thus throwing it away.

The blind man provides not only the occasion for a satirical social commentary. He is symbolic, with mythological overtones, and is conjured up with as much regard for his imaginative power as for his probability: the scene in which he figures provides insight into the characters of both Emma and Homais and points a moral without stating it. Here, then, is an instance of the romance precisely in the manner that Hawthorne describes. Nor is this an isolated incident, either in *Madame Bovary* or in the realist tradition as a whole. In the last fifty pages, which Martin Turnell claims have "the traditional excellences of the finest European novels . . . the characters . . . become symbolic figures, and we see them crowding in on Emma with hostile faces: Homais ("the progressive"), Bournissien ("the ecclesiastic"), L'heureux ("the Usurer"), the beggar ("Death, or . . . the Devil"), Rodolphe and Léon ("variations of the Faithless Lover")."[31] Is *Madame Bovary* then a romance? If not, how are scenes like this or indeed, if one accepts Turnell's account, the last fifty pages of the novel to be exempted from Hawthorne's use of the term? And if we accept the fact that *Madame Bovary* is *the* realist novel, how is realism to be exempted as well? But if *Madame Bovary* is, as it has always been considered to be, a novel of classic intention, how seriously can we take Hawthorne's belief that he was not writing traditional novels?

The last question receives more point when we examine the third and most important way in which Hawthorne spoke of the romance. Having delivered, in the preface to *The House of the Seven Gables,* his plea for poetic license he added that "the point of view in which this tale comes under the Romantic definition lies in the attempt to connect a bygone time with the very present that is flitting away from us." This complements Hawthorne's remarks in the preface to *The Marble Faun:* a location with an ancient past—hence Europe's privileged position—is a setting more appropriate than a location without one. More important, however, is Hawthorne's mention that both his subject matter and his theme are historical: "the wrong-doing of one generation lives into the successive ones, and, divesting itself of every temporary advantage, becomes a pure and uncontrollable mischief."[32] In Hawthorne's novels the historical and moral interests are fused. By his account it is only through historical understanding that the contemporary action of *The House of the Seven Gables* will yield its meaning. As a result, it is not difficult to understand why Kaul believed that *The House of the Seven Gables* is undisputably "a regular novel." First, Hawthorne's statement of the moral nature of his work is consonant with Trilling's belief in the moral nature of the novel (and at odds with Chase's view that the romance is less concerned than the novel with moral judgment). Second, the idea that history underpins the content, the theme, and the moral of *The House of the Seven Gables* is at odds with those critics (Chase in particular) who claimed that it is precisely history (and social experience in general) that the classic American novelists are supposed to have bypassed in their exploration of the human condition.

This, however, does not suggest that Hawthorne was confused. His three uses of "romance" define a particular kind of work. The romance, first of all, should not be judged by its relation to actual events. Second, it uses poetic license—within, however, "very moderate" limits—to heighten characterization and to imply a moral. Finally, not only its moral but its subject and theme are in essence historical because they connect the past and the present. Of this conception the only question is why Hawthorne should have bothered (and why writers such as Henry James should have accepted) to call his fiction romance in the first place. For there is nothing in it to support Kaul's belief that he had proposed something different from the practice of the European romantic realists.

7

The Case of Hawthorne:
History, Manners, and the Idea of Community

The reason why Hawthorne used the term "romance" is given by the kind of novel that influenced him. This was not chiefly the gothic romance. Although Hawthorne used gothic conventions in his fiction, and had read most of the gothic writers, it is a mistake to make too much of the gothic in his novels. The gothic romance was in vogue in his youth; nearly every aspiring writer of Hawthorne's generation was familiar with the genre, and Hawthorne turned his knowledge to account in many of his short stories. But, as he later implied, he became dissatisfied with his stories; when he turned to the novel he wanted something else. The "very moderate" limits he set for poetic license in the "romance" indicate this. The major influence on the novels—the writer whom he names, in his early correspondence, as a model—was in fact the novelist who, more than any other, "displaced writers like Mrs. Radcliffe in the affections of the public":[1] Sir Walter Scott.

This is not surprising. As Neal Frank Doubleday, in his study of Hawthorne's early tales, observed, "there is no parallel in American literary history for the pervading influence of the Waverley novels." It was so large that the *American Quarterly Review,* in 1827, spoke of a "complete French Revolution" of the novel "in England, and, by a natural consequence, in this country."[2] As the *Review* suggested, Scott was equally influential on the continent, and he is generally regarded now as one of the founders of realism. "One might say," Walter Allen claimed, "that he made the European novel and say something much more true than such sweeping generalizations normally are."[3] His influence was also divided. That which stemmed from his medieval romances—although I must confess that I still enjoy *Quentin Durward*—was bad. These romances led to a tradition of historical fiction as an empty pageant—"from history as change" wrote Raymond Williams, "to history as spectacle, the spectacular past, as most clearly in Lytton."[4]

The novels set in the more recent past, the seventeenth and eighteenth century, chiefly in Scotland—*Waverley, Rob Roy, Old Mortality, The Heart of*

Midlothian among them—are usually held to be of a different order. In these novels, according to Allen, Scott was led to

> the portrayal of man in his public and social aspects . . . conditioned . . . by his place and function in society, his relation to an historical past. . . . Historic and social processes crystallize out in his dramatis personae. It is in that sense that he made history live, but the history lives because of the characters.[5]

His achievement was both limited and enormous. Limited because he did, after all, confine himself to the past, dealing with "life as a finished thing, a completed process," and so is inferior to Tolstoy; yet "the comparison is not irrelevant, for Scott, too, is one of the great extroverts of literature, like Tolstoy a master of the normal . . . [and in] great scenes of action . . . one sees immediately what novelists like Tolstoy and Stendhal owed to him."[6]

Although I think that Allen overrated Scott a little—the good service he did the novel has overshadowed his actual accomplishment—the good service should not be denied. Scott taught the European novelists something he himself had not tried to do: to see the present as history—to take "the organic relationships between man and man, man and society, and man and his past"[7] and transpose these to the present. George Lukacs believed that Scott advanced the composition of the novel beyond the methods of the "great writers of the eighteenth century [who] composed much more loosely." These writers could be loose "because they took the manners of their time for granted and could assume an immediate and obvious effect upon their readers." When Scott introduced history into the novel something new emerged—"certain crises in the personal destinies of a number of human beings coincide and interweave within the determining context of an historical crisis . . . [carried] deep into their personal lives."[8] When writers such as Balzac and Stendhal learned to achieve the same thing in the present the novel of critical realism was born: manners gained in symbolic intensity, owing to their association with larger events.

It was this Scott—the precursor to the realist novel, the teacher of Balzac—who was also admired by cultivated readers in the United States. It is true that in the South, as Mark Twain remarked in *Life on the Mississippi,* the influence of Scott's medieval romances was disastrous. However, "it was not the chivalric novels that influenced northern literary theorists."[9] In the more civilized North, and especially in New England—which had many affinities with Scotland itself—it was the Scottish novels that were taken seriously.[10] It was these that influenced Hawthorne, whose first novel, *Fanshawe,* echoed *Waverley* because its events took place "eighty years since," whose *Scarlet Letter* fulfilled Scott's program in the historical novel, as described by Lukacs and Allen, as no other American novel had done (it was perhaps the association with Scott that led James to compare Lockhart with Hawthorne), and whose preface to *The House of the Seven Gables* announces, in a manner consonant with the aims of the European realists influenced by Scott, the intention to examine contemporary events in the light of their connection with the past.[11]

Why then, did Hawthorne not call *The House of the Seven Gables* a novel—since, by nearly everyone's account, this is what it is? In his study of Hawthorne, Henry James provided the answer. Hawthorne's distinction between the romance and the novel is confusing rather than useful because, as James observed, Hawthorne "was not a man with a literary theory"; indeed, "he was guiltless of a system," and probably "had [not] even heard of realism."[12] If Hawthorne was unfamiliar with realism he could not have had realism in mind when he spoke of the novel. For Hawthorne, "the novel" could only be the novel he knew: that of the eighteenth century. This hypothesis receives support from Matthiessen's account of Hawthorne's style. Although Hawthorne's subject matter and his manner of treating it were derived from Scott, his style was formed by the "eighteenth-century rhetoricians." The reason for this Matthiessen attributed to "the frequent American cultural lag . . . the eighteenth century lingered in America."[13]

Because of his familiarity with eighteenth-century literature and his unfamiliarity with the novel of realism, Hawthorne's use of the term "romance" loses the meaning the romance theorists imputed to it.[14] The position taken here is this: Hawthorne, like contemporary European novelists, wished to break away from the traditions of the eighteenth-century novel. He did so, again like the Europeans, by following Scott's example: he invested his fiction with a historical dimension that the eighteenth-century novel did not have. This meant that the naive or merely shrewd observation of manners in Defoe or Fielding—who "took the manners of their time for granted and could assume an immediate and obvious effect upon their readers"—had to be abandoned. While it is perfectly reasonable to say that Hawthorne, more than these earlier writers, departs from observation and makes use of a certain symbolism, we should not say that in this he is very different from Dickens, and is anticipating modernism. Hawthorne's slim, historically oriented volumes do mark a departure from the eighteenth-century novels that he knew best (he is not, like Scott, interested in "great scenes of action"). For this reason it is obvious why he should choose to distinguish his works by calling them romances in emulation of Scott. Had he been familiar with another term, he might have used that. Hawthorne's use of the term "romance" is most easily explained by his provinciality. He needed a term for what he had done, and he took it from Scott (or he took it from common usage). When the theorists of the American romance used Hawthorne's prefaces to establish a pedigree for an American genre, they made very heavy weather of this choice, perhaps falling victim to a similar provinciality.

This is brought out in another way when we turn to Kaul's cardinal point: the idea that the classic American novel differs in form from the novel of manners because it incorporates a vision of an ideal reality: a concept of community life. We recall that he differed with Trilling about the American novel's social concern. In addition, most American novels begin with an extended portrayal of society, in the manner of the novel in its classic intention.

> But this is not the point at issue. The distinctive characteristic of American fiction is not that it wholly disregards existing social reality but that it is not wholly preoccupied with it. Unlike European fiction, it is not confined within the limits of a given social field. It often projects and examines an imagined alternative: a construct like Blithedale, Serenia, or the raft community of *Huckleberry Finn,* or simply a new human relationship, such as the one between Natty and Chingachgook, which the novel invests with significance as the nucleus of a new social order.[15]

In short, according to Kaul, the classic American novel begins as a novel of manners but at decisive points its attention turns from "actual" to "ideal" society.[16]

Although Kaul overestimated, I believe, the role of friendship in the classic American novel (for this is what some of the "ideal societies" he described amount to) he was right about the novel's characteristic movement. *The Scarlet Letter,* for example, can demonstrate his case. Its early chapters trace the lineaments of seventeenth-century New England society. Hawthorne's portrait of the society is highly stylized, but is not, in the light of Perry Miller's studies, historically inaccurate.[17] The first chapter introduces some of Puritan society's characteristic institutions and implies their interdependence. The sardonic point is that the prison is as integral a part of Puritan society as are the cemetery and the meeting house. Chapter 2 takes us to the marketplace—"no great distance from the prison door"—and introduces us to the Puritan population. It contrasts the stern attitude of the older women towards Hester to the softer one of the younger women, thereby hinting that Puritan discipline is beginning a process of decay, of which Hester's adultery and atypical individualism are also symptoms. Chapter 3 is a melodramatic picture of Puritan justice in action: it makes the point that the lower classes are more sympathetic to Hester than the elite:

> She seemed conscious, indeed, that whatever sympathy she might expect lay in the larger and warmer heart of the multitude; for, as she lifted her eyes to the balcony [where the members of the elite had assembled], the unhappy woman grew pale and trembled.

The chapter also introduces us to members of that elite: Governor Bellingham, John Wilson, the eldest clergyman, and of course Arthur Dimmesdale about whom "there was an air . . . as of a being who felt himself quite astray and at a loss in the pathway of human existence, and could only be at ease in some seclusion of his own." Like Hester, Dimmesdale exhibits an individualism at odds with his position in the tightly knit Puritan hierarchy: in his way, he is a precursor to "the man of feeling." The following chapters sketch in the details of Hester's solitary life, emphasizing her artistic talent—which sets her further apart from society—and, finally, introduce Pearl, "beautiful and brilliant, but all in disorder." It is Pearl who provokes the first conflict in the early part of the novel, in the chapters "The Governor's Hall" and "The Elf-Child and the Minister." Although "The Governor's Hall" has Hawthorne's dizziest piece of writing (it has competition), the notorious encounter between Pearl and the Puritan children—"Behold verily, there is the woman of the scarlet letter; and, of truth, moreover, there is the likeness of the scarlet letter running along by her side! Come, therefore, and let us fling mud at them!"—these chapters are impressive as a whole. The elegance of the Bellingham mansion, the polished brilliance of Bellingham's armor, and the motley garden about the house, mixing cabbages and roses, invite a complex response. What kind of civilization, we wonder, is going to grow here? So does the contrast between Bellingham's severity and "the appliances of worldly enjoyment wherewith he had evidently done his utmost to surround himself." Hawthorne's gloss is ambivalent and satirical.

> But it is an error to suppose that our grave forefathers—though accustomed to speak and think of human existence as a state merely of trial and warfare, and though unfeignedly prepared to sacrifice goods and life at the behest of duty—made it a matter of conscience to reject such means of comfort, or even luxury, as lay fairly within their grasp. This creed was never taught, for instance, by the venerable pastor John Wilson, whose beard, white as a snowdrift, was seen over Governor Bellingham's shoulder; while its wearer suggested that pears and peaches might yet be naturalized in the New England climate, and that purple grapes might possibly be compelled to flourish against the sunny garden-wall.

Then comes the interview between Bellingham, Wilson, and Pearl, which leads to a crisis because the Governor and the clergyman, although disposed to be kind to the child—Wilson tries to pat her cheek—simply do not know how to respond to her almost literal outlandishness. Bellingham, with a nervous jocularity, likens her to the "children of the Lord of Misrule" in holiday time in old England, and Wilson follows suit, likening her to a figure thrown "when the sun has been shining through a richly painted window, and tracing out the golden and crimson images across the floor." Adding, "but that was in the old land." Both men, by their comparisons, reveal their fear of, and sensual yearning for, the richer but rejected past of their youth, which Pearl, in her naturalness and flamboyant dress, has evoked in them. They are unable to place her in their present world, and when Pearl refuses to answer her catechism, she defeats their initial sympathy. Confronted by one who violates the conventions of which they are the chief guardians, Bellingham and Wilson can do nothing but fall back upon the conventions of manners in which they have been trained.

> After putting her finger in her mouth, with many ungracious refusals to answer good Mr. Wilson's question, the child finally announced that she had not been made at all, but had been plucked by her mother off the bush of wild roses that grew by the prison-door. . . .
> . . . "This is awful!" cried the Governor, slowly recovering from the astonishment into which Pearl's response had thrown him. "Here is a child of three years old, and she cannot tell who made her! Without question, she is equally in the dark as to her soul, its present depravity, and future destiny! Methinks, gentlemen, we need inquire no further."
> Hester caught hold of Pearl, and drew her forcibly into her arms, confronting the old Puritan magistrate with almost a fierce expression. . . .
> . . . "God gave me the child!" cried she. "He gave her in requital of all things else, which ye had taken from me." . . .
> . . . "My poor woman," said the not unkind old minister, "the child shall be well cared for!—far better than thou canst do it."

They are brought to their senses, and tragedy averted, only by the intervention of Dimmesdale.

The Scarlet Letter, until this point, relies upon the study of manners. To see this more clearly, let us turn to a famous example of the novel of manners, the "Red Shoes" scene from *The Guermantes Way.* This is especially pertinent because it was used by both Trilling and John W. Aldridge (who was defending Trilling against Delmore Schwartz's attack on *The Liberal Imagination*) to demonstrate the European novel's difference from the American.[18] The scene begins with an exchange between the Duchesse of Guermantes and Swann, who has called on her just as she and her husband are about to go to dinner. When she asks him if he will be going to Italy with them in the following year, Swann startles her with the news that before then he will be dead. The Duchesse finds herself at a loss.

> Placed for the first time in her life between two duties as incompatible as getting into her carriage and showing pity for a man who was about to die, she could find nothing in the code of conventions that indicated the right line to follow, and not knowing which to choose, felt it better to make a show of not believing that the alternatives need be seriously considered, so as to follow the first, which demanded of her at the moment less effort, and thought that the best way of settling the conflict would be to deny that any existed. "You're joking," she said to Swann.

Swann assures her that he is telling the truth, but with exquisite politeness urges her not to be late for dinner, having realized that "for other people their own social obligations took precedence over the death of a friend." The Duchesse, divided as before (having perceived "in a vague way" that she shouldn't be) continues to walk to her carriage even as she tells Swann that her dinner is "not of any importance."

The Duke, meanwhile, although he has overheard Swann, hurries his wife along until he notices, as she steps into the coach, that she is wearing black shoes with her red dress. He demands that she return to fetch her red shoes, and when she does he asks Swann to leave, so as not to delay their departure further. Then comes the famous display of callousness:

> I shan't be at all sorry, not at all sorry to sit down to dinner. Five minutes to eight! Oh, women, women! She'll give us both indigestion before tomorrow. She is not nearly as strong as people think." The Duke felt no compunction at speaking thus of his wife's ailments and his own to a dying man, for the former interested him more, appeared to him more important. And so it was simply from good breeding and good fellowship that, after politely showing us out, he cried "from off stage," in a stentorian voice from the porch to Swann, who was already in the courtyard: "You, now, don't let yourself be taken in by the doctor's nonsense, damn them. They are donkeys. You're as strong as the Pont Neuf. You'll live to bury us all!"

As Aldridge observed, "what is most striking about this scene is the extent to which the code of manners of the Duke and Duchesse makes possible their bad behavior to Swann." The irony is that a code of manners, "while ostensibly designed to make true humanity continuously possible, ends by making life frequently cruel." Both the Duchesse and the Duke, that is, surrender their humanity to their conventionality. "The code of conventions or manners . . . [is the] binding and compulsive force out of which, when it is violated or when there is brought up against it a more transcendent necessity, conflict and drama are generated."[19]

This is still an admirable formula for how the novel of manners proceeds. But, as we have seen, this is precisely how Hawthorne proceeds in "The Elf-Child and the Minister," thereby undermining Aldridge's controversial point, and highlighting how right Kaul was to have rejected the idea that American novelists do not turn their minds to society. Like the Guermantes, Bellingham and Wilson are caught between their natural sympathies and their social code. Unable, again like the Guermantes, to allow their natural sympathies to triumph, both men fall back upon convention: Bellingham assumes the brusque, authoritarian manner that his commanding position not only allows him, but practically dictates to him, while Wilson resorts to the pieties *his* position extends to him. Both neglect the painful condition in which Hester—here paralleling Swann—stands before them.

Nevertheless, it is certainly true that *The Scarlet Letter* "projects an imagined alternative" to the actual society it examines. This is evoked through a direct report of Hester's imagination. Hester, in her isolation has turned from "passion and feeling to thought." Unable and unwilling to retrieve her social place, she transcends the conventional wisdom of her society.

> The world's law was no law for her mind. It was an age in which the human intellect, newly emancipated, had taken a more active and wider range than for many centuries before. Men of the sword had overthrown nobles and kings. Men bolder than these had overthrown and rearranged—not actually, but within the sphere of theory; which was their most real abode—

the whole system of ancient prejudice, wherewith was linked much of ancient principle. Hester Prynne imbibed this spirit. She assumed a freedom of speculation, then common enough on the other side of the Atlantic, but which our forefathers had they known it, would have held to be a deadlier crime than that stigmatized by the scarlet letter. In her lonesome cottage, by the seashore, thoughts visited her, such as dared to enter no other dwelling in New England.

Had it not been for Pearl, Hawthorne speculates, "she might, in one of her phases, have been a prophetess." A prophetess, although a melancholy one, of feminism:

Indeed, the same dark question often rose into her mind, with reference to the whole race of womanhood. Was existence worth accepting, even to the happiest among them? As concerned her own individual existence, she had long ago decided in the negative, and dismissed the point as settled. A tendency to speculation, though it may keep woman quiet, as it does man, yet makes her sad. She discerns, it may be, such a hopeless task before her. As a first step, the whole system of society is to be torn down, and built up anew.

Hester, who has "imbibed [the] spirit" of those men who "had over thrown and rearranged . . . the whole system of ancient prejudice" is a precursor to the enlightenment. As the references to the overthrow of kings and nobles and her speculations on the position of women suggest, she embodies a democratic, indeed revolutionary, spirit. Her very isolation from conventional relations has been the precondition of her speculative freedom and has strengthened the antinomian tendencies of her character. (It is not for nothing that Hawthorne compares her with Anne Hutchinson.) Hester has broken free of the Puritan (in fact, premodern) mold in which character was formed to be a function of social place in an integrated civilization. She exists, above all, as an individual, and foreshadows in her person the liberal transformation of American society. Yet Hester, as a representative type, is not only forward-looking but Janus-faced. Like many who look forward to a time when "the whole system of society is to be torn down and built up anew" she also looks nostalgically backward to an imagined Golden Age, represented by her own sensuality, her artistic talent, evinced in her embroidery, and her memories of "her native village in Old England and her paternal home; a decayed house of grey stone, with a poverty-stricken aspect, but retaining a half obliterated shield of arms over the portal, in token of antique gentility." These things evoke what Hawthorne, in "The New England Holiday," describes as "the sunny richness of the Elizabethan epoch; a time when the life of England, viewed as one great mass, would appear to have been as stately, magnificent, and joyous, as the world has ever witnessed." The ideal society suggested by *The Scarlet Letter* would combine the creativity, color, and richness of aristocratic Elizabethan culture with the speculative freedom and egalitarianism of the democratic enlightenment. In addition—and this too is a subject of Hester's passionate speculation—the personal happiness of individualists like Hester and Dimmesdale would be secured.

The Scarlet Letter vindicates Kaul's description of the characteristic movement in the form of the American novel. First, the observation of manners in an actual society; second, the evocation of an ideal society against which the actual is judged. And as Kaul suggested, a part of the ideal is a belief in democracy. Yet once this has been said, a problem remains. It is not that *The Scarlet Letter* is atypical. Most of the classic American novels do take the turn to utopianism that Kaul described. The problem is that many, perhaps most, of the great European novels of the period do as well.

Hawthorne and James: Dissolution of the Theory of the American Romance

Unwittingly, Kaul demonstrated that the form of the classic American novel and the European novel were the same. Hence his book, despite its cogency, marked the dissolution of the theory of the American romance. If this was not perceived at the time, it was acknowledged that he had helped restore the social dimension to the study of the American novel. By doing so, he prepared the way for the energetic, if inconclusive, attacks on the theory by Martin Green, David Hirsch, Nicholaus Mill, Robert Merrill, and (less directly) Richard Poirier. As mentioned before, these critics were not occupied, as I am, with metacriticism, that is, with the inner development of the idea of American exceptionalism. As a result, although some did address Kaul's book, it is not surprising that its central idea—the utopian aspiration for an ideal society—although the weakest part of the argument for exceptionalism, should have gone unchallenged. Its weakness was not that it was untrue, but that the ideal was simply not American. It was a synonym of that critical idea of "culture" which sustained the novel of bourgeois society: culture that is, as a "whole way of life," a "court of appeals where real values could be determined." The American "concept of community life" is simply a national variant of this.

It was not the only national variant. The idea of a whole way of life or community (whatever we call this one thing) changed from nation to nation just as nationalism did. In America, democracy informed the idea of culture, more than in any other country at the time. But that Americans as a distinctive nation had a distinctive idea of culture that informed the American novel is not the point in dispute. The question is whether American novelists, because they incorporated a concept of community life into their novels, were being exceptional. The answer to this question is no. Nor is this surprising. It was after all Kaul, among the romance critics, who abandoned the idea of consensus because he realized that American and European societies had the same problems. Just as the rise of bourgeois society triggered a critical response in European writers, so it did in the United States. What is surprising, of course, is that Kaul should not have noticed this similarity.

In this he was probably hindered by the restrictive interpretation of the novel implied by other romance critics. For the "novel of manners," while an accurate term, can obscure the variety of the novel. As George Lukacs pointed out, modern criticism of the novel often tends to run together disparate moments in the novel's history, such as the eighteenth-century novel of manners proper, the novel of critical or bourgeois realism, and the naturalist novel.[1] All of these may be termed novels of manners, but, unless we distinguish each, our account will be too syncretic to have much descriptive value. The converse is equally true: if we take one kind of novel as a model, we are likely to make some odd exclusions. And if large and restrictive definitions are changed as the focus is changed, we can make some factitious distinctions. This is what the romance critics did too often. Even Trilling was not immune from this: Cooper's mind was not turned to society; his characters embody ideas; he wrote romances. But, in another place, Scott is a "founder of realism."[2] Yet Cooper, all his creative life, was called "the American Scott," and Scott usually called his own novels romances. For William Dean Howells, the guardian of verisimilitude, both novelists wrote romances.[3] And both were equally admired by Balzac, who did not think he was departing from them. If strict verisimilitude is the criterion, half the novelists on both sides of the Atlantic would not pass muster, especially in the first half of the nineteenth century—as I indicated when discussing Hawthorne's prefaces (and shall mention again in a moment). Kaul's idea failed for a similar reason. In both the European and the American novel, the characteristic movement is from the satiric and ambivalent study of manners to the contemplation of idealized alternatives to actual society.

We can see this clearly enough in Proust, whom Trilling offered as a representative European novelist. Proust's great novel is concerned only intermittently with society. We have, in addition to the study of society, the long reveries of its protagonist who imagines not one but a series of ideal worlds, the first symbolized by aristocratic society, the last by the world of art, in which life is redeemed from its meanness and incoherence. Proust, indeed, is almost too easy an example if the point is to show that the European novel is not exclusively concerned with manners in a narrow sense. Besides, his work is in part undeniably modernist. But if we turn to European novels contemporaneous with the classic American novels the point still stands. To demonstrate this, let us turn to *The Charterhouse of Parma* (1839), and compare it with *The Scarlet Letter* (1851). My choice of *The Charterhouse* is very nearly arbitrary, but this has its own interest. *The Charterhouse* and *The Scarlet Letter* are as different as novels can be and yet, in Kaul's terms, they have the same form.

There is no need to examine the means by which Stendhal establishes his credentials as a classical novelist: this is universally acknowledged. The duchy of Parma is sketched with relevant detail, and like Hawthorne's Boston, it is a stylized portrait of a hierarchical society under strain. The society is that of restoration Europe. We see the whole of it, although the focus is at the top: the dictator, the prime minister, the minister of justice, the governor of the citadel, the duchess, the archbishop, the heir-apparent, the reactionary marquis, the futile party politics, and the relations between the classes—the nobility, the bourgeoisie, and the populace. The satirical note of the novel is given by the situation of the governor of the Citadel who, although the head of the liberal party, has designed especially uncomfortable cages for the liberal prisoners in order to obtain a weekly audience with his sovereign.

Concomitant with satirical observation is another theme: the idealized world of excited reverie in the attractive hero, Fabrice, in which he imagines a life worthy of his talents, here frustrated by the pettiness of a corrupt world. (In this Fabrice is like his creator: "I see" wrote Stendhal, "that *reverie* has been the thing I have preferred to everything else, even to passing for a wit.")[4]

The ideal world that Fabrice imagines, and in his character partially embodies, is a complex one. First of all it would welcome that genius and heroism which Stendhal associated with Napoleon and his revolutionary armies. These are brilliantly evoked in the novel's first paragraphs:

> On 15 May 1796, General Bonaparte made his entry into Milan at the head of that youthful army which but a short time before had crossed the Bridge of Lodi and taught the world that after so many centuries Caesar and Alexander had a successor.
>
> The miracles of a gallantry and genius that Italy had been witness of in the space of a few months aroused a slumbering people. . . .
>
> In the Middle Ages the republicans of Lombardy had given proof of a valour equal to that of the French, and had deserved to see their city razed to the ground by the German Emperors. Ever since they had become *loyal subjects* their main business had been the printing of sonnets upon little handkerchiefs of rose-coloured taffeta. . . . It was a far cry from such effeminate manners to the deep emotions aroused by the unexpected arrival of the French army. Very soon a new and passionate standard of manners sprang into being.

Stendhal was a radical liberal, but he did not believe genius and heroism were exclusively liberal virtues, as the reference to the Milanese of the Middle Ages makes plain. Stendhal's heroes, not only Fabrice in *The Charterhouse,* but Julien Sorel in *The Red and the Black,* look back to the Renaissance, when heroism was more prominent and genius more richly rewarded than in the present. Fabrice, in his prison cell, wonders: "Can I be one of those men of valor of whom antiquity has furnished the world with certain examples?" Yet despite the nostalgia of Stendhal's heroes for the golden age of the French aristocracy, a revival of conservative politics is never suggested. For it was indeed the revival of conservative politics after the fall of Napoleon that created the stifling society in which his heroes make their way.

Finally, as Turnell notes, Stendhal's view is that "genius is absolute and inexplicable." The environment has its importance, however. "Environment does not determine a man's *character,* but it does determine his *fate.*" In the wretched society in which he lives, Fabrice can rarely express his heroic talents. He, like all of Stendhal's heroes, is an *étranger,* "the Janus-face who emerges in periods when the sensitive individual cannot identify himself with any of the different groups of which society is composed."[5] The result is curious. Although attractive to others, Fabrice protects his real self through ruse, and plays a variety of parts, some rooted in folklore. (And in romance?) He is a "parody of a Knight Errant" when disguised in a red wig, he pursues La Fausta and seduces her maid. As a churchman, he is an "ironical portrait of an eighteenth-century ecclesiastic." At times he is "the youthful hero of romance trying to win a bride belonging to the world of fairy-tale." Most characteristically, however, he is an innocent, almost unconscious of the great world. Hence, despite his instability and real hypocrisy, Fabrice is never condemned by his creator. He has a core of character, brought out when he fights at Waterloo and falls in love with Clelia.[6]

Second, in addition to genius and heroism, the ideal world of Fabrice's imagination would incorporate that passionate freedom to which all of Stendhal's heroes in their finest moments aspire, and which lies behind their behavior even when they conform. The ultimate triumph of this spirit of liberty, however, could only be in the distant future, perhaps at the very time, Stendhal wryly suggests, when his books will be widely read. Meanwhile, liberty will be the covert possession (along with the virtues of genius and heroism) of "a happy few" such as Fabrice and, to a lesser extent, such characters as Sanseverina, Mosca, and Palla, the mad liberal bandit, revolutionary, and poet. The spirit of liberty may be expected, however, to break out from time to time and to shatter the complacency of a decaying world—as it does in the climactic scene of *The Charterhouse* when Sanseverina, having made common cause with Palla in order to liberate Fabrice from prison, stages a palace coup. The signal for Palla to assassinate the tyrannical prince is the opening of Parma's reservoir. The water that floods the streets of Parma and cleanses the city of its despot represents the momentary triumph of both political liberty and the passions of the novel's sympathetic characters.

Finally, there is Stendhal's emphasis upon happiness through personal relations, which is one with his recognition that the society of his day was not going to be overthrown in the foreseeable future. The tragedy of Stendhal's heroes is that, estranged from society because of their superior character and their willingness to break with convention, they come to live only for personal relations, although they realize that these alone cannot sustain "a whole way of life." This, we recall, is Hester's insight too in *The Scarlet Letter,* even as she is willing to stake her future on a flight with Dimmesdale. In "a whole way of life" personal relations would have their important place, but they would not be the entire focus of energy. Moreover, happiness could be guaranteed only through an ideal society: in the social life of actual society even personal relations are doomed to frustration.

Stated abstractly, the utopian ideals of *The Charterhouse of Parma* and *The Scarlet Letter* are similar. Janus-faced, both Hawthorne and Stendhal evoke an ideal society that would strike a balance between the virtues of a largely aristocratic past and those promised in the future by the revolutionary and democratic enlightenment. In addition, they would like society to encourage the fulfillment of romantic love. Certainly Hester's situation—her isolation and her dream of happiness through private relations—parallels that of Stendhal's *étrangers,* who are also representative of the typical hero in the novel of manners: "the Young Man from the Provinces." (A difference: Hester has come to the Provinces.)

I am not suggesting any particular affinity. The novels of Hawthorne and Stendhal, in style, plot, characterization, and the actual societies they examine, are not much alike. Moreover, since the ideal society of each is made vivid not only in abstraction, but as embodied in the character of the hero, their utopian visions are ultimately as dissimilar as Hester and Fabrice. And there is a further difference, in the manner in which utopian vision is evoked. As noted, in *The Scarlet Letter* this is largely through a report of Hester's reveries. By contrast, the political side of Fabrice's ideals is indicated more by Fabrice's actions than by his thoughts, most of which are given over to his love of Clelia—although his republicanism is declared when he tells Sanseverina that he would like to go to New York and become an "American citizen and soldier of the Republic." It might be thought that Stendhal's concreteness here supports the idea that American novelists were less interested in society than Europeans. In fact, Hawthorne's relative abstraction comes not from "romance," but from the fact of Hester's isolation: a report of her thoughts is the only way we can know them. In this, Hawthorne is more typical than Stendhal. As George Steiner has mentioned, throughout the history of the novel ideas tend to be presented abstractly whenever they touch upon politics. We need only think of Book VIII of *Anna Karenina,* "with its unpremeditated polemic and its tractarian intent," as Steiner puts it, or of "the close of *Nana* or of the epilogue to *The Magic Mountain.*"[7] In fact, the difference between Stendhal and Hawthorne here challenges a conventional idea about the alleged formal differences between the American and the European novel. According to the theory of the American romance (in Chase's view), the novel of manners typically treats social life and politics. The romance, by contrast, is concerned with intensely personal quests. Yet it is Stendhal, the great political novelist, who communicates a portion of his utopian ideal in intensely personal terms while Hawthorne, usually not thought of as a political or social analyst, communicates his ideals more objectively, in political and social terms.

The Scarlet Letter and *The Charterhouse of Parma* are after all very unlike and of unequal merit: because of its greater substantiality *The Charterhouse* is the greater novel. Regarding their similarity, they are alike only, but significantly, in their elemental form. Each novel critically studies an actual society by examining the relation of society to extraordinary people alienated from it. Each novel departs from the observation of manners in order to evoke an ideal society—the measure by which society and the heroes may be judged. The departure from the observation of manners, in each case, leads inevitably to what one critic has called, in reference to *The Charterhouse of Parma,* the "devaluation of reality"[8]—by which he means social reality—a characteristic that the theory of the American romance mistakenly attributed to the classic American novel alone. Taken together, all of these characteristics do signal that a new departure in the novel had been made. Hawthorne, comparing his novels with the eighteenth-century fiction that he knew, realized this. So did his European contemporaries, such as Stendhal, with the difference that they did not call their own fiction romance quite as consistently as Hawthorne did. But they dramatized ideas just as much. And this (to return to an earlier theme) gives the lie to the idea that they were less involved with the human condition than American novelists. It is difficult to say, indeed, where society leaves off and the human condition begins, but certainly if ideas indicate this, the Europeans went as far. (With sex—another element of the condition—they went farther.) Kaul failed; given this formal "identity," the question of insubstantiality remains.

But if this is true, whence descends that traditional sanction for calling the American novel romance? The answer is that it descends not only from a misreading of Hawthorne, but from Henry James' study of him. Why did James accept Hawthorne's use of the term? This question demands that we note that the realist novel, which replaced the eighteenth-century novel of manners per se, had two moments before giving way to the more mundane, if sometimes more frenetic, novel of naturalism. To the first of these moments belonged writers such as Stendhal and Hawthorne. To the second belonged writers such as Flaubert and Henry James himself. In *Madame Bovary* and *Sentimental Education* an imperfect society is closely studied and, as in the novels of Stendhal, is judged from an ideal perspective. But in Flaubert the ideal is no longer an ideal society, but art itself. Estheticism replaces utopianism as the controlling attitude of the novelist. Hence there is, in Flaubert, no attempt to suggest an idealized alternative to actual social life, despite Flaubert's contempt for the society he observes and the satire he expends upon it. In Flaubert there is much judgment, but this judgment is not based on an ethics. (This is to his detriment:

without an interest in a social alternative, contempt for society is unearned.) The novel itself, as a work of art, is Flaubert's ideal.

Because utopianism has been excised, the social novels of Flaubert are less visionary than those of Stendhal, and more prudent in their exercise of the imagination. (He made up for this, alas, in *Salammbô* and *The Temptation of Saint Anthony.*) As a consequence, they tend toward stricter verisimilitude and journalistic observation—characteristics often wrongly thought of as the essence of the tradition of the novel. Although, as shown by the scene of the blind beggar in *Madame Bovary,* Flaubert retains a sense of symbolic wonder, the drift of his novels is toward the mundane. Sympathetic heroes like Fabrice are not present in Flaubert's fiction. There are fewer sympathetic characters altogether, and, such as they are, they tend to be "simple hearts"—Felicité in *A Simple Heart* and Dussardier in *Sentimental Education*—or detached professionals such as Dr. Larivière in *Madame Bovary.* Once the step toward strict verisimilitude, journalistic detail, and mundanity had been taken, the next step was taken by Zola. Hence the estheticism of Flaubert played midwife to the sociology of naturalism. Once the utopianism of early realism had been abandoned, art for art's sake could be born, to expire at the hands of science. Dr. Larivière is succeeded by *Dr. Pascal.*

Why was the utopianism of early realism abandoned? George Lukacs thought that the waning of the revolutionary spirit of the bourgeoisie after the revolution of 1848 meant that European writers after this event either could not or would not conceive of "the great good place" as a social ideal.[9] Lukacs' idea is old hat now, but Henry James, closer to the events, saw something similar; the thesis, modified to include the effects of industrialization, I think still stands.[10] The difference may be seen in Stendhal and Flaubert. Stendhal is skeptical about the future of his social ideals, but he does not abandon a certain idealism. Gramsci would have embraced him as a pessimist of the intellect and an optimist of the will. Such poise is beyond Flaubert, whose social despair leads him to lose ambivalence toward his subjects and to handle them more crudely, despite the famous style. ("Why, why *him?*" Henry James would complain of the nullity of Frederic Moreau.)[11] His imagery, for example, as Proust and critics since Proust have pointed out, is impoverished.[12] And this must be seen as the consequence, not of a lack of talent, but of a lack of attentiveness to that world which he was so anxious to transcend. Despite the real loss of power and subtlety in later realism, however, it is not difficult to see why its advocates, such as Flaubert—whose relation to George Sand, as Henry James pointed out, presents the case[13]—could see it as a real advance over the "naive" novel of the earlier part of the century, that is to say, the novel of writers such as Stendhal and Balzac. Less pessimistic than he, their imaginations were more excited by the present, hence their willingness to abandon verisimilitude and adopt a certain expressionism.

With this distinction between the realism of Stendhal and that of Flaubert, we can understand why James accepted Hawthorne's description of his novels as romances. For James' relation to Hawthorne is like Flaubert's to the earlier realists, whose art Flaubert tried to supercede. James, as mentioned, took careful note of Flaubert's ambition to write a new kind of novel: it is not difficult to find a similar ambition embodied in his study of Hawthorne.[14]

This may be understood most easily through James' curious, but often convincing, discussion of Hawthorne's attitude to life, a discussion so curious it should have aroused more comment than it did from the romance critics, since it contradicts the idea, advanced by some of them, that American novelists were pessimistic about the human condition. This, for example, was the view of Harry Levin and Richard Chase, for whom the classic American novel possessed, as we saw, "the Manichaean quality of New England Puritanism" and embodied a "romantic nihilism, a poetry of force and darkness." James thought the contrary about Hawthorne,

> Puritanism projected from above, from outside, a black patch over his spirit, and it was for him to do what he could with the black patch. . . . But Hawthorne, of course, was exceptionally fortunate; he had his genius to help him. Nothing is more curious and interesting than this almost exclusively *imported* character of the sense of sin in Hawthorne's mind; it seems to exist there merely for an artistic or literary purpose. . . . But *his relation to it was only*, as one may say, *intellectual;* it was not moral and theological.[15]

We should not, James added, take too seriously "Hawthorne's relish of gloomy subjects," and "to speak of Hawthorne . . . as a *romancier pessimiste,* seems to me very much beside the mark." Neither an optimist nor a pessimist, Hawthorne is "ironical . . . but neither bitter nor cynical . . . rarely . . . tragical." From his books the "dusky preoccupation with the misery of human life and the wickedness of the human heart is totally absent."[16]

The reason for this, James finally concluded, was that Hawthorne belonged to an America that had vanished, an America that had rendered its inhabitants uncritical in their attitude to their society:

> Our hero was an American of the earlier and simpler type. . . . The generation to which he belonged, that generation which grew up with the century, witnessed during a period of fifty years the immense, uninterrupted material development of the young Republic; and when one thinks of the scale on which it took place, of the prosperity that walked in its train and waited on its course, of the hopes it fostered and the blessings it conferred—of the broad morning sunshine, in a word, in which it all went forward—there seems to be little room for surprise that it should have implanted a kind of superstitious faith in the grandeur of the country, its duration, its immunity from the usual troubles of earthly empires. This faith was a simple and uncritical one, enlivened with an element of genial optimism, in the light of which it appeared

that the great American state was not as other human institutions are, that a special Providence watched over it.[17]

Even the institution of slavery, although it cast "a faint shadow" in this picture was not sufficient "to darken the rosy vision of good Americans," a rosy vision that Hawthorne shared when he insisted that Pierce was right to resist "the mistiness of a philanthropic theory" and to defend the South's constitutional rights. This, contended James, demonstrated the naiveté of pre-Civil War Americans, which was "shattered by a social revolution as complete as any the world has seen."[18]

Let us set aside the possibility that Hawthorne, precisely because he was less optimistic than the abolitionists, foresaw that the attack upon slavery would lead to the horrifying Civil War, and opposed abolition on this humane ground. According to James, the Civil War was a decisive turning point in American history and in the mind of Americans because it introduced "a sense of proportion." In the future, the "good American" (he is thinking of himself) will be more "critical," hence, more of an "observer" than the good American of Hawthorne's day, who was "uncritical."[19]

James' discussion retains its brilliance, and in other chapters I shall return to it. I think it holds the key to many classic American novels—to their interests, their intensities, and their failure of insubstantiality. Here I want mainly to show how it bears on the idea of romance. In the preface to *The American* James stated that there is only one attribute, very like the one Hawthorne named, that distinguishes the romance from the novel. It is "experience disengaged, disembroiled, disencumbered, exempt from the conditions that we usually know to attach to it."[20] Romance arises from the portrayal of experience that is not a direct, minute expression of the actual social world as we know it. By this he does not mean, however, that the romance deals with completely arbitrary and improbable experience, for *The American,* which he believed to be a romance, is certainly no more arbitrary or improbable (it is a good deal less so) than, for example, *The Charterhouse of Parma.* James' remarks, however, can apply to that heightened imaginative projection, shading into the expressionism of Balzac, through which writers such as Stendhal and Hawthorne suggested both actual and ideal societies, especially since *The American* itself is notable for its melodramatic aura. If this is so, then, what distinguished the romance for James was that utopian vision which often stylized manners, and which was an attribute exemplified by many earlier novelists. This suggests that James would have used "romance" to designate not only the novels of Hawthorne, but most continental realism before Flaubert as well. As a matter of fact, he did so use the term, often without invidiousness: Stendhal was "the most powerful . . . of romancers," Balzac a "realistic romancer," George Sand wrote "romances."[21]

This is plausible not only because James himself remarked upon Flaubert's position in the history of realism, but also because, by James' own testimony, the Civil War represented for him the same thing that the revolution of 1848 did for Flaubert: the end of social and political optimism. It is true that he became less of an aesthete than Flaubert and had harsh words for most of Flaubert's work apart from *Madame Bovary*. Nevertheless, it is also true that James sometimes turns toward aestheticism.[22] Hence his novels, like Flaubert's, are less visionary and rely more upon verisimilitude than those of his predecessors. He is, as he said that good Americans of the post-Civil War period would be, an observer. Hawthorne, by contrast, is unpessimistic and uncritical not in any absolute sense, but because he, unlike James but like the pre-Flaubertian novelists, couches his ideals in social and political instead of aesthetic terms. Lacking James' "pessimism" he is not content to play the role of mere observer. By James' standards, which sometimes approach Flaubert's, Hawthorne may be considered a writer of romances but so, as suggested, would many of the early European novelists such as Stendhal. In other words, one part of the distinction was simply the result of a wish to appropriate the term "realism."

This view, however, is crossed and complicated by a second, invidious, yet related usage. We find it in James' belief that one of Hawthorne's characteristics is the use of fancy: "Hawthorne was a man of fancy," a little too often possessed of "a taste for conceits and analogies, which bears . . . the fanciful stamp." Because the "deeply imaginative" *House of the Seven Gables* "comes nearer to being a picture of contemporary American life"—that is to say, nearer to later realism—than any other of Hawthorne's novels, it is fair to conclude that for James, fancy and conceit, as opposed to the imagination, are attributes of the romance, the very attributes that make it inferior to realism. By this account "romance" does not name a form separate from but equal to the novel. It merely names an inferior habit into which Hawthorne, unfortunately, lapsed too often: "Hawthorne, to say it again, was not in the least a realist—he was not to my mind enough of one." What would have made Hawthorne a realist? James' answer is given as an objection to the title of an article on Hawthorne— "Un Romancier pessimiste"—when he observed that "pessimism consists in having morbid and bitter views . . . not in indulging in shadowy fancies and conceits."[23] The point is plain: had Hawthorne been more of a pessimist he would not have indulged in fancies and conceits. He would not, in other words, have been a writer of romances. Rather, he would have been—like James—"an observer," less "uncritical." In short, he would have been a realist of James' kind. But of course, if James' account of the impact of the Civil War is correct it is impossible that Hawthorne should have been other than what he was. His lack of pessimism was a function of his happy time and place—America before the Civil War—and his position as a "good American." Here, I believe, James finds the key to much of Hawthorne's insubstantiality, and therefore that of the tradition as a whole: insubstantiality is a function of an uncritical attitude toward

America itself. Hawthorne's fancies and conceits are a substitute for sustained, critical and imaginative observation.

We cannot take this too far; James was very far from saying that Hawthorne failed, nor would he have said that Hawthorne was unpessimistic or uncritical in an ordinary sense. Many of Hawthorne's characters, some of them sympathetic, have unpleasant fates. And it is undeniable that Hawthorne criticizes Puritan society in *The Scarlet Letter,* bourgeois society as embodied by Pyncheon in *The House of the Seven Gables,* the utopian commune and the city in *The Blithedale Romance,* and the circle of American expatriates in *The Marble Faun.* James' description of Hawthorne as unpessimistic and uncritical makes sense, however, in two ways: when we contrast the relative insubstantiality of Hawthorne's portrait of contemporary America in *The House of the Seven Gables* to that of, say, France in a novel such as *The Red and the Black;* and when we recall that James had the same relation to pre-Civil War American novelists that Flaubert had to the realist writers who were active before the revolution of 1848. In part, then, this second invidious usage, despite its often valid application, rejoins the neutral first.

"Romance," then, was not used by James as it is by the theory of the American romance, to distinguish between different artistic forms. We can allow it two meanings that slide into each other a little ambiguously. First, it refers, sometimes without invidiousness, to the novel of the first half of the nineteenth century—the novel of romantic realism. Second, "romance" means some bad fanciful habits that lead to a relative insubstantiality.

As he grew older, James came to regret that he had made the distinction in the first place. This is shown in "The Art of Fiction" when he criticized Walter Besant's discussion of the "modern English novel" because of Besant's "odd literal opposition of description and dialogue, incident and description." Such oppositions James argued, are "as little to the point as the equally celebrated distinction between the novel and the romanc—to answer as little to any reality." Not only did he state that the distinction is spurious, his remarks on the alleged difference between "the novel of character and the novel of incident" might almost have been written in anticipation of Richard Chase's contention that the classic American novel, because it is romance, "tends to prefer action to character," to the extent that "character becomes . . . somewhat abstract and ideal, so much so in some romances that it seems to be merely a function of plot."[24]

> When one says picture one says of character, when one says novel one says of incident, and the terms may be transposed at will. What is character but the determination of incident? What is incident but the illustration of character? It is an incident for a woman to stand up with her hand resting on a table and look out at you in a certain way. . . . At the same time it is an expression of character.[25]

He went on to call "romance" a "clumsy" term of "convenience," or else a conceit "simply for the pleasantness of the thing, as for instance when Hawthorne gave this heading to his story of *Blithedale*."[26] By this account, "romance" is without substance—a convenience that has lost its convenience for James. In what is perhaps his last reference to Hawthorne, in "Honore de Balzac" (1902), it has disappeared: "All painters of manners and fashions, if we will, are historians . . . Fielding, Dickens, Thackeray, George Eliot, Hawthorne among ourselves."[27] (James was not alone here; Nancy Mitford had written Hawthorne that *The Blithedale Romance* reminded her greatly of Balzac.)[28] In James, there is no traditional sanction for the view that the classic American novel is romance, in the sense of a separate, national form.

9

The Social Origins of the Classic American Novel

Let me summarize my criticisms. In its first and classic form—developed by Trilling, Bewley and Chase—the theory of the American romance was based upon consensus history. Like consensus history, it had two variants. It began with the idea that the novel arose with bourgeois society and incorporated its salient feature, cultural tension between its classes: first, between the aristocracy and the bourgeoisie; second, between the bourgeoisie and the working class. The United States, by contrast, had never known such tensions. It had never had an aristocracy, and the conflict of capital and labor had never had a cultural dimension. The theory depended upon a convincing distinction between class tension that is not cultural and one that is. Here, however, for the nineteenth century, the theory broke down.

One possibility was that American society had not been based upon class. Hence its social tensions had been insignificant. But neither variant of consensus history established this. Had American society lacked an ideology, this would suggest that class, after all, had been its basis. But even the presence of a single ideology would not have been important unless ideology itself had been the basis of society. This was unlikely, because ideological society, as Trilling observed, requires a powerful modern state and bureaucratic agencies—which did not exist in the America of the classic novelists.

Another possibility was suggested by the common denominator in the interpretation of Trilling, Bewley, and Chase: the absence of conflict between political ideologies. Perhaps, in Europe, ideological struggle had given class conflict its cultural dimension. However, if this is true, ideology, not class, had been the basis of culture there. For had the society been based on class, ideology would never have had this importance. Given that importance, Europe already would have had, in the nineteenth century, an ideological society—although one divided by opposing ideologies. Here, however, a contradiction arose. For the novel is traditionally thought to have grown from a society based upon class. The theory began with this traditional view. Then, unexpectedly, to contrast the novel to the American romance, it shifted its ground. Even if we ignore this, we still remain faced with three insoluble problems. First, conflict between political ideologies is not often evident in the classics of realism. Second, as American naturalism shows, this need not be present at all for respectable novels to be written. Third, as we shall see, so far as it was present in the European novel, it was present in the American.

In the second form of the theory, that of Kaul, the inadequacy of consensus history was assumed. Although Kaul allowed that American society had possessed distinctive features, he argued, reasonably, that these could not account for the development of a new form. However, he noticed that the American novel incorporated a concept of community—a standard by which the actual state of society might be criticized. This, and references of Hawthorne and James to Hawthorne's novels as romances, led him to believe that American novelists, under the influence of nationalism and utopianism, had deliberately turned from the European novel. However, their nationalism was unremarkable, even when it proved chauvinistic, since even chauvinism was not uncommon in Western societies at the time. Moreover, their utopian vision—the concept of community life—was merely a national variant of the vision of culture that informed the novel in Europe. Finally, "romance" for Hawthorne and James was in each case different from that supposed by Kaul. Hawthorne's prefaces define a "romance" that was consonant with the "novel" in Europe. For James "romance" was a term of convenience for a tradition of the novel earlier than his own (and for weak fanciful writing); and as he grew older he renounced even this usage.

The conclusion is inevitable. If the classic American novel is romance, its theory has yet to be developed. As a result, two alternatives present themselves. The first is to make another attempt. Some contemporary critics are doing this, and I shall come to them presently. The second is to abandon the theory. This is what I recommend, in the light of my fourth criticism, to which I now proceed. Contrary to the theory in its first version, Americans have, since the earliest settlements, known cultural tensions. Contrary to Kaul's version (in part), these actually were the basis of the American novel. The bourgeoisie (or middle class), of course, was one of the contending parties in these. In tension with it were classes, subclasses, and societies that were, if not aristocratic, distinctly not bourgeois: not in relations or culture, and not in ideology. Even when not "conservative," they were decidedly illiberal. In other words, the theory suffered not only from inconsistency, but from historical error. The social basis of the novel existed in America as in Europe, and in the same form. Kaul, in a sense thought so too, but he was so intent upon salvaging the theory that he did not discuss, except in a general way, the features of American society that had lent themselves to the novel. In particular he did not answer Trilling's contention that American society had not been marked by cultural tension between classes. It is time to do this now.

Before we begin, however, one more observation about the novel must be made. Trilling, when discussing its basis, always linked cultural tension with class, and rejected an ethnic alternative. Taken literally, this is too narrow; and certainly Trilling was aware of this: it was occasion that determined his emphasis. Nevertheless the point, although very simple, deserves some clarification.

It is true that in most novels the cultural tensions are those of class; but this is not always the case—as witness Tolstoy's *The Cossacks,* whose place in the tradition may be assumed. There, the cultural tension arises from the sojourn of Olenin, a cosmopolitan member of the gentry, late of Moscow, in Cossack society. The tension between Olenin and his hosts, which generates the drama of the novel, is not between classes in a single society, but the tension between different societies. This does not prevent it from being the basis for a brilliant study of manners, seen with satiric ambivalence. The point, once again, is to set a limit to historicism. For while changes in consciousness may be initiated by circumstance, they need not remain the slaves of circumstance: a discovery, once made, may become a permanent acquisition even in an alien environment, if it finds a receptive home. While the novel did not become important until the society that sustained it had itself become important, satiric ambivalence, once claimed by the novel, could be sustained by the novel itself. Tolstoy's Russia was by no means a developed bourgeois society: *The Cossacks* is a kind of international novel, comparing different societies that happened to reside in a backward, polyglot empire. But relations, ideas, and literature from the West had civilized that part of the gentry to which Tolstoy (and Olenin) belonged. As a result, Tolstoy could bring to his subject the ambivalent observation that the novel requires. *The Cossacks* is pertinent because, in subject, it resembles so many American novels.

With this qualification, we can mention classes, subclasses, and societies that were neither bourgeois nor liberal, and whose presence created cultural tension with the advance of American society. (1) First, tribal societies: among them the Indians; later, when American merchants had begun far-flung expeditions, the peoples of the Pacific. There is no doubt that the presence (and sometimes resistance) of these groups caused ambivalence among American writers. This was partly, of course, the result of a bad conscience: the romantic age liked to find the noble savage in any society too primitive to pursue profit. In addition, however, there was an awareness that tribal societies had virtues of their own: heroism, loyalty, knowledge of nature, woodcraft, honor, a sense of community, and dignity. Their institutions, moreover, were traditional in a sense not reserved for the term "liberal." Tribal societies, whether in the United States or not, had civilizations that deserved, and occasionally received, sympathy (*à la The Cossacks*) from writers such as Cooper and Melville.

(2) Next, the Puritans, although the choice might seem dubious, since the Puritan revolution brought the modern age to England. The Puritans were mer-

chants, farmers, villagers, and owners of private property. In what sense were they not bourgeois? The question might take the form of a riddle: when does a middle class not act like a middle class? The answer: when it is the New England patriciate.

The reason is given by Weber's distinction between two kinds of bourgeoisie: one traditional and "conservative," bearing the marks of the feudal past, with a corporate life, a passion for hierarchy, and often a passion for theocracy; the other modern and revolutionary—the entrepreneurs of popular imaginaton, the ones that "built America"—competitive, individualistic, and innovative. The distinction rests upon two kinds of capitalism: "political" and " modern industrial" (or "bourgeois"). Political capitalism, the older of the two, took profits from war, conquest, and political power. Although it passed through several phases, which Weber names imperialist, colonial, adventure, and fiscal, it was tied to the past. For whatever the phase, profit and expansion were subordinate to political directives, the goals of which were never only economic in aim. Bourgeois capitalism was its successful rival, based on the market, free labor, and the fixed plant: this was the capitalism of the political economists, the capitalism of unrestrained expansion.[1]

The Puritan patriciate, although American, was not in this sense bourgeois. Its economy was political capitalism, originally in its colonial form, with "prerogatives over conquered territories . . . politically guaranteed trading monopolies, shipping privileges, the politically determined acquisition and exploitation of the land as well as compulsory labor." As the colonial Puritans developed mercantile habits, they turned to the adventure form: "to charismatically lead raids on foreign countries" or to pacific, but still flamboyant, enterprises such as the Caribbean or the China trade. Weber's examples of political capitalists are the "the Italian city-states during the Middle Ages, the Hanseatic League, and the merchant adventurers of England."[2] The Puritans, if different, were closer to these than to the classes that displaced them. For unlike their brothers in Old England, they were little obliged to compromise with the age; their doctrine retained a pristine severity, and they laid it down in law. As a result their culture, especially in its early phase, was in most respects conservative, if we mean by this a culture hostile to private enterprise in almost every sense of the term. For a summary statement of how conservative it was, we can turn to the greatest historian of New England. As Perry Miller wrote "to understand Puritanism we must go behind . . . eighteenth-century developments to an age when the unity of religion and politics was . . . axiomatic."[3] What we find when we do go behind these developments is a society that is corporate, theocratic, hierachical, and dictatorial.

> Puritan philosophy demanded that in society all men, at least all regenerate men, be marshaled into one united array. The lone horseman, the single trapper, the solitary hunter was not a

figure of the Puritan frontier; Puritans moved in groups and towns, settled in whole communities, and maintained firm government over all units. Neither were the individualistic business man, the shopkeeper who seized every opportunity to enlarge his profits, the speculator who contrived to gain wealth at the expense of his fellows, neither were these typical figures of the original Puritan society. Puritan opinion was at the opposite pole from Jefferson's feeling that the best government governs as little as possible. The theorists of New England thought of society as a unit, bound together by inviolable ties; they thought of it not as an aggregation of individuals but as an organism, functioning for a definite purpose, with all parts subordinate to the whole, all members contributing a definite share, every person occupying a particular status.[4]

What we find, in short, is the world Hawthorne portrayed in *The Scarlet Letter* and in many of his tales.

(3) Next we come to the New York patroons and the North-eastern gentry for whom they set the tone. Here is one group in America like the European aristocracy, for the very good reason that its position, as Marius Bewley observed, was based upon "feudal tenure." This sustained "the vast manorial system that New York had inherited from colonial days," the jewel of which was "the great estate of Rensselaerwyck on the Hudson, covering an area of nearly eleven hundred square miles, and containing a number of villages and thousands of small farms."[5] The patroons, who established themselves not only in the countryside, but in New York city as well, evolved a life almost wholly at odds with the liberal culture around them: "all had their coats of arms, and history of knights and squires and manor houses." Theirs was "a spirit of aristocracy . . . foreign to the custom of the country; while others made their way into the wilderness to be rid of every vestige of the feudal system, these came to perpetuate so much of that tradition as could be saved."[6]

The patroon system was overthrown by the Anti-Rent War of the 1830s and 1840s chronicled by Cooper in the Littlepage trilogy. The victorious opponents were the tenants, who broke up the estates and turned the land over to themselves (and of course to a good many speculators), thereby establishing bourgeois property once and for all. The fall of the patroons, then, is a classic example of a cultural struggle of the kind Trilling named as the basis of the novel—between a conservative aristocracy and a rising bourgeoisie. The patroons of course, are an extreme case, but the gentry associated with them were less so, and their culture finds an echo not only in Cooper, but in Melville and Wharton among major novelists and in Irving and Brackenridge among minor ones.

(4) More important than the patroons, in both literature and history, were the Southern slaveholders. Because the production of the plantations was directed, in large measure, toward the market, efforts have always been made to see the slaveholder as a kind of entrepreneur, not very different from his Northern counterpart. These efforts have been unpersuasive, and the last notable

attempt, *Time on the Cross,* provoked a controversy that in the end discredited the book's thesis. In general, historians who have treated the slaveholders as a separate class have carried the day. In their view, the slaveholders were just what they thought themselves to be: "the closest thing to feudal lords imaginable in a nineteenth-century bourgeois republic."[7] That they were also culturally crude, does not, as W. J. Cash believed, count against this view in the least. As Eugene Genovese has sensibly observed, in their early stages most ruling classes, aristocracies among them, have been crude as well.

> It was, as I recall, Saint Jerome who observed that a rich man need not be a thief; he might be the son of a thief. . . . The question remains: What social vision informed these men's dreams? What kind of life did they seek for their children? Parvenus are parvenus, but bourgeois parvenus are not necessarily slaveholding parvenus once one gets beneath appearances.

> Whether or not they ought to be called "aristocrats" is a matter of definition, if not of taste. The essential point is that their acquisitiveness did not make them bourgeois.[8]

Nor is this all. The presence of the polemicist George Fitzhugh challenges the argument that the United States has never developed an influential conservative ideology. Fitzhugh's essays, as Genovese has demonstrated, were "the logical outcome of the Slaveholder's philosophy."[9] That this philosophy was the antithesis of liberalism is evident in its cardinal points: that one is human through dependence upon the wills of others; that men owe everything to society; that there are no inalienalble rights, but that rights, on the contrary, come only through the willingness of the many to alienate their property in their persons to others—which is the organic essence of society; and that only those with property in others should rule the state, with policies that sustain its natural order.

In other words, America developed a conservative and aristocratic tradition—but this was obscured by consensus history and ignored because it defended slavery and because the Civil War obliterated it. Yet it was impressive enough to have led the South to secede, and it commanded the respectful attention of writers as different as Twain and James.

(5) With the slaveholders, of course, is their complement, the slaves. It may be fairly wondered if, in culture, they have been adequately portrayed by either novelists or historians. In the pages of Genovese's *Roll, Jordan, Roll* (by most accounts, and in my opinion, a persuasive portrait), they have the look of a peasantry—collectivist, communal, with a strong sense of mutual aid, an aversion to economic calculation, a love of folk custom and song, and an abiding religion often laced with superstition. But that their culture had its own shape has been always allowed, and whatever it was, it was not middle-class. It generated, moreover, an ambivalent response in nineteenth-century Ameri-

cans. And this ambivalence found its way into literature, as *Uncle Tom's Cabin, Huckleberry Finn,* and *Pudd'nhead Wilson* make plain.

(6) Although the Civil War and the advance of capitalism destroyed the foundations of conservative culture in America, the American middle class continually sought contact with the European aristocracy. There is of course no need to establish aristocratic cultural difference, but to mention aristocratic influence despite its foreigness. That the aristocracy was foreign did not prevent it—any more than did the foreigness of tribal peoples—from leaving its mark on American culture. The international novel, of which Americans have been the chief practitioners, would be proof of this alone. But in other matters —for example, the passion of the robber barons for European art—the aristocracy had at least a negative influence, in that it stimulated a sense of cultural rivalry.

(7) The upper class itself was divided in a manner suggested by Weber: two corporate patriciates, the Brahmins of Boston and the merchants of Old New York, with ideals of republican virtue and civic humanism, were culturally at odds with the flamboyant entrepreneurs who represented the American future. They developed, especially the Brahmins, an urbanity not often associated with America: a paternal involvement in the life of their cities that was not purely economic, but organized for cultural ends in the arts, education, and urban design. Politically the influence of these two groups on the course of American history ended early, but in literature their significance lasted much longer, as expressed in the novels of Wharton and James.

(8) Finally, mention should be made of cosmopolitan communities standing apart from middle-class America, with little social significance, perhaps, but with distinctive cultures that did attract the attention of American novelists. I am thinking chiefly of two groups: first, the semi-bohemian society of artists, expatriates, and adventurers who wander through the novels of Hawthorne, James, and Wharton; second, the society of sailors, as we find in the novels of Cooper and Melville. In Melville's novels, especially, they appear as an international group with a life of its own, so self-defined that admission to it requires a painful initiation, and so little national that Melville, like Conrad, could write as an insider even when, as in *Billy Budd,* all the characters belong to a nation not his own.

Here then, is a list, admittedly schematic, of classes, subclasses, and societies that were neither (typically) middle class nor liberal, and that stood in odd relation to the march of liberal culture. In principle, novels could have been written about the tensions between members of these groups and members of that culture. The mention of novelists in the foregoing discussion suggests some that were. The only questions that remain are these: were such novels widespread and were they typical?

It cannot be an accident that all of the classic novelists sympathetically acquainted themselves with some of these groups. Cooper with the Indians (and the frontiersmen who had partially assimilated to them), the patroons and the European aristocracy; Hawthorne with the New England patriciate and the European aristocracy; Melville with the South Sea islanders, the slaves, and the patroons; Twain with the Southern aristocracy, the slaves, and the European aristocracy; James with the patriciates in New York and New England, and the aristocracies of the South and Europe; Wharton with the same groups as James. It is also a fact that these groups are found in a high percentage of notable American novels. The tensions between the Indians and the encroaching settlers—with the frontiersman Natty Bumppo caught between them—is one focus of Cooper's Leatherstocking tales. The intrusion of an American sailor into the culture of the South Sea islanders is the subject of Melville's *Typee;* a similar subject informs *Omoo;* and in *Moby Dick* it is Queequeg who establishes one of the novel's moral centers. The moral decline and fall of the New England patriciate is charted by Hawthorne in *The Scarlet Letter, The House of the Seven Gables,* with a slight displacement, in *The Blithedale Romance,* and in a large number of his tales. The rise and fall of the patroons and the related landed gentry are chronicled by Cooper in *The Pioneers* and the Littlepage trilogy, while Melville's *Pierre* examines the wretched career of one of the decadent scions of a patroon-like family. Members of the Southern aristocracy have central places in some of the greatest American novels: James' *The Bostonians;* Twain's *Huckleberry Finn, Pudd'nhead Wilson,* and (once removed by fantasy, in which they merge with the European aristocracy) *A Connecticut Yankee in King Arthur's Court.* Slaves occupy equally important positions in *Huckleberry Finn, Pudd'nhead Wilson,* and *Benito Cereno.* The European aristocracy finds its way into the novels of every single classic American novelist: Cooper's *Homeward Bound, Home as Found,* and *Satanstoe;* Hawthorne's *The Marble Faun;* Melville's *Redburn;* Twain's *Connecticut Yankee, The Prince and the Pauper,* and *The American Claimant,* and the majority of the novels of Henry James and Edith Wharton.

The presence of these groups in the classic American novel suggests that their relations, between themselves and with middle-class Americans representing the larger cultural tendency, were the social basis of the novel itself. From the cultural tensions they initiated, the American novelists found one motive that led to their search for a reforming cultural vision.

Another motive was tied to it. This was an abiding concern for the fates of "knowable communities" in the crisis of transformation: social, economic, and political.[10] American society, it is true, possessed some singular features: between the settlements were often vast tracts of wilderness, while, on the frontier, society itself sometimes hardly existed. But the classic American novels, when they are set at home, are chiefly concerned with the settlements, not with the spaces between them. New York and New England, already older than the Midwest is now, nurtured all the major American novelists except Twain. Their novels, accordingly, are very often set in the traditional, although changing, Northeast, or in places more ordered still; and only Cooper and Twain ever turn their attention to the frontier dispersal. But with Cooper, a case can be made that he was a better novelist in the "culture-making"[11] *Satanstoe* and *The Pioneers,* which describe the foundation of the communities that he knew and loved, than in the later Leatherstocking tales, so often unconvincing because, as Mark Twain argued, their characters and their actions lack credibility. As for Twain, it is true that in *Roughing It* we have an authentic frontier classic; but *Roughing It* is not fiction, and is exceptional in Twain's work. No one can fail to notice that the St. Petersburg of *Tom Sawyer* and *Huckleberry Finn* and the Dawson's Landing of *Pudd'nhead Wilson* are portrayed as substantial and rooted places—far more so, in fact, than the actual Hannibal upon which they were based. With Cooper's Templeton, they take their place beside Melville's New Bedford and Nantucket, and his floating communities, with Hawthorne's Salem, Hawthorne's and James' Boston, James' and Wharton's Old New York, and Wharton's Berkshire towns. The best of Cooper, and almost all the novels of Hawthorne, Melville, Twain, James, and Wharton, transpire in densely woven societies similar to those in European fiction.

The transformations the novelists examined were various, and, as in European fiction, they were rarely the obviously dramatic ones—unless, like the American Revolution (*The Spy, Israel Potter*), they were also removed in time. Nor are they often dealt with directly: their echo is caught (as in European novels) in personal relations and experience. One, however, deserves mention here, because I have alluded to it before, and because my point is the parallel between American and European cultural tensions. In *The English Novel from Dickens to Lawrence,* Raymond Williams argues that in England, in the late 1840s, there was a recognition of a crisis in society, owing to the massive changes wrought by industrializaton, urbanization, and increased democratizaton. This crisis provoked an astonishing creativity in the novel: within twenty months, in 1847–48, *Dombey and Son, Wuthering Heights, Vanity Fair, Jane Eyre, Mary Barton, Tancred, Town and Country,* and *The Tenant of Wildfell Hall* were published.[12] Now, the American novel never had such a simultaneous flowering, but the American Renaissance in all the *belles lettres* did, and almost at the same time. This argues, I believe, for a similar recognition of crisis, and one that continued to haunt the imaginations of American writers, especially the classic novelists, long after it had passed away. The Littlepage trilogy, *The Blithedale Romance, The House of the Seven Gables,* the majority of Melville's novels, and *Uncle Tom's Cabin* belong, both in composition and setting, to the 1840s and early 1850s. So, in setting, do *Tom Sawyer, Huckleberry Finn, Pudd'nhead Wilson, The Europeans, Washington Square,* and, in part, *Old New York.* What was the transformaton that drew the novelists to this time?

I believe Henry James, in *Hawthorne,* gives the answer when he speaks of "Old America"—as I shall henceforth call it—that republican period of great expectations destroyed by the Civil War. But if the Civil War was its quietus, its ending was long in preparation, and the novels that treat the 1840s and 1850s mirror the beginning of the end. The Littlepage trilogy's climax is the dispossession of the patroons, whose ineffectuality has a muffled echo in the flounderings of Melville's *Pierre.* The novels of James and Wharton capture the brittleness of the Northern urban patriciates in the breakdown between generations—the promising children dead, dispersed or defeated, the others too conventional to shoulder the burden of old republican distinction. Stowe and Twain probe not only the horrors of slavery, but the moral disorder among the slaveholders themselves: the weak gentility, the outbursts of violence, the inertia that erodes benign intentions. Melville's middle-class sailors, Hawthorne's middle-class communards and bohemians, Twain's subversive waifs and slaves—all testify to a great social and cultural restlessness, a breakdown and transformation of traditional roles. The crisis of "Old America," then, brought on by the pressures of development—Jacksonian democracy, slavery in the South, entrepreneurialism in the growing cities and on the land in the North, the settlement of the West—provoked the novelists to intense speculation on the state of American society and its culture—a speculation that also led them far afield, to investigate other societies and cultures. I do not say that the novels I have mentioned attempt a panoramic survey of the times: what I do claim is that the tensions of the times in society and culture were their animating force. And in this the American novelists were at one with their European contemporaries.

If all of this is true, a consequence follows: the social basis of most American novels was that of the novel in its classic intention. If this says nothing about the value of the novels, it says everything about the standards by which they should be judged. It suggests that Henry James was right after all, in a sense more literal than perhaps he intended: "I can think of no obligation to which the romancer would not be held equally with the novelist."[13]

There is no place here to test this austere precept on a large number of classic novels. Nevertheless, if we turn to one of them, Cooper's *The Pioneers,* we can find support for its view.

10

Cooper: Realism and "Romance"

"The 'cultivated American' at the present day has an old-time fondness for Cooper, which makes the smile in which he indulges on finding there are people who still read him a very kindly smile."[1] Thus Henry James in 1875, when Cooper's reputation (among writers) was in decline. James never undertook a criticism, but it is easy to infer why he held the opinion he did: like Scott (whom James much preferred), Cooper belonged to an earlier generation of writers for whom careful craft and verisimilitude were not priorities. James, Howells and Twain—our Victorian trinity—spanning the spectrum of later realism, were, in effect, agreed on the lack of artistry, the failures of characterization, the rank improbability, the melodrama, the "romance" to be found in Cooper's tales.

Cooper's defenders have generally carried the day, to the extent that he is still read and studied. At the least, he is usually thought (and I find him so myself) an attractive historical figure: intelligent, cultivated, cosmopolitan, and a writer of impressive energy—probably the most distinguished man-of-letters to precede the American Renaissance, and the most interesting novelist before Hawthorne.

There has been an ambiguity to the reputation, however, for his admirers have been of two kinds. Beginning with Brownell's *American Prose Masters,* one kind grants some of the faults that Mark Twain, for example, found in him, or argues that Twain was in error.[2] This defense has often conceded that Cooper is not a great writer, but that his faults are balanced by virtues the realists themselves approved. Cooper, in this view, is a social novelist—with Scott, a writer of "romance" only in the sense of romantic realism, and therefore a precursor to later realism, and belonging in this sense with the realists themselves. His novels are valued for the quality, supposedly un-American, of substantiality: that is, for their systematic, critical, and interesting observations of custom, class, and social relations. They are, indeed, preeminently concerned with cultural struggle, and contain a large amount of detailed social history—a fact almost sufficient in itself to refute the idea that American society was unsuitable terrain for the novel.

The other admirers were the romance critics. They also often admitted Cooper's faults, but found his compensating virtues not in realism, but in myth. The myth they admired (for its effects) was the myth of the frontiersman. This, as Richard Chase argued, "imaginatively recaptured and enhanced" Cooper's social ideal: a "shared harmonious social order in which a hereditary aristocracy dwells in country mansions while on the border of its lands Natty Bumppo stalks the forests." And this was especially so when accompanied by the writing admired by the romance critics themselves, with "ideal and abstract" characters who are "two-dimensional types . . . not complexly related to each other or to the past . . . [but] in ideal relation," and whose origins are often "envelop[ed] in mystery." They tended to admire, in other words, some of the characteristics other admirers have not. Chase himself—although be did not overrate Cooper—threw down the gauntlet when he claimed that Cooper had "some of the gifts of a true novelist and more of those of a romancer."[3] His talents, in short, were really mythopoeic instead of realistic. When Cooper wrote of the frontier, he wrote romance, and approached greatness; when he wrote of a settled society, and especially of his own class, he wrote realistically, and usually poorly— although *Satanstoe* received some esteem.

In fact, this account was misleading, although not simply because of the emphasis on myth—which, as we shall see in a moment, had a legitimate place. Cooper sometimes wrote romance when he treated society and sometimes wrote realistically of frontiersmen and Indians—even of Natty and Chingachgook. My view is that, whatever the distribution of "romance" and realism in his work, the passages of realism are usually the more successful. (His landscapes are claimed by both kinds of his admirers.) This is not to say that Cooper is never successfully mythopoeic, but that his myths are stronger when they are not abstract. If this is so, a question follows: Why did the romance critics often like Cooper at his weakest?

The answer can be seen most clearly in *The Pioneers,* whose virtues are all realistic. It benefits, first of all, from the vividness, widely acknowledged, of Cooper's recreation of Templeton and its frontier way of life. The testimony of D. H. Lawrence has often been quoted for its beauty; it is so beautiful that here it is again:

> Perhaps my taste is childish, but these scenes in *The Pioneers* seem to me marvelously beautiful. The raw village street, with woodfires blinking through the unglazed windowchinks on a winter's night. The inn, with the rough woodsman and the drunken Indian John; the church, with the snowy congregation crowding to the fire. Then the lavish abundance of Christmas cheer and turkey-shooting in the snow. Spring coming, forests all green, maple-sugar taken from the trees: and clouds of pigeons flying from the south, myriads of pigeons, shot in heaps; and night-fishing on the teeming, virgin lake; and deer hunting.[4]

More important (and here Cooper's reading of Austen served him well), the inhabitants of Templeton are convincing precisely because no one is idealized or rendered abstractly. Judge Temple, for example, because his circumstances resemble those of Cooper's father, is often taken to be Cooper's spokesman, and, in social vision, he largely is, but neither his background nor his character is sentimentalized. The Judge is a man of great estate, but in chapter 2—a fascinating account, worthy of Balzac, of the rise of the post-revolutionary ruling class in the tidewater hinterland—his position is shown to be of purchase, not descent, and his money has not been won entirely by ability. His family's fortunes have been checkered and he himself has risen through commerce, an alliance with a bona fide landed gentleman—a combination familiar in the eighteenth century—and the hazards of revolution, in which the role he played was equivocal. The Judge, in fact, is a *parvenu,* and some of his pretensions are exposed with a wit that anticipates Veblen. His house, for example (Cooper is often good with houses), in which he takes much pride, is not perfectly appointed:

> The walls were hung with a dark, lead-coloured English paper, that represented Brittania weeping over the tomb of Wolfe. The hero himself stood at a little distance from the mourning goddess, at the edge of the paper. Each width contained the figure, with the slight exception of one arm of the General running over on to the next piece, so that when Richard essayed, with his own hands, to put together this delicate outline, some difficulties occurred, that prevented a nice conjunction, and Brittania had reason to lament, in addition to the loss of her favorite's life, numberless cruel amputations of his right arm.

Nevertheless, despite its grotesqueness, the house succeeds in its purpose: it does impress upon the community that the Judge is its leading citizen.

The Pioneers, then, has the satiric ambivalence of a true novel. Its major and minor characters are at once socially typical and individualized: very rarely are we invited to pass simple judgment upon them. Judge Temple, *parvenu* that he is, nevertheless has an abiding concern for the welfare of his community. His interpretation of that welfare, conditioned by his status, is self-serving, but not at all hypocritical. Nor does the Judge abuse the popular understanding of his prerogatives. His attempts to impose the rule of law, to develop the economic potential of the town, to direct its expansion while restraining the entrepreneurial ambitions of Richard Jones and Hiram Doolittle, and to protect the ecology of the countryside are clearly submitted for our approval. The Judge has personal failings, and Cooper—as shown in the Judge's first encounter with Natty and Effingham—highlights his insensitivity. But in his public role as Templeton's leading citizen, the Judge's lack of breeding is balanced by his developed sense of noblesse oblige; and the potentially exploitative nature of his position is insignificant beside his positive role in reconciling the conflicting interests of Templeton's inhabitants, thereby establishing a sense of community among people of disparate backgrounds lately thrown together in a single location.

Something similar can be said, for once, about his antagonist, Natty Bumppo. (Despite his greater antipathy, Oliver Effingham is hardly that. As the scion of a landed family upon whose ruin the Judge's fortunes have been built, his interests and the Judge's are reconcilable, as his marriage with Elizabeth makes plain.) It is always a pleasure to find Natty here, not yet the idealization he was to become, so vividly characterized: at once a figure of fun and a tragic representative of a dying way of life. His personal failings, unlike those of the Judge, are a lack of formal education and rough manners: he never understands the Judge's rationale of law, and his appearance and manners provide the occasion for some humorous observation, but his conduct is often superior to the Judge's, as is his sense of dignity. His personal superiority has led some readers to suppose in Cooper a confusion of purpose, but Cooper's handling of the conflict between Natty and the Judge is convincing. Natty's individualism is shown to be admirable, but rooted in a life made obsolete by the advance of the civilization that Cooper finally endorses. Cooper's social theme is the dispossession of the native Americans (represented by Indian John) and the quasi-anarchistic frontiersmen by the plantations of those squires who, in alliance with the patroons (with whom they tended to merge), became the ruling class in upstate New York. This process is made poignant by the presence of Natty; but the Judge has not only civilization, but history on his side. Cooper's success in rendering Natty's virtues while exposing their impotence against historical advance allows us to understand why Balzac, for example, took Cooper as one of his masters. It is a measure of the quality of *The Pioneers* that Natty's self-imposed exile, which the Judge does not understand, does not appear as capricious self-denial, but as the appropriate end of an irreconcilable conflict between two goods. Natty's mythic presence does indeed enhance Cooper's social ideal, which is beautifully suggested, and is all the more persuasive because its fragility has been realistically observed. Emerging from its defeat in actuality, it indicates the limitations of the society that denies its possibility. In such moments, Cooper is an admirable tragi-comic and realistic artist.

The disabling romance of *The Pioneers* comes from an unexpected source—unexpected, as we are accustomed to finding romance in the woods and realism in the salon. It is introduced by Oliver Effingham, whose failure to come to life is generally admitted, but usually on the grounds that he is one with the flat gentlemen and "females" who litter Cooper's work. To an extent this is true, and provides an issue to come back to: it is strange, after all, that Cooper should often fail with the class he knew best. But Effingham stands a little apart from the ordinary Cooper gentleman: he emerges from the forest, his origins cloaked in mystery and the subject of coy speculation. What we learn about his past is fantastic in detail; and his language is abstract and stylized. Owing to his woodcraft, a heroic aura surrounds him. While he is given the faults of youth— rashness, a tendency to prejudice, and so on—none of these are social in origin: otherwise, he is a paragon. And as the long-lost avenging heir come back to reclaim his usurped patrimony, Effingham plays an archetypal role. He is, in other words, a figure of romance. The difference between his presentation and Natty's can be illustrated by two passages. First Natty:

> He was tall, and so meagre as to make him seem above even the six feet that he actually stood in his stockings. On his head, which was thinly covered with lank sandy hair, he wore a cap made of fox-skin. His face was skinny, and thin almost to emaciation; but yet bore no signs of disease; on the contrary, it had every indication of the most robust and enduring health. The cold and the exposure had, together, given it a colour of uniform red; his grey eyes were glancing under a pair of shaggy brows that overhung them in long hairs of gray mingled with their natural hue; his scraggy neck was bare, and burnt to the same tint as his face. . . . A kind of coat, made of dressed deerskin, with the hair on, was belted close to his lank body. . . . On his feet were deerskin moccasins . . . after the manner of the Indians, and his limbs were guarded with long leggings of the same material as the moccasins, which . . . had obtained for him . . . the nickname of Leather-stocking.

This is at once concrete and realistic in its critical examination of social experience. The details are not only vivid, but so selected that, with the half-humorous, half-heroic phrasing, they suggest at once an intensely independent, idiosyncratic character, and the way of life he represents. To put it another way, his humanity and his social existence are simultaneously evoked; to a large degree they are shown to be mutually dependent. Here, by contrast, is the initial description of Oliver Effingham:

> On entering the apartment he had mechanically lifted his cap, and exposed a head, covered with hair that rivalled in colour and gloss the locks of Elizabeth. Nothing could have wrought a greater transformation, than the single act of removing the rough fox-skin cap. If there was much that was prepossessing in the countenance of the young hunter, there was something noble in the rounded outlines of his head and brow. The very air and manner with which the member haughtily maintained itself over the coarse, and even wild attire, in which the rest of his frame was clad, bespoke not only familiarity with a splendour that in those new settlements was thought to be unequalled, but something very like contempt also.

> The hand that held the cap, rested lightly on the little ivory mounted piano of Elizabeth, with neither rustic restraint, nor obtrusive vulgarity. A single finger touched the instrument, as if accustomed to dwell on such places. His other arm was extended to its utmost length, and the hand grasped the barrel of his long rifle with something like convulsive energy. The act and the attitude were both involuntary, and evidently proceeded from a feeling much deeper than that of vulgar surprise.

The difference can be seen at once: Natty has a "skinny face" and Effingham has a "prepossessing . . . countenance." Effingham's is an abstract description. Instead of the closely observed and evocative details that sustain the portrait of Natty, we have "something noble in the rounded outlines of his head and brow," "the single finger accustomed . . . to dwell in such places," the hand that grasps "with convulsive energy," the flabby rhythm and alliteration of "neither rustic restraint, nor obtrusive vulgarity," and the vulgar concern with "vulgarity" itself. We never know exactly what was prepossessing, never see that noble something on the brow, or understand just what it was about that finger that suggested it was accustomed to dwell in such places. As a person, Effingham is not there: he lacks substantiality.

He is there symbolically. Like Hester Prynne, Fabrice del Dongo, and many central characters of the nineteenth-century novel, he is a Janus-faced figure who embodies an ideal world—the very myth, in fact, that the conflict between Temple and Natty has evoked. At home with the rifle and piano, glossy locks under a hunter's cap, he is a myth, Cooper's social ideal incarnate—or would be, if we could believe in him—a "world historical" figure, of the kind described by Lukacs:

> Not a hero like others but one who concentrates in himself all the forces at a particular time: as a character he brings certain influences to the point of action and becomes himself a determining influence . . . the hero [is] one who brings to dramatic focus the social forces that are embodied in himself and thus opposes them.[5]

There is a difference, however, between Hester, Fabrice, and Effingham. Unlike Effingham, but like Natty, Hester and Fabrice are not only symbols; each lives as a human fact; each is particularized, hence personalized—and yet each retains all of, indeed more than, Effingham's symbolic force. Nor can the difference be explained by saying that Effingham is a romance character, hence abstract and two-dimensional. For here the inadequacy of the idea of "abstraction" and "two-dimensionality" in the idea of the American romance becomes evident.

In the great medieval romances, the characters are often abstractly and two-dimensionally conceived, as is, for example, the Green Knight in *Sir Gawayne and the Grene Knight*. But, first of all, this is not always true: Sir Gawayne himself really does approach three-dimensionality. He may be *the* courteous knight, but he is also Gawayne, and his courtesy is bought at the price of more anguish than Effingham (or, to anticipate, Natty after *The Pioneers*) is ever allowed: his response to the Green Knight's wife is acute, and acutely observed. Second, even the Green Knight himself, although abstractly conceived, is not abstractly executed: every gesture, every detail, down to the shade of his color, is vividly noted—and again, his symbolic value is not compromised. On the contrary, the better medieval romancers seem to have realized that if a character was going to be mythic, symbolic, *and* divorced from social fact, there was a greater, not a lesser, need to individualize him. Realism can sometimes get by, with minor characters, by neglecting personality, and by portraying characters in their typical functions. But this is impossible when a character is like the Green Knight. And if the Green Knight is not quite three-dimensional, he does not, in any case, represent a human possibility. Finally, the strangeness of characters like the Green Knight, and the bizarre, often magical events they initiate, although disruptive of situations (the Green Knight certainly startles Arthur's court), take place in an extraordinary universe where such things "naturally" happen.

By these criteria, neither Oliver Effingham, nor I believe, very many so-called romance characters in American literature pass inspection. (One that does, I believe, is the white whale.) What would it have cost Cooper to have particularized Effingham's description, to have shown him as a person as well as a symbol? For especially in a world not governed by heaven or magic, it is when ideals are incarnated in character that we begin to take ideals seriously, that we say to ourselves, "yes that might be possible," even when its actual possibility is denied in the story, as in *The Scarlet Letter* or *The Charterhouse of Parma,* and as in the rest of *The Pioneers.* However, in letting a character live, an author faces two difficulties: first, he has to believe, imaginatively, in the character's possibility; second, he has to release him to readers who will respond to him as a person and as a member of a class, that is to say, with a measure of ambivalence. In the case of Effingham (and, I believe, in the case of many "romance" characters, by Cooper and other authors), both difficulties may have been at work. Almost certainly Cooper did not believe in the reconciliation Effingham offers—that the conflict between Temple and Natty is irreconcilable would seem to suggest this. But I think it even more likely that he did not wish to risk ambivalence, for fear of inviting ambivalence toward what Effingham represents. In either case, character is sacrificed to symbol, but at the price of the reader's interest (this reader's interest, at any rate) in what the symbol represents. And when symbol is insisted upon in this way, we can say that the imagination has been abandoned for ideology, in the definition of Trilling: "the habit or the ritual of showing respect for certain formulas to which, for . . . reasons [of] emotional safety, we have very strong ties of whose meaning and consequences in actuality we have no clear understanding."[6] Is not romance character, as the romance critics defined it, just this—a formulaic abstraction, without a clear link to actuality, whose virtue (or lack of it) is insisted upon? Does not this evoke James' criticism of Hawthorne as well: that uncritical fancy substitutes for sustained and critical imagination? Effingham, then, is an ideological symbol, a symbol of emotional safety, and he is the precursor to other such symbols, not only in Cooper, but in other novelists as well. What meanings does he have that Cooper does not want to put at risk?

There are two, I believe. The first is the more local and concerns Effingham's class existence. Effingham, as an abstract character, does not invite an ambivalent response. He is there to be accepted or rejected out of hand, and once it is clear that his motives are pure we are urged to accept him uncritically, with the things he represents. One of these things, it turns out, is a significant part of the landed gentry: that part whose position has been inherited rather than won. This differentiates him from Judge Temple, and it marks him rather than Temple as the precursor to the wooden heroes of Cooper's novels of contemporary life, all of whom are to the manor born. This touches upon the reason why many (not all) of Cooper's gentry are uninteresting. Here, from *Home as Found,* we see the gentry's conception of itself in the mind of Eve Effingham, a descendent of Oliver's:

> Eve actually fancied that the position of an American gentleman . . . had no superior, with the exception of those who actually ruled . . . this fact, she conceived, rendered him more than noble, as nobility is usually graduated. She had been accustomed to seeing her father and John Effingham moving in the best circles of Europe, respected for their information and independence, undistinguished by their manners, admired for their personal appearances, manly, courteous, and of noble bearing and principles, if not set arbitrary rule connected with rank. Rich, and possessing all the habits that properly mark refinement, of gentle extraction, of liberal attainments, walking abroad in the dignity of manhood, [they had] none between them and the Deity.

Cooper's gentlemen are usually all of this; unfortunately they are often only this. (We see "their etiquette instead of their manners,"[7] as Chase put it.) If Cooper rarely shows them warts and all, it is because he doesn't want to show the warts. It is not that the gentry lacked manners, but that Cooper downplays their manners, which are at one with their class and their humanity, and, by abstractly idealizing, he empties the gentry of their humanity. Like Effingham, they are insubstantial. In *The Pioneers,* and in other novels, there is a tendency to hypostatize the world of the gentry—on Effingham's mythic coattails, as it were—out of social history altogether, and to deny their class traits, for all that they are also a class. The problem, however, is not simply Cooper's belief in an oddly republican version of the myth of the aristocracy—the idea that aristocratic rule represents the natural order of things. Most, if not all, of the great nineteenth-century writers needed some kind of "myth": it was after all one with their reforming vision of culture. Indeed, as readers, we want them to evoke their vision vividly, whatever it may be, in order that we may measure our own way of life against it. The problem is that, when characters are not only abstractly conceived, but abstractly executed, we are not allowed to see, or to judge, what the reality they represent would actually mean. Myth, when thus abstractly offered, is not used as it is in *Sir Gawayne,* as a means of exploring experience more fully; it is a vehicle of ideology.

The myth of the aristocracy does, however, pose a fatal problem of form for *The Pioneers.* On the one hand, we have the plot of Natty and Temple, of which one meaning is that history is inexorable and sweeps all antiquated forms, however attractive, into its notorious dustbin. On the other hand, in the Effingham subplot (subplot, for that is how we remember it), we have an attempt to exempt from history a historical order: a society governed by a "hereditary" gentry. The meanings of the two plots are irreconcilable. In *The Pioneers,* at least, the Effingham subplot is not important enough to destroy the value of the novel. But in his contemporary novels—such as *Homeward Bound, Home as Found,* and *The Redskins*—which attempt to analyze the dispossession of the gentry and, at the same time, to affirm the gentry's natural right to its position, Cooper defeats himself before he begins. His failure is striking when we consider that *Homeward Bound* and *Home as Found* are sequels to *The Pioneers,* while *The Redskins* is the third of a trilogy whose earlier volumes, *Satanstoe* and *The Chainbearer,* are two of the works upon which Cooper's reputation rests. Two reasons for the failure of the contemporary novels are clear. They are thematically (hence formally) incoherent, and their aristocratic characters often fail to live, even as Cooper insists upon the superiority of their way of life.

It is not only his aristocratic characters who fail to live. In the other novels of the Leatherstocking saga it is often Natty and Chingachgook. Natty and Chingachgook are, of course, larger creations than Oliver Effingham, and I would not want to insist upon their absolute failure. But I think it inconsistent that critics who allow that Cooper fails with Effingham in *The Pioneers* and with many of the gentry elsewhere also insist on the general success of the later Natty. For the problem is the same:

> Notwithstanding his years, and his look of emaciation, if not of suffering, there was that about this solitary being however, which said that time, and not disease, had laid its hand heavily on him. His form had withered, but not wasted. The sinews and muscles, which had once denoted great strength, though shrunken, were still visible; and his whole figure had attained an appearance of induration, which, if it were not for the well known frailty of humanity, would have seemed to bid defiance to the further approaches of decay.

This is the opening description of Natty in *The Prairie.* We see only the state of his muscles—everything else is simply imputed to him ("There was that about this" . . . "an appearance of" . . .). It might just as well be Oliver Effingham grown old. Natty becomes an abstract symbol, and therefore less of a person, just to the extent that he is deprived of specific traits, among them, class traits. This means that he is even deprived of a believable language. As Twain remarked, *à propos The Deerslayer,* he slides from the genteel to the primitive so incongruously that we sometimes attend to him with comic expectation.[8] Now this was no more of a necessary process than in the case of Effingham: as Temple and Natty himself in *The Pioneers* show, class traits were readily available to Cooper and he had them firmly in hand: here Temple and Natty are successful as characters and symbols.

What changes is Natty's role. No longer rancorous, as in *The Pioneers* (although he continues to avoid civilization), he becomes the helper, instead of the antagonist, of the gentry, preserving them from ferocious Indians (*The Last of the Mohicans*), or, as it may be, squalid plebeian squatters (*The Prairie*). Again, the failure is not that he has a new role, but that Cooper withholds his humanity. This is one reason, I believe, that all the later Leatherstocking tales are tales of violent action and pursuit: the animation is compensation for this. As Chase put it (triumphantly): "Natty Bumppo begins as a real man, and then, by gradual accretion, legendary tales and folklore gather about him until he and his adventures and companions are transformed into general myth."[9] Just so: but again, if Don Quixote, with whom Chase compared him, could succeed as both man and myth, why not Natty Bumppo? The answer, I believe, is the same: we are not to be ambivalent toward Natty in his role as preserver of the gentry. As a paragon and protector whose virtue is never in doubt, and whose talents, nearly magical, ensure his potency, he too becomes a symbol of emotional safety. Nor, as we shall see in a moment, is he alone.

Why did Cooper feel obliged to abandon the realism for which he was genuinely gifted for romance? F. R. Leavis thought that, despite real talent, he was spoiled by the bad influence of Scott.[10] I believe the answer lies in the history of his times, which returns us to a theme of the last chapter: the crisis of "Old America." Cooper was himself a member of that great landed gentry, comprised of wealthy squires, the patroons, and the Southern aristocracy, which had, through the Virginia dynasty and the Adams faction of the Federalist party, controlled the political parties and the political life of the early republic. Its peculiar synthesis of democratic politics, both capitalist and seigneurial economics, and aristocratic manners was a transient combination at best, despite the tears that have been shed for it by generations of nostalgic historians. Between the date of *The Pioneers* (1823) and the time Cooper turned to the writing of contemporary fiction (1838), this class, or rather, coalition of similar classes, had begun to lose its grip. The symbolic date is the election of 1824, when neither of the major candidates (Quincy Adams and Jackson) shared the gentry's Jeffersonian vision of an enlightened yeoman republic in which slave labor would have quietly disappeared, but not the moral restraints upon rapacious entrepreneurs. (Although Quincy Adams represented something perhaps compatible with this, his presidency would be a failure.) Thereafter, as the nation drifted to crisis, the gentry in the North was displaced by a new ruling class of industrial capitalists in alliance with yeoman farmers, not of the self-sufficient and morally restrained variety imagined by Jefferson, but of the ordinary entrepreneurial kind that broke up the estates of the patroons. Here democratic politics, bourgeois values, and capitalist economics triumphed. In the South, the gentry lost its Jeffersonian patina and attachment to the enlightenment as it transformed itself into a class romantically and aggressively attached to slavery. Here the spread of seigneurial agriculture and aristocratic values triumphed.[11] Because Cooper was a very self-conscious New Yorker, only the Northern development finds a place in his fiction, but even though he knew his subject at first hand, and had grasped its importance immediately, he was incapable of persuasively rendering it. Faced with the prospect of recording the decline of his own class, Cooper, in his contemporary novels, imaginatively broke down, as the Littlepage trilogy, which chronicles the rise and fall of the patroons, shows: it is generally agreed that as it approaches the present it becomes increasingly tendentious. (Marius Bewley, who claimed greatness for Cooper, called *The Redskins* "a declamatory failure.")[12] One strength of *The Pioneers* is the connection it makes between the rise of the gentry, as exemplified by the fortunes of Judge Temple, with the movement of history. However, it is exactly this movement that Cooper is unable to treat dispassionately and ambivalently whenever it points to the gentry's demise. As a result, Cooper cut himself off from one of his strengths in his contemporary novels, which nobody believes are successful. He became incapable of seeing the struggle of the gentry and its opponents in complex social, historical, and moral terms. He came to see it only in the simplistic terms of the romance, as Chase described them—an opposition of Manichaean dichotomies and categorical alternatives.

In order to have succeeded in a contemporary novel Cooper would have had to have examined the representatives of the gentry with the satiric ambivalence and dispassionate objectivity that he ' displayed towards all the major characters (save Effingham) in *The Pioneers*. This he could not do because of his partisan refusal to acknowledge the logic of the gentry's decline. Only when his materials did not suggest that decline was Cooper secure enough to treat the gentry critically. He succeeded only when his novels were set in the days of the gentry's rise—in other words, in the past. The fact that the vast majority of his novels are historical seems to indicate his recognition of this difficulty.

The Pioneers remains Cooper's closest approximation to a successful contemporary novel. But its action is set at a generation's remove, and a generation represents a more significant span in this novel than it does, for example, in European novels such as *The Charterhouse of Parma* and *Middlemarch*. For when we speak of the historical novel as opposed to the realist novel what is at issue is not an amount of time, but the relative continuity of the society an author writes about with the one in which he lives. Historical fiction rather than realism is the result whenever a fundamental social change has intervened between the period of the action in the novel and the time when the novel was written. By this standard *The Pioneers,* with its primitive and "remote" setting, is a historical novel—as is *The Chuoans*—while *The Charterhouse of Parma* and *Middlemarch* are not, even though the time between the actions of all these novels and the dates of their composition was roughly the same.

Even in a generally successful work such as *The Pioneers,* as the example of Effingham shows, Cooper was not immune to the temptation to idealize inherited class, but Judge Temple is such a splendid creation that we forgive this. But the tendency toward "romance" remained, and appears in other parts of his work. Not only the gentry and Natty, but other frontiersmen and often the Indians are perceived in the terms of abstract myth. So are events: not only Natty's exploits, a fact which rightly vexed Mark Twain, but some turns of plot, the improbability of which is not mitigated, as in medieval romance, by their taking place in a magical world. (Cooper's world is heavily furnished, and it is historical.) This tendency has its strangest manifestation in *The Redskins,* when the patroons are brought to the threshold of doom. Here, where an impossible alliance between frontiersmen, Indians, and gentry saves the day (for a moment), Cooper comes to see, irrationally, the fate of the Indians and the frontiersmen to be bound to that of the gentry—as if he had not, in *The Pioneers,* already shown that the rise of the gentry had determined the fate of the frontiersmen and the Indians in the first place. The key to Cooper's failure here, as with the later Natty, is to understand not only that he admired the frontiersmen and the Indians, but that he was able to admire them because, although opposed to the gentry, they posed no threat to the gentry in the present. Meanwhile, they were also opposed to the groups that really did threaten the gentry's way of life. This, and the fact that the frontiersmen and Indians had not despoiled the wilderness before it had been properly appropriated, allowed them to be enlisted, symbolically, as mythic protectors in Cooper's cause against the entrepreneurs, bounty hunters, and squatters—the Hurry Harrys, the Bushes, the Newcomes, The Thousandacres—he really feared. The irony is that these despised characters are often his vivid ones. Opportunity Newcome (wonderful name) is the liveliest person in *The Redskins,* while the portrayal of the Bushes in *The Prairie* deserves all the praise it has received. What is common to all of them is not that they are less mythic or symbolic than his good characters, but that Cooper does not transform them into abstractions.

This, of course, does not dispose of Cooper, nor am I trying to do so. When he was able to relax, as he was in *Satanstoe,* secure in the knowledge that the dispossession of the patroons was far away, he was able to create a believable hero, in Cornelius Littlepage, along the lines of Oliver Effingham. He was even able to satirize his gentry gently, as when he shows the heroine's prudishness turning her from her English suitor (who shocks her with a performance of *The Beaux Stratagem*) and to the hero. In *Wyandotté,* the satire goes deeper: the naiveté of the gentleman hero leads to his murder; the struggle for the land is viewed almost cynically; some of the important characters settle in England. Even Natty, in *The Deerslayer,* recovers some credibility: his youth lends his unformed character a dramatic appropriateness. All I have tried to do here is to identify a weakness in Cooper's work that has sometimes been taken as a virtue because it is "romance"—when I think it really is an unwillingness or inability to put certain ideals at risk by embodying them in credible characters who might invite an ambivalent response. That is why I have called the symbolic embodiments of these ideals ideological, or symbols of emotional safety. This is no brief for verisimilitude, but it does challenge the idea, odd, to my mind, that abstract conceptions require abstract execution in order to be mythic. An abstractly executed myth is a pale myth, and medieval romance suggests no warrant. This is one reason why I do not believe we can call American "romance" a genre. In addition, the classlessness of characters reflects not the relative absence of class in American society, as the romance critics supposed, but is, in part, a response to fears very much rooted in class.

It would be unfair, however, to leave the matter simply in class terms, although Cooper is indeed one of the more class-conscious American novelists. For in addition to class, there is in Cooper a genuine concern for social harmony (Effingham suggests this too) and for civilization—for a society that would provide the means and leisure to allow contemplation, the life of the spirit, and (although Cooper is weak here) sensual pleasure—at the least, the visual delight in art and nature. The genuine link between his gentry and Natty is that both have the means to pursue these things—the gentry, because they are rich, and Natty, because he is self-sufficient and has avoided the routine of ordinary labor. This concern is merged with Cooper's democratic hopes and fears, and I think it is partly our sense of these things that prevents us from simply dismissing Cooper's criticisms of the restless lower orders as class prejudice. Indeed, his criticisms are often convincing. This is the second of the meanings I mentioned earlier that Cooper wishes to protect: Effingham and the later Natty not only further the cause of the gentry, they establish social harmony (Effingham in his person, Natty by defeating malign forces) and protect civilization itself. But if the concern is part of Cooper's quality, his way of presenting it often is not.

Cooper, in both his virtues and his defects, is an important and representative figure. He instances what would be, in the nineteenth century, a central problem for the American novel. Henry James had identified it in *Hawthorne:* the unstable mixture of realism and uncritical, because abstract, "romance." Some of his difficulties—for example, the inhibitions that his class consciousness imposed upon his imaginative freedom—are of course his own. Nevertheless, the conflict between a meretricious kind of "romance" and an artistically impressive realism extended throughout the century. We find, I believe, in the work of later writers, similar symbols of emotional safety or incidents that suggest the need. We need think only of the lucky death of Pyncheon in *The House of the Seven Gables,* or the burlesque that nearly ruins the ending of *Huckleberry Finn.* In each case a social conflict that has been central to the novel (as in *The Prairie)* is too easily resolved. It is things like these, with the abstraction that often empties characters of their class traits, making them insubstantial, that made it plausible for the romance critics to claim that American novels aren't really interested in society and class, and social conflict, but in the human condition. If one doesn't think the social issues of *Huckleberry Finn* important, as Trilling did not, then the burlesque will not seem a crucial failure, as it did not to Trilling. The next logical step, which the early romance critics took, that social conflict and class tensions must not have been culturally important in American society, is not far away. Having passed through the social and political debates of the thirties and the early forties, having rightly rejected, sometimes with anguish, Stalinism, it is not perhaps surprising that the romance critics would have found a charm in abstract myths, devoid of class traits, suggesting social harmony, rugged individualism (in Natty), and offering emotional safety from the conflicts of an overpoliticized youth and the influence of a barbarous politics. In short, the very defects of the American novel had an ideological appeal.

What of the human condition, and why could not the American writers have illuminated it? It should be evident that the human condition, no less than the social condition, requires from the writer a dispassionate—or at least not a partisan—treatment of political and social subjects, when he touches upon them. For if there is such a thing as a human condition that transcends history, its problems can hardly be amenable to ordinary political or social reform. Although in principle no single kind of writer can claim possession of the imagination that can treat it, certain kinds have a clearer title than others—among them, the religious, and members of classes or societies whose position is so hopeless, so secure, or so marginal that its members are not preoccupied by the prospects of political success. Cooper, although he belonged to a class whose decline he clearly saw, was preoccupied by the prospect of its political success. He continued to hope for his class's political and social triumph. His partisanship eroded his satiric ambivalence, disabling him as a novelist and turning him to "romance," but to no avail. For to have written effective genuine premodernist romances—to have intelligently explored the human condition—Cooper would have had to have abandoned the very political fervor that had led him to "romance" in the first place, and his work does not suggest that intention. What it does suggest, when it fails, is what Philip Rahv called "the cultism of myth . . . the fear of history . . . [that] powerhouse of change which destroys custom and tradition in producing the future."[13] In short, he did not despair of society enough, and so demonstrated that Hawthorne, unwittingly, was right when he wrote that the romance needed ruin to make it grow. Although the classic American novelists might occasionally approach the imagination that could create effective romance, in the sense of a distinguished premodernist genre, they were in general—as befit the citizens of a militant and confident republic— too committed to a progressive conception of society to look beyond the promise of history.

In the United States, a concern for the human condition did have a flowering in some short stories, chiefly by Poe and Hawthorne, but like nearly every other nation, it had to wait until the twentieth century before it produced interesting novels whose major concern was the naked human condition. It is no accident that it was the South, whose distinctive way of life had suffered irreversible disaster in the Civil War, that led the way in the development of this literature. It could do so precisely because some of its members *had* given up hope of any restoration of the past, and also expected nothing from the future.[14]

My discussion of Cooper allows me to offer a suggestion about the significance of the element of "romance" in the classic American novel. It has been noted that national literatures have national vices. F. R. Leavis claimed that the English novel's failing is its tendency to sacrifice a carefully organized moral drama for a lengthy and slapdash—if colorful—treatment of plot, character, and event. This failing, he thought, has been unrecognized owing to the uncritical acceptance of the picaresque by the English "critical tradition."[15]

In contrast to the English novel is the French, which, for its part, rarely neglects to articulate a thesis. It tends toward just the opposite failing. As Martin Turnell has noted, "its issues are sometimes . . . too much a matter of black and white . . . [with] little room for the kind of moral drama which is peculiarly the sphere of the tradition in England—George Eliot, Henry James, and Conrad."[16]

We should hardly expect the classic American novel, whose achievement is less than that of either the English or the French novel, to avoid a singular fault of its own. This is the element of "romance"—indicated not only by the example of Cooper but by every other classic American novelist. The writings of each that most closely approximate the romance as defined by the romance critics—*The Marble Faun* and *Mardi,* for example—are among their inferior productions. These novels suffer from failures similar to Cooper's. In each case the writer's imagination is frustrated by programmatic biases—hence the flight from the concrete, three-dimensional portrayal of character and event, with a loss of substantiality, and a move toward abstract myth without, however, a compensating insight into the human condition.

11

The Ideology of the Theory of the American Romance

I shall now suggest an alternative reading of the classic American novel and try to explain why the theory of the American romance had appeal despite its erroneous interpretation. I begin with the idea that there was, in the nineteenth century, a fundamental continuity in Western civilization on either side of the Atlantic.

This idea suggests itself because, when we look beyond the First World War, we are at a loss if we try to draw a sharp line between Europe and the United States. Europe was too heterogenous—in politics, society, and culture—to permit many generalizations. It was divided politically between the conservative empires of the East, the liberal nation-states of the Northwest, and the ambiguous and mercurial Mediterranean lands. It was divided in religion, and some denominations were separated geographically. It contained different social and economic formations: industrial capitalism, whether liberal or not, agrarian feudalism, and attempts (as in Germany) to combine the two. This collocation cannot be contrasted *en bloc* to the United States—which certainly, in politics, society, and culture, had more in common with England and France than these countries had with the Russian or Austrian empires.

More important, in historical development there is not much contrast, until the First World War, between Western European countries and the United States, save that in the United States, in the Civil War, there was more concentrated political violence. England and France, for example, through bourgeois revolution, had moved from conservative feudalism to liberal capitalism as the economic foundation of their societies. Then came the industrial revolution and urbanization, and with these the disenchanted intellectuals who originated utopian socialism (and later, Marxism) and the concentrated proletariat that, through the trade union movement and socialist politics, eventually began (by the end of the nineteenth century) to challenge the rule of the elites. In the United States the pattern was essentially the same. Although its colonial society was not feudal, it was decidedly conservative in many of its social and economic practices and institutions. Capitalism was (putatively) regulated by the Crown, unfree forms of labor (indentured servitude and slavery) made up perhaps a third of the labor force,[1] and there existed a powerful landholding class in both the North and the South, aristocratic in all but name, that jealously guarded its privileges. The American Revolution swept much of this away in the North, and industrialism, a degree of urbanization, and a utopian socialist response were among its results—although it took the Anti-Rent War in upstate New York and the Civil War to destroy the landed aristocracy once and for all. Thereafter, the liberal bourgeoisie and laissez-faire capitalism had a free rein until, at the end of the century, the trade union movement began to get off the ground, while the Socialist Party of America, the Populist, and the Progressive movements became important political forces, until circumstances brought about by the First World War and the reaction to the Russian Revolution destroyed them.[2] The culture of the United States had specific features, but so did the culture of every European nation. It is not that the European peoples lacked a common heritage. It is simply that the heritage of Europe and the United States was the same. If we want a term to describe it, "Western civilization" will do as well as any other. (R. R. Palmer's "Atlantic civilization" is perhaps more precise.)[3] In any case, in the nineteenth century the United States and Europe did not, in their social, political, and economic developments, behave like different civilizations. This is why I believe that the attempt to define an exceptional basis, before the First World War, for either American culture or its novel is grounded in illusion.

The classic American novel, because it was nurtured in conditions typical of Western civilization, took the form that was typical of most of its fiction. This was, in the nineteenth century, the novel in its classic intention—of manners, or of realism, broadly defined. In the novel an actual society (or societies) is examined critically, with satiric ambivalence. The mainspring of its action is cultural tension between different social groups—chiefly, although not exclusively, classes. The tension is embodied in the relations of characters who typify aspects of social life. As revealed by manners, each character suggests an actual culture and cultural aspiration. Taken together, the characters indicate the constellation of cultural (and moral) alternatives that the novel presents. The hero is likely to be a world-historical figure: a figure who embodies historical development. Often he finds himself ambiguously related to the groups examined, to the present and the past, and to the potential future of his society as a whole. Since the novel's intention is critical, it usually incorporates some ideal of civilization, of community life or "culture," which provides a measure against which the society of the novel can be judged.

Because each Western nation had its own culture, the novel in each nation had national features. This was so, first of all, because society varied from nation to nation. Second, the ideal community or culture envisioned was likely to vary from nation to nation as well: different societies, having different failures, invited different kinds of criticism. Finally, the failure in achieving critical perspective tended to be different in different societies. The classic American novel was no exception to these generalizations. The social formations it treated were often peculiar to America; at the same time it had an international emphasis; its ideal of community was, to a singular extent, concerned with the idea of democracy, and its typical failure was the habit of "romance"—the failure to bring out fully the social, especially the class, traits of its characters. (The English celebrate differences, the French moralize about them, the Americans hide them.) The virtue of the romance critics is that they often identified the American novel's distinctive features. They overshot the mark, however, in arguing that these created an exceptional form, when in fact all they indicate was that the American novel, after all, had its peculiar failure, the one older critics had identified long before. Because of their zeal to spell out the singularity of the American novel, they overemphasized and overvalued its least significant, but most eye-catching trait—most eye-catching, because it was the glaring defect. At the same time they failed to establish that American novels had interests and insights not found in European novels—at least to the extent that they constituted a new form. In order for the American novel to have been exceptional, both the experience and the ideas it treated would have had to have been more singular than they were. The failure of the romance critics to see that the features they identified were either minor, or failures, or, in one case—a special American concern for the human condition—erroneous, convicts their theory of provinciality.

This provinciality, a belief that one's nation has a culture that sets it apart, grew out of nationalist sentiment present everywhere in the West in the nineteenth century. At that time, however, nationalism was not provincial, but an element of the sensibility of an entire civilization—that of bourgeois society in the liberal age. We have to ask why that sentiment continued in America in modern times, long after it had declined in the rest of the Western world. The answer, I believe, is given by a glance at the destiny—the peculiar destiny—of both nationalism and liberalism in America since the end of the First World War.

Before the First World War, as I have mentioned, exclusive national sentiment was not provincial, but was indeed the rule everywhere in the West. Each of the Western nations tended to think of itself as unique. This, however, should not lead us too quickly to equate the belief with the truth. National differences existed, of course, but nationalist ideology was, in large measure, one of the illusions of the bourgeois and liberal epoch: the Western nations were interdependent in many aspects of their cultures. In time these nations paid for their nationalist exclusiveness: World War I, the depression, and World War II shattered the confidence that the nation-state was a self-sufficient unit. When Europeans emerged from their thirty-year cataclysm in 1945, they were determined to transcend the heritage of the liberal nation state, and in the transnational associations that followed the East-West partition they proceeded to do so— although a sharp distinction in ethics and politics must be drawn between the East and the West.[4] This determination applied to culture no less than to politics: an appropriate symbol for the change can be found in Thomas Mann, who had so far repudiated the nationalism of his youth that his decision to settle in Switzerland upon his return to Europe was taken as a stand for a transnational Europe.[5] Even across the East-West divide Europeans were to learn a language more cosmopolitan than before. In the West especially this civilized effort would be sustained, despite such minor, if very noisy, regressive offshoots as the fashion for populist third-world tyrannies among the ultra-left intelligentsia in the sixties and early seventies. All of this, it need hardly be mentioned, was in the tradition of Western development, in which—in contrast to Oriental accretion before colonialism—cultural transformations have been punctuated by revolutionary upheavals.

The case was different with the United States, which emerged from the Second World War with its confidence in the liberal nation-state intact—not to mention its confidence in the justness of the imperium it acquired at the moment when the Europeans were about to liquidate (not without reluctance) the legacy of colonialism. In contrast to European intellectuals, who were attempting, in submerging their national differences, to find a basis for a cosmopolitan civilization, American intellectuals turned to intense speculation upon the alleged exceptionalism of the American heritage. In contrast to the rest of the Western world this *was* an anomaly. It was part of the transformation, in the United States, of a dynamic cultural tradition into a static one—the same that had led the West (Americans included) from absolutist regimes to the nation-state, and then to the internationalism of the post-liberal age. America had become, with New Deal touches, the petrified embodiment of nineteenth-century nationalist and liberal ideology. Yet the point about nationalism and liberalism is that they had not been conceived in this conservative spirit. They were, at their inception, creative and, in a literal sense, revolutionary responses to an unprecedented situation: the decay of that transcendent ethos, rooted in medieval civilization, whose last gasp had been the absolutism of the *anciens régimes*. In short, the meaning of nationalism and liberalism in the nineteenth century was not the same as in the twentieth century. In the nineteenth century they had been linked to the idea of progress. In the twentieth century, in the West, they became linked, when they retained their old-fashioned forms, to a politics of (mild) reaction. The new universalism that emerged from the Second World War had robbed nationalism and liberalism of their original progressive impetus. However, the significance of this escaped the perspective—especially the consensus perspective—of American intellectuals. It is not that Americans were unaware of post-war transnational impulses: the contribution of the United States to the formation of the EEC is well known.[6] It is just that Americans interpreted their destiny in terms appropriate to the vanished liberal age. Take, for example, the unwillingness of Americans to recognize that they had emerged from World War II as an imperial power with imperial interests. What George Lichtheim has observed of Roosevelt was generally true for Roosevelt's compatriots:

> It did not occur to him that American interests could be imperialist . . . like all American liberals, he identified imperialism with European colonialism. That there might be such a thing as liberal imperialism . . . was plainer to Churchill than to Roosevelt. . . . The Americans did what the British had done before them: they rose to world eminence in the name of liberalism.[7]

This was symptomatic. The Americans continued to persist in oldfashioned nationalist and liberal ideas long after the circumstances that sustained them had disappeared, and were recognized to have disappeared, in Europe. The consensus interpretation of American history and the theory of the American romance were two examples of this exceptional survival.

We must inevitably ask how this happened. The answer is given by the nature of ideology as it has been understood since Marx as a mode of thought that both reveals and conceals important truths. The reason that twentieth-century Americans persisted in the nineteenth-century belief that their national culture was exceptional was because their national culture had indeed become exceptional—in the twentieth century. Again we must observe that the idea of the liberal nation-state was not in America, as it was in Europe, a casualty of the world wars. The choice of suburbanization instead of, as in Europe, urban renovation, with the subsequent collapse of urban government and the decay of the inner cities; the failure of American trade unions to organize more than a third of the labor force, and its steady decline thereafter; and the failure of social democracy to become more than a private philosophy—these are three obvious indices of post-war America's singularity, which was a function of American society's archaism. Alone in the West, the United States continued to preach, and largely to practice, the unadorned nineteenth-century liberal virtues—as is evident in the aversion to centralized (public) planning and to some of the more ordinary forms of welfare (i.e., socialized medicine) in force almost everywhere else. In addition, the United States retained, in the largely (but by no means entirely) Black and Hispanic urban ghettoes a genuine proletariat, indeed a sub-proletariat—without money, property, or a place in the larger society—living in conditions of squalor unrivaled in even the poorer Western European countries.

With a concept of arrested development as a starting point we can, I believe, understand how America has a claim to be exceptional among the democratic nations, and how consensus history can provide some insight into American culture—not, however, in the nineteenth century, but in the twentieth.[8] Especially relevant is the idea that the United States has had a society without ideological struggle. I have argued, first of all, that even had this been true in the nineteenth century, the presence or absence of ideological struggle would have had little significance because ideology, in bourgeois society, was an epiphenomenon. Second, I have pointed out that it was not true that American society had been without ideological struggle. The case is different, however, in both respects, in the twentieth century, and Trilling's just remarks about the supersession of bourgeois society—based entirely upon class—by modern ideological society tells us why. In modern society ideology has ceased to be the epiphenomenon that it was, and has become instead a basis of culture and society alike. As a result, the presence or absence of ideological struggle is a matter of decisive cultural importance. A characteristic of Western Europe is that it entered the ideological age with several competing ideologies: these tended to perpetuate the class-based cultural pluralism and politics of the nineteenth century. In contrast, the United States, after the First World War, did not, with the result that in America, class-based cultural pluralism tended to decompose, and out of its detritus an unprecedented mass consumer culture took shape under the aegis of a fossilized liberalism.

This is not the place to examine the process by which this came about. Suffice it to say that just at the moment when political radicalism in the United States—represented by the left-wing of the Progressive movement, the Socialist Party of America, and the syndicalism that led to the founding of the IWW—looked as if it might coalesce into a major ideological alternative to liberalism, the First World War intervened and radicalism was submerged under a wave of patriotic sentiment. That America's entry into the war had a wholly successful outcome, combined with the widespread fear engendered by the Russian Revolution, ensured that the end of the war brought no radical revival. Then, when the popular response to the depression seemed to promise a rebirth of radicalism, the New Deal, the Second World War, an understanding of Stalinism's horrors, and the Cold War intervened. If our world is, as Trilling claimed, one whose societies are structured, at least in part, by political ideology, then the great fact that separates America society has been the political failure of the democratic left, or conversely, the triumph of liberalism. As a result, the United States has now—and only now—an exceptional society and culture based upon a liberal consensus. In Western Europe, by contrast, society was modernized so far as class divisions tended to erode under the often left-leaning auspices of the developing welfare states. In this context the perpetuation of class-based cultural pluralism and politics was genuinely liberating because forms of cultural and political activity formerly class-bound were now available, often through public institutions, to many who would not have had access to them before. In the United States, however, society remained in some degree archaic, in that public services remained at a minimum and private wealth retained its authority: even the idea of a public welfare remained undeveloped and unsupported by powerful associations and institutions. In this context, the decomposition of class-based cultural pluralism represented a slide toward a gentle barbarism—since the mass consumer culture that replaced the old class-based cultures was no more creative than the petrified liberalism that sustained it. In short, if America, through consensus, ceased to be a province of a great civilization, this is because it became not less provincial, but less civilized. However, because the liberal consensus has been a development of the twentieth century, we can indicate the failure of consensus history (as used to interpret the American novel) and the theory of the American romance, both in the earlier version based upon consensus history, and in the later version developed by Kaul.

The failure was this: because American critics did not perceive how modern a development, in culture, the liberal consensus was, they projected a unitary culture upon an era when it had not in fact existed. They failed to understand that in the nineteenth century the culture of the United States had been class-based, and, therefore, pluralist—even if it were true (as it was not) that in this period the United States had either only one or no important political ideology. As a result, they passed on a mistaken idea of cultural exceptionalism in the American novel that deformed the work of later critics—even one such as Kaul, who rejected the very consensus idea upon which the case for exceptionalism had been based.

Of course we must now ask ourselves why this group of intelligent and dedicated men could have made such an error. Two possibilities suggest themselves, and they are not mutually exclusive. The first is indicated by an element of the modern liberal consensus: the hypostatization of both nationalist sentiment and old-fashioned liberalism. We should not expect that the guardians of this culture would have had a very developed historical understanding. The second possibility is, I believe, more compelling: it suggests that American intellectuals were led astray by one of their important motivations. I have mentioned this motivation before: it was anti-communism. Let us turn to two statements of principle, one by the consensus historian Daniel J. Boorstin, and the other by Lionel Trilling, in which each author attempted to relate the historical accuracy of his work to the demands of the contemporary political situation. The statement by Boorstin has been cited before:

> [One form of my] opposition [to the Communist party] has been an attempt to discover and to explain to students in my teaching and in my writing, the unique virtues of American democracy. I have done this partly in my Jefferson book [*The Lost World of Thomas Jefferson* (New York, 1948)] . . . and in . . . *The Genius of American Politics* (Chicago, 1953).[9]

The second, by Trilling, has also been partially cited. Let us take him up where he mentions the cultural situation that animated *The Liberal Imagination*.

At our distance in time the significance of this situation is perhaps not easily recalled. I speak of the commitment that a large segment of the intelligentsia of the West gave to the degraded version of Marxism known as Stalinism. No one, of course, called himself a Stalinist; it was the pejorative designation used by those members of the class of advanced intellectuals who were its opponents. At its center was the belief that the Soviet Union had resolved all social and political contradictions and was well on the way toward realizing the highest possibilities of human life. . . . The Stalinists of the West were not commonly revolutionaries, they were what used to be called fellow-travellers. . . .

. . . The opposition I offered . . . was of the simplest kind, consisting of not much more than my saying to the people who prided themselves on being liberals that liberalism was (1) a political position and (2) a political position which affirmed the value of individual existence in all its variousness, complexity, and difficulty.[10]

It is clear that Boorstin and Trilling were quite self-consciously engaged in fighting the Cold War (in Trilling's case *avant la lettre*). Both men, by recalling the liberal virtues of a former age, were hoping to inoculate their audience against the intrusion of communism—seen by both as alien to American culture. In the light of this motivation it is evident what kind of political purpose the idea of American exceptionalism, born of liberal consensus, was intended to serve.[11] It was intended to promote in Americans a sense of national identity that would serve as a bastion for liberal politics. Boorstin and Trilling had a political interest in finding that the American past had been exceptional. A cynic might respond that it was no wonder each believed that American exceptionalism was an incontrovertible fact.

Before we concur in this response, however, some qualifications must be made. First of all, I agree with their rejection of communism—and especially the communism of the period, although I also believe their worries about communist influence in the United States were exaggerated. (In addition, anti-communism has always furthered the provincial American habit of equating anything to the left of the Democratic Party with communism itself, witness the reaction to the Progressives.) Second, I do not believe that the study of the past from a political perspective is to be condemned. A coherent politics can cohere the mind. That both Boorstin and Trilling were politically motivated, and that their political motivation may have led both to hope to find that the United States had been culturally exceptional, does not, in my view, count initially against their arguments at all. Their ideas count first; the origins of their ideas second—and a long way back.

Yet a moment does come when we have to consider the politics of a historian or a literary critic and the interpretation he has to offer, for politics and literature are most obviously related in their concern with ethics, although even here their relations are complicated, not direct. It is perfectly possible to have a decent and insightful politics and to blunder in an understanding of literature. Worse, it is possible to blunder because of, not despite, a decent and insightful politics through a misplaced emphasis. If an interpretation accords with political hopes and yet is mistaken, we can describe the effort as ideological—in the negative sense of the term. At this point I should like to set aside consideration of the merits of the consensus interpretation of American history—for reasons advanced earlier—except as the interpretation concerns the theory of the American romance. The theory of the American romance, so far as it embodied the political purpose of Trilling, did indeed have a political motivation. Even in its more modest incarnations, it turned its back on the Progressive tradition. In its interpretation of American culture and the classic American novel, it did accord with the liberal political hopes of the Cold War, as advanced by critics such as Trilling. I have tried to show that its interpretation of both American culture and the classic American novel was unconvincing. Under the influence of a defensive nationalism and a modern consensus, it carried the reaction to the Progressives too far—so far, that it began to value just those elements in the American novel that served an ideological need for emotional safety, and both a triumphant and a melancholy patriotism (such as Marius Bewley's) could take comfort in the American novel's unique greatness. If I am right, then despite the many merits of the critics who contributed to its development, the theory of the American romance should be placed, not among the ranks of the truly illuminating criticisms of the period, but among the more sophisticated and convincing (convincing in part because the creators believed it themselves) examples of ideological persuasion not always initiated by, but sustained by, the Cold War.

Ideological Criticism and the Revival of the Theory of the American Romance

As we have seen, the theory of the American romance was originally advanced by critics opposed, in some measure, to the ideas of progressives such as Parrington. In its earlier version—that of Trilling, Bewley, and Chase—the insubstantiality of the classic American novel was taken to indicate a lack of social concern, owing to an exceptional consensus in American culture and society. This view was modified by Kaul, who claimed that the American difference in the novel was chiefly (and narrowly) formal. Abandoning the idea of consensus, he argued that the American novel was as socially concerned as the European; its form was merely a function of its utopian aspiration—a concept of community life. In the late sixties and seventies, Kaul's ideas provided the framework for most of the books that continued to describe the American novel as romance, such as Porte's *The Romance in America,* but because Kaul had diminished the distance between the American and European novel, he left the idea of romance open to the criticism it sustained as the seventies unfolded, and to the criticism advanced in these pages.

One of the odder developments in recent critical history is the revival of key elements of romance theory, especially the idea of an exceptional consensus, by critics of the new (now middle-aged) left. These are the "ideological critics," who bid fair, with the publication of *Ideology and Classic American Literature* and the forthcoming *Cambridge Literary History of America,* to establish a new orthodoxy in academic interpretation of American literature. In this chapter, I examine the persistence of romance theory in the writings of the two most important ideological critics, Sacvan Bercovitch and Myra Jehlen. I discuss them together not only because of their editorial collaboration, but because their interpretations are so close that Bercovitch, in *Ideology and Classic American Literature,* can describe Jehlen's essay there with a passage from an essay of his own, when his subject was not Jehlen, but himself—and the ideological school in general. We shall come to this passage very soon, for it contains important ideas, but first we must look at ideological criticism itself in order to lay bare the significance of its project.

Ideological criticism is, above all, the expression of a relativist and historicist perspectivism. Because it is willing to evaluate literature on the quality of its vision, it is similar to the old criticism, with its view of literature (and of criticism itself) as a criticism of life.

> But [adds Bercovitch] there is a crucial difference. For, say Philip Sidney and Matthew Arnold, the ideals embodied in literature convey the abiding norms of morality and the spirit, by which life invariably falls short. For [ideological criticism] these ideals, considered as a criticism of life, serve to engage us in the dynamics of history.[1]

Neither literature nor criticism (nor, as it turns out, anything else) can lead us "into a Canaan of unmediated truth. Quite the contrary: [ideological criticism] is the recognition that that promise is itself a function of ideology."[2] Although often of Marxian (indeed Gramscian) provenance, ideological criticism rejects the distinction between truth and ideology—the ideas of subjective, false consciousness—the distinction through which Marx retains his connection to classical philosophy. Although ideological criticism acknowledges "the special capacities of language to break free of social restrictions and through its own dynamics to undermine the power structure it seems to reflect," it has "abandoned [Marx's] dream of absolute knowledge"[3] and embraces instead "Mannheim's Paradox": the idea that moral and political judgments must be made even though they remain ideological because "no analysis can rise above the level of its own ideology"—which is always dependent upon "an historically and socially determined set of meanings." Taken in this light, ideology ceases to be the illegitimate offspring of the world of ideas and becomes the world of ideas itself, in Weber's terms "not only rationale but reason," and reason of a very powerful sort.[4] Fusing Gramsci's notion of cultural hegemony with Weber's notion that ideology makes men, the ideological critics, as Jehlen puts it in an approving reference to Daniel Bell, hold that "ideology represents not meaning, but the realization of meaning in the world."[5] Bercovitch is even more emphatic: "I hold these truths to be self-evident, that there is no escape from ideology: that so long as human beings remain as political animals they will always be bounded in some degree by consensus."[6] Ideological criticism, as one of the "new historicisms," either defends an existing consensus or wishes to establish a new one, not, however, on the basis of justice (which presumes a knowledge of truth), but of interest. From its perspective, all art and thought is groundlessly interested—in the sense that truth is denied—and the very "attraction of an ideological analysis is that it permits interested study of what has reemerged as interested art."[7] Ideological criticism, then, is an attempt to combine the moral, social, and political concerns and the valuative habits of the old criticism—the criticism of life—with the epistemology of postmodernism. However, it would be a mistake, Bercovitch claims, to see its purpose as wholly subversive (like deconstruction's): the aim of ideological criticism "is not to reduce [artistic] achievement to ideology." On the contrary, "ideologically-aware analysis . . . will help us to see what we have found to be extraordinary, irreducible, and uncontained about our major texts."[8]

So much for the premises of ideological criticism: what of the classic American novel? Let us turn to the recycled passage I mentioned, in which Bercovitch states the view of Jehlen, himself, and their school.

> In [our] view, our classic texts re-present the strategies of a triumphant middle-class hegemony. Far from subverting the status quo, their diagnostic and prophetic modes attest to the capacities of the dominant culture to co-opt alternative forms to the point of making basic change seem virtually unthinkable, except as apocalypse. This is not at all to minimize their protest. The point is not that our classic writers had no quarrel with America, but that they seem to have had nothing but that to quarrel about. Having adopted the culture's controlling metaphor—"America" as synonym for human possibility—and having made this tenet of consensus the ground of radical dissent, they redefined radicalism itself as an affirmation of cultural values. For the metaphor, thus universalized, does not transcend ideology. It portrays the American ideology, as all ideology yearns to be portrayed, in the transcendent colors of utopia.[9]

The key terms are "middle-class hegemony" and "the American ideology." They indicate that the United States has been exceptional, throughout its history, in the consensual force of that hegemony and that ideology. According to Bercovitch, "the central fact of [American] development" has been "the steady (if often violent) growth of middle-class American culture," a growth that has had several stages, to be sure, but that was, in "every one of these stages, including the War of Independence . . . historically organic." This organic growth was unique because the society was unique: "a new hierarchical order ranging not from peasantry to aristocracy, but from lower to higher levels of a relatively fluid free enterprise structure."[10] The society was unique not merely sociologically, however, but also because of its intellectual glue: "the American ideology," a set of ideas that established

> an ideological consensus—in moral, religious, economic, social, and intellectual matters—unmatched in any other modern culture. And the power of consensus is nowhere more evident than in the symbolic meaning . . . infused into the term America. Only in the United States has nationalism carried with it the Christian meaning of the sacred. Only America, of all national designations, has assumed the combined force of eschatology and chauvinism.[11]

Because religious sentiment informed the spirit of its nationalism, America avoided the factiousness and alienation of other bourgeois societies. As Jehlen puts it, borrowing from Lukacs, "middle-class America was an integrated society ... like Athens and Renaissance London, and very unlike nineteenth-century London and Paris."[12] As a further consequence (Bercovitch here) "the development of what we now call America shows no significant ideological warfare ... of the kind that marked "the rise of European capitalism [which] was attended by a clash of cultures, a lingering struggle of emergent middle-class values against traditions inherited from an ancien regime."[13]

This led to a literary tradition different from the European. The writers of the American Renaissance—essayists, poets, and novelists alike—had a vision more limited than writers in Europe: "the symbol of America functioned as an ancestral taboo, barring them from paths that led beyond the boundaries of their culture." Although some European writers were equally nationalist in their visions, in Europe "the spirit of the nation (or 'the people') antedates modern society." Hence, even when nationalist, Europeans were endowed with a larger spirit. As for "aesthetic withdrawal" or the "romantic-antinomian declaration of superiority to history and 'the mass'"—these too were European phenomena. "What distinguishes the American writer is his refusal to abandon the national covenant."[14] In other words, although the writers of the American Renaissance criticized the quality of American life, their sense of possibility was limited by America. The ideals they deployed against American actuality—"independence, liberty, enterprise, opportunity, individualism, democracy, 'America' itself"— were drawn "from the ideology of the early republic," which has been "variously identified with agrarianism, libertarian thought, and the tradition of civic humanism." Hence (and unfortunately, but necessarily) these ideals were not, as the writers believed, universal at all. They were, indeed, "no more or less true to the laws of nature and the mind than the once eternal truths of providence, hierarchy, and the divine right of kings."[15] Even Melville—Bercovitch's favorite American writer it seems—"simply could not envision a different set of ideals ... beyond that which his culture imposed."[16] Because of this, "the case for social constraint, for law and order, for conformity to conventional roles is very powerfully argued throughout American fiction." Not for the protagonists of American fiction the social defiance of Julien Sorel or Rastignac, whose "moral autonomy" and rejection of conventional values "would have seemed blasphemy to Cooper, Hawthorne, Melville, Howells, James, and even, it can be argued, Twain."[17] Despite the American novelists' "remarkable gift for seeing ... metaphysical issues ... their insight was attended by an equally remarkable blindness to social limits."[18] Hence a myopic vision.

> What our major writers could not conceive, either in their optative or in their tragic-ironic moods, was that the United States was neither utopia at best nor dystopia at worst, neither "the world's fairest hope," as Melville put it, nor "man's foulest crime," but a certain political system; that in principle no less than in practice the American Way was neither providential nor natural but one of many forms of society.[19]

This argument seems, on the face of it, to be an indictment of classic American literature—at least that of the Renaissance. And, indeed, at times Bercovitch does strongly imply a revaluation, as when he suggests that America, perhaps, "has yet to produce a work of undeniable international greatness," and that a comparative perspective may "eventuate in a shift in the literary center of gravity, from the nationalist American Renaissance to the transatlantic enterprise of a later era: James, Norris, Dubois, Wharton, Adams, Eliot, Pound, Stevens, Stein, and the neglected 'ethnic' writing of the early twentieth century."[20]

Because I am going to argue against the ideological critics on various grounds, I had better say right away that I find several of their ideas convincing. I think it true (but notice how "true" declares a difference) that there has been an "American ideology," although not quite as these critics define it, that the ideals of the early republic were of the first importance, that there is little American literature of international greatness, and that some of the late-nine-teenth- and early-twentieth-century transatlantic writers do deserve more attention than some of the writers of the Renaissance. These ideas, I find, can support my conclusion that "romance" has been a term that has often disguised failed writing.

This conclusion, however, the ideological critics do not themselves draw. As a result, it is impossible to discuss their idea of American literature without mentioning their criticism's first weakness: its inconsistency in evaluation. Bercovitch, after discussing the limited vision of American literature suddenly gives back with one hand what had been taken by the other. For he goes on to "add, as emphatically as possible, that the argument I have just outlined does not in any sense diminish the aesthetic power of the texts." No more than we would blame Chaucer for his "commitment to the 'medieval world view'" need we blame Whitman and Emerson for "their failure, if such it was, to see through the rhetoric of free-enterprise democracy." For "the emotional and conceptual ground of the rhetoric, was profound, humane, and exhilarating, a set of beliefs and promises which may rank among the most liberating, most energizing ideas produced by any culture, past or present." It adapted the spirit of revolution to a sense of continuity, its definition of self-interest as individualism allowed for "mutuality and continuity;" it invested "the dream of progress with moral as well material imperatives," and "translated the spirit of expansion into a vision of growth, experimentation, and constant renewal; and which, summarily, created in the word 'America' the most compelling cultural symbol of the modern era, nationally and internationally."[21]

A similar oscillating uncertainty occurs in Jehlen's essay, "The Novel and the Middle-Class in America," where it is unclear whether Jehlen is condemning the social conformity she perceives in Hawthorne and Melville, or whether she simply means to describe a characteristic of a genre. Certainly the second possibility is affirmed when she resurrects the term "romance" to say that American novelists, Henry James aside, "seem not to have written novels at all." The salient features of American fiction, she argues, are owing to the conformist intentions imposed by America's exceptional consensus, itself both cause and (chiefly) consequence of the American ideology. We should not be deceived by the many stories of "extravagant individuals in flight to the wilderness and beyond while, until recently anyway, the [European] novel has explored the everyday lives of people at home." Despite its "lack of sociability"—that is, substantiality—the American romance does "lead us back to society," for the story it tells "is the story of a defeated, a downed, flight." Rejecting (rightly in my opinion) Chase's idea that the American romance is more rebellious than the European novel, Jehlen claims that the American romance is less critical of the world it depicts. Hence, although Ahab is "mysterious, archetypal, rather than socially typical, abstractly conceived, perhaps universal but certainly not of the everyday world" it remains true that Melville is "less aggressively individual than, say, Balzac, since his intention is to show that 'the wages of blasphemy are death.'"[22]

But even if all this is true, the problem remains: Jehlen conflates mutually exclusive definitions. If the American romance "is not a novel at all," but a separate genre, then its traits cannot be held against it. Yet, in the end, this is what she does: there are, she believes, "frustratingly few real achievements" in the American novel, and these occur only when the writers attempt an "independently critical stance" like that of the European novelists.[23] But if this is true, then the romance is really not a genre at all, for its typical feature—its recommendation of social conformity—is held to be a defect. "Romance" becomes, therefore, simply a term for a kind of bad novel, except when redeemed by a critical stance—in which case, however, "romance" is no longer romance.

The same muddle pervades ideological criticism's attitude to American literature as a whole. We can begin with the flat contradiction in Bercovitch's view that (1) American literature never transcends the American ideology, which (2) itself has no universal values (because nothing does), and yet (3) succeeds in achieving something "extraordinary, irreducible, and uncontained." The contradiction is evident: if the last statement is true this means that American literature does succeed in achieving universality (what else can "irreducible and uncontained" mean?) on one of two grounds: either the literature transcends the American ideology, or the ideology, which the literature does not transcend, does indeed contain universal elements. But if either (or both) of these grounds are true they refute one (or both) of the first two claims. If we stand on these, however, we cannot go on to claim that American literature ever does achieve the irreducible and uncontained condition that Bercovitch says it does. Moreover, if ideology is, as ideological criticism claims, "the realization of meaning in the world" then how can one claim that ideological limitation does not "in *any* sense (italics mine) diminish the aesthetic power of texts themselves"? This could be true only if aesthetic power had a non-ideological meaning, a possibility that has been denied ("there is no escape from ideology"). But even if we grant this possibility in the interests of consistency, our troubles will not have ceased. For aesthetic power is the central fact that criticism addresses. If separated from ideology, aesthetic power, then, is clearly not what ideological criticism addresses—in which case ideological criticism becomes peripheral to criticism itself. But Bercovitch insists that it is ideological criticism that can discover the extraordinary, irreducible, and uncontained aesthetic power of American literature. These are some, but not all, of the conundrums in which ideological criticism is enmeshed—and I shall return to them later. At the moment, however, I want to turn to the criticism's idea of the American novel, which allows us to greet our old friend, the theory of the American romance, in a nearly traditional guise.

For, regarding the novel, ideological criticism is hardly as original as it seems. The idea that the United States has had a consensual ideological society was adumbrated by Trilling and spelled out by Bewley and Hartz. The idea that America has had a consensual, organic, and non-ideological society was also adumbrated by Trilling and argued by Chase and Daniel Boorstin. Ideological criticism's original contribution is to fuse these formerly opposed views by substituting "the American ideology" for Hartz's liberalism and, by according the ideology a religious dimension, to bridge the gap between Hartz's uni-ideological interpretation and Boorstin's non-ideological interpretation of American history. Boorstin was right to have claimed that no political ideology had dominated American history, but wrong to claim that no other ideology had been dominant; Hartz was right to claim that America had been knit by a dominant ideology, but wrong to claim that this had been merely a political liberalism (although liberalism in a larger sense, as Jehlen notes, typifies it).[24]

In a similar manner, ideological criticism is able to bridge the gap between the early and later versions of the theory of the American romance. Trilling, Bewley, and Chase were right to argue that the classic American novel is abstract and metaphysical—so far as it represents a flight from society and portrays highly individualistic characters in situations without much social relation. But the defeat of these characters and the message of social conformity advanced by the novel highlights its social concern: to this extent the interpretation approaches, in a small way, Kaul's. It resembles Kaul's more clearly in its insistence on the importance of nationalism. In other words, the American novel dramatizes and criticizes the individualism of the middle class. It presents that individualism in abstract isolation; it criticizes individualism by portraying its defeat. Yet it affirms the middle-class conformism of America. Although its vision is admittedly more limited than that of the European tradition, the American novel does have one claim to a greater wisdom in its self-reflective criticism of its own ideological limitations. Speaking of Melville, Jehlen writes: "if Melville is less tolerant of romantic rebellion than his European counterparts he is also probably better aware than they of just what it can entail."[25]

In the form revived by Bercovitch and Jehlen, the theory of the American romance can be summarized in three points. (1) The American romance was the exceptional outcome of an exceptional consensus established by the American ideology, whose mixture of nationalism and religiosity was unique in the nineteenth century—in its nature and its power. (2) The American romance, like American literature in general, was unable to transcend the perspective of the ideology, hence its limited scope, in contrast to the European novel, and hence the defeated career of its rebellious protagonists. (3) Because it was caught up in the problems of extreme individualism, making "heroic myths out of the ultimate efforts of characters to conquer structural constraints,"[26] the characters of the American novel are, more than European characters, abstract and metaphysical—characteristics that indicate neither artistic success nor failure, but the status of the American romance status as a separate genre. However, a positive evaluation arises from the profundity of the American romance's narrow insights—an evaluation that echoes the greater profundity accorded it by earlier romance theorists.

All of this is well argued and plausible, not least because of its traditional affiliations. As I have mentioned, I am uncertain how aware the ideological critics are of these: when Jehlen, for example, invokes Lukacs' idea of an integrated civilization, she does not seem to realize that this had been implicit all along in consensus history and most romance theory. But precisely because of these affiliations, ideological criticism's understanding of the American novel is open to the same objections as the theory in its older versions.

13

The Failure of Ideological Criticism

Let us take up in turn the three major ideas of the revived theory of the American romance. The first of these is the idea of an American ideology. I believe that the ideological critics have identified something important—and they deserve credit for this—but that they have an unhistorical understanding of its nature and power. Regarding its nature, Bercovitch insists that of all symbols of national identity, "only *America* has united nationality and universality, civic and spiritual selfhood, secular and redemptive history, the country's past and paradise to be in a single synthetic ideal."[1] This seems to me untrue, for the reason given in chapter 6: the ubiquity of Western nationalism in the nineteenth century. To extend my discussion there: the Poles who thought of Poland as "the Christ of nations," the Slavophiles who thought of Russia as "the third Rome," and the Germans who conceived first, of a teutonic *Mitteleuropa,* and then, in our century, of a Third Reich, all had similar synthetic ideals. To claim that the American ideology was exceptional in its nature is highly dubious. Its survival into the twentieth century is a different matter, and is, I believe, exceptional— but it owes more, as I have argued, to America's rise to world power than to the power of ideological continuity. In any case, the survival is irrelevant to a consideration of the nineteenth-century novel.

But, granting the existence of the ideology, are we not obliged to concede its great power? Perhaps in having such an ideology Americans were not unusual, but perhaps the force of that ideology was greater in America than elsewhere. This suggestion, however, has to confront, first, the evidence that German and Russian nationalisms were far more influential, and second, American social and political tensions and conflicts, some major (mentioned in chapter 9), involving groups not at all enchanted by middle-class liberal ideology. The most obvious of these is the Civil War, followed at some distance by the overthrow of the Puritan oligarchy, the Indian Wars, and the New York Anti-Rent Wars between the patroons and their tenants. To these we can add international confrontation, if not actual conflict, between Americans and other cultures having attitudes that may be said to have entered the American consciousness.

Now, both Bercovitch and Jehlen recognize this problem, but I find their efforts to solve it unconvincing. Bercovitch argues—unsuccessfully in my opinion (of which more in a moment)—against Perry Miller's belief that the Puritan oligarchy was opposed to the currents that shaped America in the eighteenth century. Referring to the South, he treats it as a society separate from the rest of America, quoting Louis Hartz's, William Taylor's and C. Vann Woodward's respective descriptions of it as "an alien child," "dissociated from the nation at large," "shot through with un-American experience."[2] Fair enough, but what becomes of Poe's stories, Twain's novels, *Uncle Tom's Cabin,* and, in our century, the fiction of Faulkner and the Southern school? The conclusion must be that none of these is entirely American. This too may be a fair description, but if so, it refutes the notion of an exceptional American literature—except in a sense very different from the one Bercovitch is advancing: a tradition including Poe, Twain, and the modern Southerners would then be imperfectly American, and it certainly would not reflect consensus. A similar objection can be made to Jehlen's description of Cooper as a "conservative burger,"[3] which may, indeed, indicate Cooper's own position fairly, but not that of the patroons, who cultivated an aristocratic patina they are allowed to wear by most historians and, more importantly, by Cooper himself.

For the rest, ideological criticism, despite its commitment to "multiple Americas," and its rejection of any "transcendent"[4] culture, oddly has little to say about the beliefs of any group other than the northern American middle class; perhaps more than liberal critics, the ideological critics define American reality in the terms of this class. This is cause and consequence of an improbably flattened version of American history, and a failure to perceive that the modern triumph of the middle-class need not reflect ideological homogeneity in the past. Indeed, to call America an "integrated society" as Jehlen does, ignores the circumstance, mentioned in earlier chapters, that in genuine integrated societies all-embracing institutions—such as the modern state, the church in the Middle Ages, the *polis* of classical Greece—not the market, are the means by which culture is disseminated. If any parts of the United States had integrated societies they were the parts that were not typically middle class: Puritan New England, the Slave South, and the Tribal West.

But what about the middle class itself? Was it, at least, dominated by the American ideology? Here, I believe, the ideological critics have a real contribution to make, not only to the understanding of the class, but to the American novel when it fails to transcend nationalist ideology. But, to anticipate, it does not always fail. And if we can trust Henry James' version of Old America as described in *Hawthorne,* we have reason to doubt that the ideology had exactly the character the ideological critics impute to it. Nevertheless, James certainly did describe an American ideology when he spoke of the faith that animated Old America. However, its religious dimension is not the one Bercovitch and Jehlen describe. It is not eschatological, nor is it a means of establishing a middle-class hegemony in the resolution of political, social, and cultural, conflict. It is, instead, a "simple," "uncritical," and "genial," means of ignoring, to the peril of all classes, that political, social, and cultural problems exist. Moreover, the country's "superstitious faith" in itself is explained by "the uninterrupted material development of the young Republic."[5] That is, James believed that this faith was not an organic continuation from the Puritan past, but was rather a spiritual epiphenomenon of material conditions existing in the early nineteenth century. Like Perry Miller, then, but unlike Bercovitch and Jehlen, James saw a radical break between the Puritan past and the nineteenth century—hence his denial that Hawthorne's ideas and attitudes had any but a residual connection with those of Puritanism. Nor did James see a continuation of the faith of Old America into the present: the Civil War, in his view, put an end to it. Why didn't James see what Bercovitch and Jehlen see? I think it unlikely that the son of Henry James, Sr., would have been blind to the kind of religiosity and conviction they describe had it existed and had great importance. I believe, therefore, that ideological criticism has read too much of contemporary America's ideology into the past, thereby repeating a failure of the traditional theory of the American romance. Having said this, however, I recall my comment above about its potential contribution: in a moment, and in the next chapter, I shall come back to it.

This brings us to the next idea—that the vision of the classic American novel is always limited by "America." Is it true, as Bercovitch claims, that the American novelists never transcended the terms of the American ideology, that "they could not conceive . . . that the American way was neither providential and natural but one of many possible forms of society?" True that, as Jehlen claims, they "lack a sense of a world elsewhere"?[6] These claims are certainly consonant with my discussion of American naturalism. But they are often untrue, I believe, for the classic American novelists—not only for the later transatlantic novelists, for whom Bercovitch half-concedes the point, but for the earlier ones as well.

In many novels, the classic American novelists took great pains to show the limitations of American culture and thought and to portray other cultures of at least comparable worth. With Wharton, I take it, there can be no dispute: although in her novels Americans such as Undine Spragg and May Welland are often victorious in their confrontations with the European aristocracy, the higher value of European culture is usually not called into question. The same is true for James (although his estimation of American culture is higher), who sometimes even allows the Europeans to triumph—rightly, as when Felix detaches Gertrude from her Old American family in *The Europeans;* wrongly, as in *The American*. As for Twain, Jehlen concedes that Huck's rejection of "civilization" can only mean a rejection of America—although she claims that Huck's "unique refusal sadly lacks conviction."[7] But Huck is not unique, even in Twain's work. When the Connecticut Yankee returns to contemporary America after his naive revolution fails, he dies mourning the loss of Arthurian England. In *Pudd'nhead Wilson,* in one of Twain's sunniest passages, the musical performance and aristocratic manners of the Italian twins are wholeheartedly appreciated by the folk of Dawson's Landing—indicating their acceptance and respect (and Twain's) for "a world elsewhere." And the magnificent, tragic Roxy, like Jim in *Huckleberry Finn,* represents a life sharply different from that of the American middle class.

Wharton, James, and Twain, of course, belong to the late nineteenth and early twentieth century. What of the novelists of the Renaissance and, before them, Cooper? Here I think ideological criticism stands on firmer ground, for the reason given above: these are preeminently the authors of "Old America." Even here however, ideological criticism overshoots the mark, especially in the case of Cooper: Natty and Indian John in *The Pioneers,* the Tories in *Lionel Lincoln,* and the patroons in the Littlepage trilogy, are not prisoners of middle-class ideology. That they are defeated is a matter of fact, but (a point to which I shall return) the value of what they represent is not removed by defeat. Something similar can be said of the sailors and South Sea islanders in Melville (although Melville and Hawthorne may well be the novelists for whom the constraints of an American ideology most counted). Yet even in *The Scarlet Letter,* which Bercovitch and Jehlen find exemplary, ideological criticism fails to account for the novel's ideological complexity. According to Bercovitch and Jehlen, Hester's resigned decision to return to live in Puritan Boston constitutes a validation of "the American way of life," and the triumph, which the novel itself endorses, of the American ideology.

This is a misreading. First, Hawthorne's Puritans are not connected organically to the nineteenth century, as Bercovitch claims the historical Puritans were, but resemble the Puritans as they have been described by Perry Miller: dominated not by an aristocracy, of course, but by an oligarchy fundamentally different from the bourgeoisie that would replace them. This is one of the points of "The Custom House," when Hawthorne writes that, although he has "a home-feeling with the past," this is owing to his Puritan ancestry, without which he would be like the "new-inhabitant . . . [who] has no conception of the oyster-like tenacity with which an old settler . . . clings to the spot." In other words, his own connection to the past is personal and atypical: for the most part, he does not see active continuity between the nineteenth century and the Puritan past. In fact, he is certain that his Puritan forebears would reject *him* out of hand. As a result, Hester's submission to Puritan New England, if that is what it is, in no way validates any American ideology that might have been current in Hawthorne's time. If anything, as I have argued, Hester's views of revolutionary revolt are far closer to the ideas of the Enlightenment—that is, to the ideology that *was* current in Hawthorne's time, than to the society she returns to. Her submission would symbolize its defeat. Of course, if we invert the ideological critics, and read her return as a gradualist triumph (she will lead the Puritan daughters to the middle-class future) we can find an endorsement of "America"—but only if we give up the Puritans themselves.

But even if we accept, for the sake of the argument, the idea that the Puritans are the bearers of the American ideology, Bercovitch and Jehlen's reading of the novel is still untenable. Hester's return to New England, even if it represents her acceptance of its society, need not be taken as a general endorsement. For in contrast to Hester is Pearl, who leaves New England, never to return. It is clear from the letters Pearl sends—"with armorial bearings unknown to English heraldry"—that Pearl's destiny is neither middle-class nor American. She abandons the national covenant and (*pace* Bercovitch) the novel endorses her as much as Hester. Whatever the faults of *The Scarlet Letter,* Hawthorne is aware that America is "but one of many possible forms of society," and that for some—even the native American Pearl—other societies are a better home. To put it this way, however, makes *The Scarlet Letter* sound spuriously contemporary, as if it were a novel that argued for a relativistic cultural pluralism: Bercovitch and Jehlen, the standard-bearers of such relativism, do not think so, and they are right.[8] As we have already seen, the utopian quest for a best life informs *The Scarlet Letter,* which imagines a synthesis of the cultural richness of the Elizabethan age and the revolutionary, enlightened ideals of Hester. This synthetic ideal is not beyond criticism, of course, but it is proof that *The Scarlet Letter* does not suffer from the ideological myopia Bercovitch and Jehlen attribute to it. In this matter, I believe, ideological criticism simply fails to illuminate the book.

However, I believe it could help illuminate one of the book's grave weaknesses—so long as it was willing to concede successes. *The Scarlet Letter* is a very uneven novel, as many have seen. Even Q. D. Leavis, who insists upon Hawthorne's greatness, observes that Hawthorne's symbolism is often intrusive and often "when trying for an archaic diction [Hawthorne] can be seen to write no language."[9] As James and Brownell remarked long ago, the characterization of Chillingsworth is a flat failure: Chillingsworth never comes to life, remaining merely a symbol—and an inconsistent one at that. For Hawthorne claims throughout the novel that Chillingsworth progressively degenerates, but, from the moment of his first appearance, Chillingsworth is already a monster, sneering and snarling melodramatically.[10] Here, I believe, ideological criticism has something important to say. If we take Dimmesdale, at least in his impulses, to be a precursor to middle-class romantic individualism—a "man of feeling" out of joint with his age, then his inertia, like that Hawthorne found in the Custom House, reflects badly upon middle-class America, especially in contrast to the energy of the orthodox Puritans. By endowing Chillingsworth with near-supernatural influence, Hawthorne lifts responsibility a little from the sad minister's shoulders. In addition, by robbing Chillingsworth, partly through abstraction, of his humanity, Hawthorne forestalls, illegitimately, an ambivalent response to him—thus further guaranteeing that all our sympathy goes to Dimmesdale. Chillingsworth, then, can be seen as an ideological symbol of the kind I mentioned in connection with Cooper, through which Hawthorne manipulates the plot in favor of his future-foreshadowing characters. Meanwhile, the novel loses (James' complaint again) its critical focus and its substantiality. If the ideological critics missed their chance with Chillingsworth, it is probably because their approach is too programmatic; having decided that the novel as a whole must be myopic, they do not find the place where it actually is.

This point brings us to the last of ideological criticism's major ideas: that the classic American novel is romance because its characters are abstract and metaphysical, and because they are defeated, with the implication that social conformity is good—characteristics that are consequences of the mythic concern of the classic American novel, which is to dramatize the individual's search for freedom from restraint.

Here, we should notice, we are not far from the ideas of Richard Chase, although he is referred to only rarely by ideological critics. But the references to Chase are telling, as when Jehlen claims his work is too abstract because "whole historical epochs [and] lines of conflict within them, dissolved into all-encompassing and non-controversial generalities."[11] Of course, it was Chase's concern for a trans-historical human condition that led him to all-encompassing generalities: Chase retained an idea of existential truth. Ideological criticism, whose historicism denies the existence of the trans-historical, and whose relativism denies the possibility of truthful generalities, can have no commerce with this. For the rest, however, Chase's ideas are "non-controversial"—they simply are not historically specific enough.

Ideological criticism, in other words, accepts Chase's description of the American novel; it merely tries to sharpen his description by reducing the degree of generality. When Jehlen, sounding much like Chase, speaks of "the ultimate efforts of [American] characters to conquer structural constraints" she indicates that these "characters abstract as they may be, are in fact symbolic surrogates for 'America's middle-class,'" whose failures, although genuinely tragic, are not universal but, [her term] "bourgeois."[12]

Now these ideas, I believe, may well be true. To the extent that they are, they contribute to the understanding of the American novel. The problem is simply that none of them indicate that the American novel belongs to a separate genre. To see why, let us begin with the idea that the vision of the classic American novel is usually, as Jehlen claims, "bourgeois." How does this separate the American novel from the European, even if we grant that the American novel makes "heroic myth" out of its material? For, when we turn to the European novel, we find the same thing. It is a cliché (but none the less true) that the European novel rose with the rising bourgeoisie. As for myth, I believe it has become clear that the European novelists were no less concerned with myth than Americans. Charles Dickens, for example, has been the subject of a wonderfully appreciative study, *The Dickens Myth,* by Geoffrey Thurley. Thurley, who believes that the novel, with its "necessary prerequisites" of "social mobility, technological expansion, and political libertarianism" is "the great art-form of bourgeois man, of the capitalist world,"[13] argues that Dickens' novels are, almost without exception, structured by a single myth, an "archetype" of that world's "most complex feelings of unrest." Its elements are "a child abandoned by feckless or unfortunate parents [who] climbs out of the abyss of poverty and darkness towards security, peace, and light." He is aided by "benevolent retired uncles," and "hindered by fearsome ogres, powerfully attractive demons from whose clutches he cannot escape until they are ritualistically slain."[14] Thurley then goes on to argue that Dickens is the archetypical English novelist, for his myth is

> the representative myth for bourgeois man—for Western man, that is, at this particular stage of his technological, economic and social development, the stage reached in the capitalist, industrial era. Man in this situation suffers from unique and novel discomforts—from uncertainties as to purpose, identity, and status. But he suffers also from a new sense of guilt and responsibility, and it is modern man's attempts to establish the limits and extent of his own responsibilities that is Dickens's main subject.[15]

If Thurley is right, then Dickens writes myths that are very close indeed to the myths American novelists are supposed to write: that is, myths of bourgeois man. Of course the myths of Dickens have an English accent: there is, no doubt, a national difference between English and American novels. But this we have always known. The question is whether the American novels belong to a different genre; whether they are, indeed, exceptional. Consider the account Thurley gives of Micawber, when he takes issue with Chesterton's idea that Micawber and Pickwick are essentially the same kind of man:

> This error is an intelligent one. There is more than a generic Dickensian benignancy in common between the two men: there is the same firm rotundity, the gentility, the baldness, the smiling grace, an energy of charm that makes people who know them feel close to the centre of things. With Micawber, as with Pickwick, life is a feast, and it is as the presiding master of ceremonies at innumerable dinner parties that we best remember Mr. Micawber. But Micawber has none of that quality of innocence Dostoevsky noted in Pickwick, and Micawber is "slippery." His gentility is backed up by no private income, his tights are shabby, his whole demeanour is in some sense founded upon falsehood.[16]

Now suppose we were to take this account and change it by substituting, for Mr. Micawber, the name of Colonel Sellers. Physical details aside (Sellers, for example, isn't bald) how much would we actually notice the change?[17] To continue in the same vein: what is the name of the novel, the hero of which is a young orphan—who manages to preserve his goodness among thieves and scoundrels, even as he is forced to suffer beatings and confinement, to witness murder, drunkenness, and all kinds of folly, and who is returned, a little ambiguously, to well-meaning, genteel guardians of a legacy that is his by astonishing good fortune? The answer, of course, is either *Oliver Twist* or *Huckleberry Finn*. (In France, it is Hector Malot's *Sans Famille*.) Or, to choose from different authors, what is the name of the novel of the social outcast, the victim of Puritan fanaticism, who lives marginally at the outskirts of a tightly knit village, who is redeemed by the love of a beautiful, illegitimate child (unacknowledged by her father, a man of great local importance), and who, after many years, is able to reenter, although only tentatively, the life of the community at last? The answer: either *The Scarlet Letter* or *Silas Marner*. Such examples imply only one conclusion: the myths of American and European novelists were the same. Hence the metaphysical and symbolic concerns of American and European novelists were also the same. As a further consequence the abstraction of characters in American novels and, by extension, the lack of substantiality in these novels as a whole, indicate not a special American quality, but simply a failure of creativity. I have already made this point in my chapter on Cooper, but will rephrase it briefly here: it is not that the numerous studies detailing the symbolic, metaphysical, and self-reflexive concerns of American fiction are wrong, it is just that they are, regarding the question of American exceptionalism and romance, beside the point.[18] Very few, if any, modes of expression or concern attributed to the American novel are absent from the European. The difference is that where American novels are often merely metaphysical and symbolic, European novels are usually metaphysical, symbolic *and* substantial.

Regarding character, European characters are as fully caught up in their symbolic myths, their quest for metaphysical meaning, as American characters are. They are also fully human, which American characters much less frequently are. Probably one of the reasons why this is often not recognized is historical. In many instances, critics began to apply mythic and symbolic analyses to nineteenth-century American fiction before they applied them to European fiction. As a result, a body of interpretation indicating mythic and symbolic qualities in American fiction developed before a similar body of interpretation of European fiction. From this began the bad critical habit of regarding the characters of American fiction as especially mythic and symbolic, when the truth is that they are simply less fully human than the no-less mythic and symbolic characters of European fiction. The insubstantiality in American literature, in other words, is a pure loss: the American novel is comparatively impoverished.

Just as weak is the final criterion for calling the American novel romance: the idea that the American novel, more frequently than the European, ends in the defeat of its socially rebellious characters, and more frequently recommends social conformity. This fails on two grounds. First, it is largely untrue, as we see when we turn to some of Jehlen's examples: among American novels *The Scarlet Letter* and *Moby Dick,* among European *The Red and the Black* and *Père Goriot.* Jehlen claims that the "European novel . . . takes the internal organization of society as its problem," while "the American romance . . . accepting the *status quo* as simply natural focuses on the difficulty of individual conformity."[19] But it simply is not true that *The Scarlet Letter* accepts Puritan society as "simply natural," nor is it true—witness again Pearl—that conformity is recommended. As for *Moby Dick*—to reject Ahab does not require accepting any single society as natural: indeed, the society of sailors is given to us, at the beginning of the novel, as an antidote to the world ashore: "with a philosophical flourish Cato throws himself upon his sword; I quietly take to the ship." Right away then, there are at least two societies in contrast: the world of the upright republican citizen (Cato) and the world of the sailor. Soon there is a third, distinctly un-American: the primitive "natural" society represented by Queequeg. If we accept, as I think we should, one of Kaul's suggestions, there develops a fourth: the little "ideal" community of Queequeg and Ishmael. And there is, finally, a fifth: the sailors' society perverted by Ahab. Which of these does *Moby Dick* see as "simply natural," and to which does it recommend conformity? Surely the point about Ahab's revolt is that it goes beyond the limits of *any* decent society: there is no indication that middle-class America is the only, or even the best, decent society. When Jehlen writes that the novel "apologizes for conventional society through Starbuck"[20]—the reply must be that Starbuck's failure to kill Ahab, or to take control of the Pequod, indicts his conventionality. Although I shall argue, in the next chapter, that ideological criticism has an important point to make about *Moby Dick,* just as with *The Scarlet Letter,* here the observation must be, as with *The Scarlet Letter,* that ideological criticism is too programmatic in its reading.

When we turn to some of the European novels that Jehlen thinks exemplary we encounter further difficulties. Commenting on the end of *Père Goriot* (which novel she contrasts to *Moby Dick*) Jehlen claims that the final isolation of Rastignac from society is applauded by Balzac: "Goriot's final agony destroys Rastignac's last feelings of obligation to conventional values . . . Rastignac's ethics are at least superior to those of Paris." As a result, "the basic thrust of *Père Goriot* . . . is just the opposite of *Moby Dick,* in which Melville depicts how cold and deadly can be the universe beyond the glow of the homefires."[21]

Now I believe this is untrue, as the final passage of *Père Goriot* indicates:

> Upon the humming hive he cast a look which seemed already to suck the honey from it, and he gave utterance to these portentous words: "Between us the battle is joined henceforward."

> And, as a first act in challenge of society, Eugene went to dine with the Baroness de Nucingen.

Unlike Jehlen, I take this to be ironic: Eugene is, in fact, morally defeated: having buried virtue (Goriot), he conforms to Parisian society, becoming a predator in the predatory world of the Nucingens. As further evidence for this view, we should recall that before *Père Goriot* had been written, Rastignac had already appeared in *The Fatal Skin* as a middle-aged cynic dispensing advice to that novel's doomed hero. He becomes, eventually, Premier of France (much to the amusement of Henry James: "Fielding was careful not to make his hero a rival of Sir Robert Walpole").[22] Rastignac, whose ethics *are* the ethics of Paris, simply is not the stuff from which social revolts are made. As for being unlike American heroes, on the contrary—Dreiser's Cowperwood would have gone into business with him.

At first sight, Jehlen is on firmer ground with *The Red and the Black*. It is true that Julien Sorel is a defiant figure unlike many we find in American literature. Although I do not agree with Jehlen that the world won't have Julien[23] (I think he, like Fabrice, rejects a world that will), Julien does go to a rebel's grave. But *The Red and the Black*, in this, is no more representative of the European novel that it is of the American. For the typical novel of the nineteenth century is the *bildungsroman*, in which the Young Man from the Provinces, through knowledge gained from a variety of experiences, seeks to achieve a place in the great world. Sometimes, as in *The Red and the Black, The Princess Casamassima*, and *Sentimental Education*, he fails. Sometimes, as in *Wilhelm Meister, David Copperfield, Green Henry*, and *Middlemarch*, he (or she) "succeeds," although often not as he first desired. But, whether his efforts succeed or fail, some kind of accommodation with society—what Jehlen calls conformity—is the goal. Julien's final gesture of defiance is atypical, just as Huck Finn's; there is nothing particularly European—as opposed to American—about it.

Yet even if we set all of this aside, and accept Jehlen's claim as largely true, one insurmountable obstacle remains. To say that the classic American novel chronicles the defeat of individualism and recommends conformity in no way entails that it is not a novel, but a member of a different genre. If it did, then Gottfried Keller's *Green Henry*, which also chronicles the defeat of its hero's efforts to achieve individualistic success as an artist, and his ultimate acceptance of a modest civil service post (symbolizing his return to responsible citizenship) would be a paradigmatic romance. The same would be true of a number of famous European novels (not to mention *The House of the Seven Gables*, by common consent the most obviously novelistic of Hawthorne's long fictions), so much so that if these were reclassified as romances we would, first of all, undercut the American novel's claim to an exceptional nature, which was what the term "romance" was supposed to indicate. Second, we would have to redefine our sense of what a novel is, since *Green Henry* (as already noted) has long been considered a paradigmatic *bildungsroman,* perhaps the greatest in the German language after *Wilhelm Meister.* By contrast, *Demian,* usually considered a romance, would become an example of the typical European novel, on the grounds that it dramatizes its hero's successful liberation from convention. This would be foolish, but unless we are willing to undertake such a redefinition, the classic American novels remain novels; which of course is what I submit they are. The problem here, in short, is that the issue Jehlen intelligently raises, while important, is thematic, not generic.

Such difficulties, I believe, are endemic to ideological criticism as a whole, and indicate why, even when we separate its metaphysical presuppositions from its practical criticism, we are obliged to stop short of a complete divorce. To understand why, however, requires a digression into the murky realm of contemporary literary theory. We must find the place named by Trilling: "the dark and bloody crossroads where literature and politics meet."[24]

A blindness seems to be inherent in ideological criticism. This can be seen most easily, I believe, in one more example drawn from *Ideology and Classic American Literature,* the essay "Sentimental Power: *Uncle Tom's Cabin* and The Politics of Literary History" by Jane Tompkins. Rejecting the (to my mind) sensible position of Edmund Wilson, who claimed, in *Patriotic Gore,* that *Uncle Tom's Cabin* has been a very underrated novel, and is at times touched by greatness, Tompkins, in the manner of the romance critics, claims that *Uncle Tom's Cabin* is not a novel, in the usual sense, at all. It has been underrated, indeed, because it has been mistaken for a novel, when in fact it is a great work of art of a different kind. Unlike Wilson, she continues to place Stowe among the sentimental writers—such as Fanny Fern and Elizabeth Stuart Phelps.

> I will argue that the work of these sentimental writers is complex and significant in ways *other than* those which characterize the established masterpieces [such as *The Scarlet Letter* and *Moby Dick*]. I will ask the reader . . . to see the sentimental novel not as an artifice of eternity . . . but as a political enterprise, halfway between sermon and social theory, that both codifies and attempts to mold the values of its time.[25]

Now it is certainly true, as Tompkins claims, that much of Stowe's novel is "significant in ways other than those which characterize established masterpieces," but the significance of this truth seems to have escaped her. To say that a discourse is "a political enterprise halfway between sermon and social theory, that both codifies and attempts to mold the values of its time" is simply to define that discourse as a work—not of art, but of propaganda. What else does the word "propaganda" mean? And who ever doubted that *Uncle Tom* was great propaganda? Here is the difference between masterpieces and *Uncle Tom* (or rather, those aspects of it Tompkins likes). What has been gained by calling propaganda another kind of art? The confusion, I believe, is owing to ideological criticism's dogmatic historicism and relativism.

The traditional distinction between art and propaganda depends upon the Aristotelian notion that art, when it achieves universality, tells the truth, and yields knowledge (or makes an honest attempt at these things) is a kind of philosophy, while propaganda is a kind of rhetoric—the rhetoric of the Sophists, which seduces rather than teaches. Ideological criticism, by denying truth, collapses this distinction and obscures the relevant terms. In fact, it redefines both philosophy and art as propaganda—sophistical rhetoric—by seizing on the one denominator common to all discourse: the power to persuade. However, it makes no distinctions between kinds of persuasion (nor can it, having denied the existence of truth), thus reducing the question of greatness in philosophy and art to the question of power in its obvious sense: philosophy, art—and all discourse—are great in the way that Hitler's speeches or television is great: they capture and move an audience.

In this matter, I believe, ideological criticism is inferior to its chief radical rival—to which I believe it is usually superior—that of the "scientific" Marxism practiced by Terry Eagleton and the disciples of Louis Althusser. Although Eagleton, like the ideological critics, does not believe in the humanistic, Aristotelian (and classical Marxist) belief that great art attains universality—this is reserved for "science"—he at least draws a distinction between art that transcends conventional opinion, and rhetoric that manipulates it (or, as he would put it, literary production that "throws into relief the 'fault-lines'" of a "hegemonic ideological formation" and other production that merely reproduces it).[26] In addition, ideology itself is not seen as the all-enveloping mist from which thought cannot withdraw itself: Eagleton and Althusser both retain Marx's notion that ideology can be understood when its relations with politics and economics are laid bare. Hence, its degree of truth and value can be measured, both in relation to its own moment and to the present. Eagleton indeed, referring to literature, proclaims a "science of value,"[27] which must, by extension, apply to ideology too. Without some such notion (or the simpler, humanist one to which I subscribe) it is difficult to see how any judgment upon or between ideologies (or works of art) can be made. Why not subscribe to a "transcendent" ideology and a "transcendent" culture when all is ideology? Why are these worse than the ideological pluralism and "multiple" cultures to which the ideological critics subscribe? These questions can only be answered by an appeal that goes beyond ideology itself.

The reason why the ideological critics do not make this appeal is, I believe, narrowly political. They desire liberty, equality, and cultural pluralism and accept the (false) cliché that these will be furthered by rejecting, through relativism and historicism, a universalist hierarchy of values—which would follow on any claim to truth. They thus remain blind to the hierarchy inscribed in this very rejection. They are not to be singled out. The blindness is a perennial one, as can be seen by glancing at Plato's *Gorgias,* where, Callicles, a "democratic" politician and disciple of the Sophists, attacks Socrates' universalist attempt to establish a hierarchy of value by distinguishing virtue from power, knowledge from opinion, happiness from pleasure, and good from bad. However, since Callicles can only object to this attempt in the name of another version of reality, better to him, he is forced, in order to justify his preference, to make use of the very categories and terms (such as better and worse) that he ought, in principle, to object to. Rejecting a universalist hierarchy of values, Callicles proclaims that, in the absence of any other right, it is a natural law that might makes "right" (and "truth" as well), and that sophistical rhetoric, which he practices, because of its unsurpassed power, is the highest art, as the foundation of "right" and "truth." As a result, he thus reveals that his love of the *demos* is a mask for his own love of power, and that his relativist rhetoric (for so it is revealed to be, despite his invocation of natural law) is a vehicle for this.

The same is true, inadvertently I believe, for Tompkins, who, in another place, has written "if we deny . . . the possibility of the existence of objective texts and indeed the possibility of objectivity altogether" then "the net result is to repoliticize literature and criticism."[28] Tompkins means, of course, to repoliticize literature and criticism to the egalitarian left, but her praise of *Uncle Tom* is inconsistent with this. She praises it not because it is "an artifice of eternity," but because it is powerful, because it successfully attempts "to mold the values of its time"—although these values can never, according to relativism and historicism, be validated. Like Callicles, in other words, Tompkins objects to universality and a hierarchy of values based upon it, and admires the claims of power, thus advancing yet another hierarchy, but with power, not virtue, knowledge, or truth, at its apex. Might makes right—and, in this case, art. This *ideological* love of power, moreover, seems to inform much of the criticism of the other ideological critics, including Bercovitch and Jehlen—again, I believe, inadvertently. It is simply that they, like most postmodernists, are blind to two related Socratic insights: that the rejection of the concept of truth removes the barrier to a tyranny of rhetoric; and that a tyranny of rhetoric is a rhetoric of tyranny.

As evidence of this blindness, let us turn to a contradiction noted earlier, when Bercovitch, having told us that "there is no escape from ideology," goes on to claim that the aesthetic power of American literature evidently does escape it—for it is not diminished by that literature's ideological limitations. What is the reason for this contradiction? It is that Bercovitch, although he clearly believes that ideology limits all expression, also wishes to make an exception of aesthetic power. The result, if we allowed this, would be an ideology that claims that all expression is ideological except the expression of power. This is the ideology of power itself. That the power spoken of is only aesthetic power should not comfort us. In Bercovitch's discussion, aesthetic power very quickly becomes political power. Indeed they are identified: the rhetoric of Emerson and Whitman *is* the rhetoric that has "created in the word 'America' the most compelling cultural symbol of the modern era, nationally and internationally." Bercovitch's praise of the American ideology, in short, is clearly a praise of its persuasive power—its ability to be (cheerfully) *"compelling."*

How else (to further the point) can we explain another oddity: the belief of Bercovitch and Jehlen that, when the protagonists of classic American novels are defeated by society, these novels recommend social conformity? The oddness of this should be obvious: we would not say that Orwell, in *1984,* recommends social conformity because his hero is destroyed. Only if we believe that power is at once the source of all value and defines "truth" (in the absence of genuine truth) could this interpretation begin to make sense. The sense that it makes, however, is a little grim: O'Brien, not Smith, is right about four fingers equalling five: one ought to yield to power because power defines "ought." Conversely, one ought to seek power for precisely the same reason. These ideas dovetail with ideas implicit in the examples given just before: the denial of truth, the praise of aesthetic power, and the identification of aesthetic power with political power, amount to a praise of rhetorical power for the sake of power. The politics this concatenation implies are not libertarian.[29]

By not grasping this, ideological criticism partakes of a contemporary phenomenon that Alain Finkielkraut, in a lively pamphlet, has called *La Defaite de la penseé.*[30] As Finkielkraut observes, modern historicism and relativism began as a reactionary response to the idea of the universal rights of man promoted by the Enlightenment and the French Revolution. In order to resist these ideals, German romantics such as Herder claimed that they were not universal, but merely French. As a result, Germany had the right to its difference, because the rights of man had no universal sanction. Later, this would become the argument of the Fascists too, in effect, for while they did claim world supremacy this was chiefly on the basis of power—"the triumph of the will"—and on the rejection of universalist values. It is no accident, therefore, that Fascism received the tacit, and sometimes more than tacit, support of intellectuals such as Heidegger, Santayana, and the young Paul De Man; for these men had also rejected the idea of universality, in the name of historicism and relativism. Unfortunately, Finkielkraut argues, democratic intellectuals have forgotten these lessons, hence we have the peculiar phenomenon of their support, in the name of democratic tolerance—"we" should not impose "our" ideals on "them"—for regimes that violate "our" ideals of human rights, among them, the ideal of tolerance itself, and the ideal of democracy: for the usual form of political difference is a bureaucratic dictatorship. It matters little whether this is nominally on the "left" (as Mao's China, supported for a time by Julia Kristeva and many in the *Tel Quel* circle) or the "right" (as Khomeini's Iran, supported for a time by Michel Foucault). One implication is that if intellectuals are tolerant of bureaucratic seizures of power in the name of "multiple cultures"—because there are no "transcendent" cultures—it is because they are insufficiently critical of their own impulses to power, and the foundations of their own power, which are also bureaucratic, lodged in the institutions in which they are employed. Their very historicism and relativism is a warrant for this: they would like "to mold the values" of their time, but without reference to fussy limitations such as a concept of truth. Historicism, with relativism, then, is an ideology of bureaucratic collectivism—(another, with which it is in conflict, is "science"): in large measure, its seemingly liberating notion of cultural *différence* is a mask for anti-democratic sentiments. Of course, the ideological critics proclaim their anti-elitism, and they are sincere, but equality could never be achieved in a context where rhetorical power—that is, propaganda power—is the key to power as such. No matter how small the units or pluralistic the organization of society, the politics of ideological criticism implies the arbitrary rule of mandarins of discourse.

> Modern criticism was born of a struggle against the absolutist state; unless its future is defined against the bourgeois state, it might have no future at all.[31]

Thus Terry Eagleton, to whom there is a ready reply: criticism against the bourgeois state has a very comfortable future in bureaucratic institutions, such as universities, that do not depend upon the state being bourgeois (or democratic for that matter). I would apply the term bureaucratic criticism to much contemporary criticism for two reasons beyond the obvious one of style: first, because it is a sociological fact that the organization of mass education in any modern ideological society, whether bourgeois or not, is of necessity bureaucratic; second, because of contemporary criticism's tendency to deny enduring insight to literature but not to its critics, thereby ensuring that the meaning of literature is expropriated, institutionalized, and administered by institutionalized interpreters. The idea that there is no unmediated truth entails that meaning will devolve upon administrators: nothing is more evident in contemporary criticism than its passion for the administration of meaning. (Ideological criticism's disclaimer of enduring insight is insufficient: it still claims to know what most literature does not.) The denial of enduring insight—by which I mean nothing more portentous than insight into nature—which we find in both "scientific" Marxists like Eagleton, and in ideological criticism, has its difficulty however: if literature is not, as humanists believe, one of the royal roads to truth, why study it?

Eagleton's answer has already been given above. For the ideological critics, the answer is that if literature is short on insight it is long on rhetorical power: to study it is an apprenticeship.

Not all literature is very insightful; both "science" and ideological criticism have much to say about the ways literature can fail to achieve insight, and both can do justice to minor works, which are wholly of a particular time and place. But their attitude flattens major works. Of course in saying this I am throwing down the humanist gauntlet, but this is unavoidable. The humanist hypothesis—that there is a common human nature which different cultures develop in different directions, with the result that great art has at once a universal and exotic appeal, in which we find both identity and difference, and a revelation of natural possibility, perhaps hitherto unknown—has not been superseded by its no less hypothetical, but usually more complicated adversaries. The problem with "science" is not that it makes a claim to truth, but that it denies the possibility of truth to any other discourse. This is not what Marx did, when he spoke (much to the vexation of "scientists" such as Macherey and Balibar) of the eternal charm of Greek art: he thought that the Greeks had insight into an element of human nature.[32] He also thought that theory had to be brought to the bar of practice—which is why, in his later years, after the failure of the Paris Commune, he moved in the direction of social democracy. By not providing the grounds for its own refutation, or allowing that other discourses might reach the truth, this "science" approaches literature in the manner of those regimes that are willing to enter into a "dialogue" with the people—so long as power remains with the regime. This tendency of "scientific" Marxism is plainly reflected in the language of one of Althusser's admirer's—from a work on literary theory: "in to-day's political arena the strategic dictates of Eurocommunism give rise to one set of literary-political calculations whereas those of an intransigent proletarianism give rise to another." "Intransigent proletarianism": whose politics are thus stirringly evoked? Not those, I believe, of the proletariat anywhere, least of all the proletariat of Eastern Europe, of Poland for example, whose intransigent politics are very much feared by the bureaucrats of "intransigent proletarianism." In fairness to Althusser (and, by extension, to Eagleton, who is later criticized on similar grounds) this quotation comes from a critical admirer who finds him too much of an "idealist," so that he did not know that "the question is not what literature's effects *are* but what they might be *made to be*." If Althusser did not know this, so much the more credit to him: the tendency of the critical admirer, if we substitute "people's aspirations" for "literature's effects" is very clear.[33]

The problem with ideological criticism is not that it is historicist and relativist, but that it is dogmatically so: it is skeptical about everything except its "self-evident" premise that there is no truth. But nothing is less self-evident than the claim that it is true that there is no truth. The concept of ideology itself depends upon the idea of truth: one cannot not presume to say that someone has missed the truth—has been ideological—unless one can also presume to say what is the truth he has missed. Even if the idea of truth is in itself no less metaphysical, it at least does not bear the burden of internal contradiction.[34] Ideological criticism, in its tendency to deny the objectivity of "texts," shares the bureaucratic intention of "science" expressed in the paragraph above. A Ciceronian skepticism—a skepticism that extended to skepticism itself, thus accepting the probable, including the probable objectivity of the voices of others, which is what "texts" are—seems to be beyond its imagination. In short, bureaucratic criticism, whether "scientific" or ideological, fails because it does not sufficiently enter into a dialectic with the "texts" it reads. It refuses to consider the possibility that the premises of its own "text" might be placed and modified by another. No doubt some utilitarians thought the same, before Dickens wrote *Hard Times*.

The result is a regression, not a progression, from bourgeois humanism—whose chief characteristic, dividing it from other humanisms (for it is false that humanism is always bourgeois), is that satiric ambivalence which Trilling rightly saw as characteristic of the novel, that glory of bourgeois society and bourgeois man. Ambivalence and the quest for universality—the first holding dogma, the second irresponsibility, in check—this is one of the advantages of the novel over other large forms, and it was one of the advantages of bourgeois humanism and bourgeois society, for all of the exploitation of which Marx, its greatest critic, rightly spoke. Bourgeois humanism was of course a fragile synthesis, and the appetites unleashed by the capitalism that sustained it may prove too much for it: in "scientific" Marxism, we find a development anticipated by Lukacs, in *History and Class Consciousness*, when he spoke, not in denigration of genuine science, of the worship of "science" as the bourgeois ideology of those who have abandoned bourgeois ambivalence. Having abandoned ambivalence, "science" represents one side of the bourgeois dissolution.

Unfortunately, ideological criticism has been touched by the other side. As in deconstruction (when benign), ambivalence touches every object except the necessity of the critic's interventions, and the idea that all is ideological. If the wildness of deconstruction is largely absent, this is because deconstruction, unlike ideological criticism, retains both bourgeois humanism's quest for certainty and its ambivalence, but in dissociation and in furious motion—a dull theorizing and indeterminism, Casaubon and Ladislaw, in a negative dialectic. Ideological criticism is firmer than this, but because of the traits it shares with deconstruction—its rejection of the category of truth and its fascination with rhetorical power—ideological criticism shares the fate of all radical anti-bourgeois postmodernisms that are not "sciences." Far from transcending the bourgeois consciousness, it has merely the other part of the bourgeois consciousness—its humanism cast aside, its ambivalence become a dogma that subverts the quest for universality, but not for rhetorical power.

We are now in a position to see how the term "romance" is used by ideological criticism, and how it contributes to the ideological subversion of that criticism's valuable insights. Let me summarize that subversion here. Ideological criticism does recover, although it overstates and complicates, the perception of Henry James (and Van Wyck Brooks, in *America's Coming of Age*) that classic American literature, because often ideologically limited (from its uncritical faith in "Old America"), is often provincial in comparison with European literature of the same period. In the eyes of James and Brooks, old critics for whom literature was a criticism of life, the provinciality of American literature was a defect. So it seems to be for the ideological critics as well—especially given Bercovitch's suggestion that no American work has "international greatness"—until these critics "recall" their dogmatic relativism and historicism, and the mandarin power they desire: their relativism and historicism, because these undercut any attempt at an enduring evaluation; their (unwitting, in my opinion) desire for mandarin power, because they cannot bring themselves to sacrifice the power that accrues to the interpreters of a great literature. Hence the major American writers (not money, land, and political freedom) "created in the word 'America' the most compelling cultural symbol of the modern era." If the classic American literature were seen to miss greatness, the prestige, hence the power, of its interpreters might diminish. In the last analysis, then, the ideological critics draw back from the full force of their own (often convincing) insights and judgments, and claim that the limitations they find in American literature do not diminish "the aesthetic power of the texts themselves."

It is partly the resurrection of the theory of the American romance that allows the ideological critics to avoid the modest evaluation of the classic American novel that their analysis implies. That is, the theory functions for them largely as it did for the earlier romance critics: as a means of denying that the evident shortcomings of the American novel—for example, its abstraction, its insubstantiality—are actual shortcomings. As a result, the problem that vexes the history of the classic American novel—Why is this novel insubstantial?—remains unsolved. Yet one answer to this problem, I believe, has been approached by several critics, including the ideological critics themselves. To this we now turn.

The Case of the Classic American Novel

Once we have decided that the classic American novelists, when they succeed, write novels of the same kind as the Europeans—socially concerned, critical, and often utopian in aspiration, in which social and cultural tensions, revealed largely through manners, play the key role—we can then speak of the American novel's difference, a difference not in genre, but in quality. We want to know why the American novelists failed—not absolutely, but in contrast to the major novelists of England, France, and Russia.

The most obvious failure, their novels' relative insubstantiality—the thin social dimension of the characters, the weak notation of manners, that is, of class traits—which sometimes initiates the more active elements of "romance," has been a constant theme in these pages. Here it must be qualified.

First, insubstantiality is a problem chiefly for the major novelists, but only under certain conditions. When we turn from Hawthorne and Melville to Howells, or, at a lower level, to De Forest, Tourgée, and the regionalists, the problem of insubstantiality diminishes: a determined, very estimable writer such as Howells had little difficulty in dealing with American manners repeatedly, at length, and with a genuine distinction. Only under certain conditions because, when we consider Cooper and James, we find that their novels are repeatedly substantial, if not in Cooper's case consistently so.

But the ways Cooper and James succeed in achieving substantiality are revealing: they reveal another American limitation. This we are often unaware of, in part because nineteenth-century fiction is now remote in time, even when not in effect. For Cooper and James are most happily substantial when their novels are set at a distance from contemporary and strictly American subjects, either because they are set in the past, at a generation's remove (or more), or are set on foreign soil (or water) and incorporate the international theme. The actual proportion of their work devoted entirely to national subjects, and at a time very close to the writer's own present, is very small. In Cooper, there is really only *Home as Found, The Redskins,* and the minor *The Ways of the Hour* (unless we count *The Prairie*—set, however, twenty years in the past, with an international theme).[1] In James, there is only *Watch and Ward, The Bostonians* and the unfinished *The Ivory Tower*. And what is true for Cooper and James is largely true for Hawthorne, Melville, and Twain. Of Hawthorne's novels, including the uncompleted, only *The House of the Seven Gables* and *The Blithedale Romance* treat the American present, of Twain's novels, only *The Gilded Age*, of Melville's novels only *Pierre* and *The Confidence Man* treat it certainly (*Moby Dick*, for reasons given earlier, seems to me a case somewhat like *The Prairie*, I shall come back to it).[2] Moreover, these works often do not represent their authors at their best. Only *The Blithedale Romance* and *The Bostonians*, in my opinion, are major successes, although *The Gilded Age* has, in Colonel Sellers, a major character. And even if we accept the old high estimate of *The House of the Seven Gables*, the modern attempts to rehabilitate *Pierre* and *The Confidence Man*, include *Moby Dick*, and bring in from outside the usual canon, *Uncle Tom's Cabin*, the number remains small. It is even doubtful that their collective value equals that of the novels of the American past—such as *The Pioneers, Satanstoe* (and much of Cooper), *The Scarlet Letter, Tom Sawyer, Huckleberry Finn, Pudd'nhead Wilson, Washington Square*, and *The Europeans* (although this is international as well). If the objection be made that these, *Satanstoe*, and *The Scarlet Letter* excepted, are *only* a generation or a little more removed—and therefore practically contemporary—the reply given in my discussion of *The Pioneers* remains: a generation in America is a long time, especially when, as in the case of Twain and James, the Civil War, industrialization, and urbanization lie between the author and his subject. All of these novels, including *The Pioneers*, are deliberately remote, either in tone or because their material makes it plain that we are reading of a vanished world.

When we consider the novels with an international theme, some of which, such as many of Cooper's novels and *Benito Cereno*, are also set in the past, we can identify the classic American novelists' second weakness, related to, although not identical with, the insubstantiality of their novels. It is not that American novelists of genius avoided American society. They did write critically and successfully of America alone, chiefly in novels removed in time, and of contemporary America, chiefly through American characters in international novels. Nor did they lack interest in writing novels on contemporary and national subjects. They all wrote such novels and Cooper and James, as their last novels show, kept this interest to the end. But something checked the interest. At their best, the major American novelists remained writers of traditional novels, but they wrote very few novels, and fewer good ones, with subjects at once contemporary and wholly American. And again we must distinguish between the writers of genius and those without it such as Howells, for whom the American present was not a problem.

The difference from novelists in England, France, and Russia is plain. By this I do not mean that the novelists of these countries wrote only on contemporary and national subjects. On the contrary, they too had the custom of setting their novels at a generation's remove, and of touching, although less frequently, on international themes. Nevertheless, we rightly are not aware of failure in relation to the present and to national settings: *The Red and the Black,* for example, is just as "typical" a European classic as *War and Peace.* And a large percentage of European novels that begin at a generation's remove are *bildungsromans,* and do reach the present when their characters' destinies have unfolded—usually not the case with comparable American novels, which, when they begin at a generation's remove, tend to stay there. Mark Twain's failure to fulfill his intention to write a novel about Tom and Huck as adults is symptomatic.

This brings me to the last qualification. Beginning with the 1890s the anomalies disappear. Although Edith Wharton will also write consistently of Europe and of the American past, she and the other important novelists will write novels at once substantial, contemporary, and entirely national in subject. In this they will be like their minor American and major European contemporaries.

The problem, then—the "case" of the classic American novel—can now be stated in all of its elements. We want to know why, until the 1890s, major American novels were at once so large (respectably so in "historical" subjects, and especially so in international subjects)—and so limited (in substantiality and, regarding contemporary America, in number and quality). We want to know why the minor novels of the time suffered less from the same limitations, and why these limitations should cease as the nineteenth century came to an end. And we want to have some explanation for the mixed quality of those major novels that do treat contemporary and national subjects: the major failures of *The Redskins, Home as Found, The House of the Seven Gables,* and (although this is contentious) *Pierre,* and *The Confidence Man;* the major successes of *The Blithedale Romance, The Bostonians,* the early scenes of *Moby Dick,* the Colonel Sellers sections of *The Gilded Age,* and those parts of *Uncle Tom's Cabin* that retain, as Edmund Wilson called it, their "eruptive force."[3]

The problem is complex enough to invite an ecumenical solution, one that includes the valuable ideas, while avoiding the excesses, of some of the critics I have been considering. The first comes from the critic who, I believe, came closest to defining the difficult position of the major novelists in nineteenth-century America.

In *America's Coming of Age,* Van Wyck Brooks ascribed the deplorable insubstantiality of classic American literature to the effects of a cultural rift—between highbrow and lowbrow, between sensitive artists and thinkers and the vulgar *hoi polloi:* American novelists, made too genteel by their Puritan heritage, failed to come to terms with American life. Some of Brooks' explanation—especially the influence of historical Puritanism (although not of "Puritan" morality)—has been unconvincing ever since Perry Miller demonstrated that Puritan culture was not as Brooks described it, and that, in any case, Puritan influence was at an end by the time the American novelists began to write. More important, the populist strain in Brook's thought led him too quickly to blame the artists; it was this populism, as expressed by Parrington, that Trilling rightly attacked in "Reality in America." And he, by denying that failure had occurred, initiated the theory of the American romance.

Yet Brooks, I believe, had a valid perception, which shows how the problem of insubstantiality and the problem of treating contemporary America, although not identical, are related. Far from being unconcerned with American society—or society at all as Trilling would have had it—the major American novelists were so concerned that they were radically alienated from it. If too much gentility was not the cause, what answer can be sought if not in consensus? Many critics, including Brooks, have identified the problem, but the clearest statement, I believe, was made by Q. D. Leavis. According to her, here echoing Kaul, American novelists were moved by a desire to prove that America was superior to Europe not only in its ability to create a high standard of living, but in its ability to create civilization—a life of the mind, the spirit, and the senses that was not a simple reflex of material need, or a simple extension of material appetites. The idea of civilization (a little neglected in contemporary criticism) rejoins the theme of culture, for civilization is the crown of a "whole way of life." For this reason, we recall, cultural tensions in society were the natural subject of the novel.

The idea of civilization is, of course, in part a very materialistic one, as Aristotle and Marx both knew. Although it does not require much technology or luxury, it does require the satisfaction of material needs, and enough surplus wealth to provide an amount of education, leisure, and freedom. The unavailability of these things is the scandal of any society, and in the nineteenth century the machinery that withheld them called down the wrath of writers and reformers in America as in Europe. But because America, then as now—and perhaps more than now—seemed comparatively wealthy and free, the high civilized hopes of the American novelists were based on plausible grounds. They had no desire to ignore social and cultural tensions—from these they would fashion their visions of culture—but they reasonably expected that the tensions in America might hold a richer promise than anywhere else. For in their eyes, the tensions and the promise were preeminently those of a prosperous democracy. The American novelists, according to Leavis—like Matthiessen, Kaul, and a host of other critics—equated America with democracy, and so equated the cultural fortunes of both. They wished to exalt democracy by praising America's cultural achievements, but there came a point when each had to confess that the honest perception was of relative failure. This arrived, no doubt, in many ways, but the most common was through a comparison with Europe, obtained either through travel—although sometimes this came late—or simply through reading, as befitted men of letters.

> [In Europe, Americans] encountered high cultures of the past embodied in visible forms . . . but more painfully, they met also a present culture embodied in superior manners and a finer social life, and in England, as even William James and Mark Twain ruefully noted, not merely internal beauty but a countryside landscaped and gardened as well as productively farmed, and with the considerable charm of countless picturesque towns and villages, an aesthetic beauty America had never achieved. For patriotic Americans, the fact that the evils of feudalism and aristocracy had resulted in immemorial beauty still being maintained and added to at that, whereas American democracy had pioneered only ugliness and destruction, was morally distressing to them.[4]

In short, the patriotic pride of Gopher Prairie collided with the perception of Carol Kennicott long before Sinclair Lewis himself ever saw the light of day. The result was a shock from which (in my opinion, here departing from Leavis) the American novelists were often unable to recover. How much of a shock can be gauged from an observation of Trilling's, which, had he developed it, might have deterred him from launching the theory of the American romance at all. It is that the novel in its classic intention, although essentially critical, often achieves substantiality not only in a spirit of criticism, but in a spirit of love:

> Mr. Pickwick and Sam Weller; Priam and Achilles—they exist by reason of their observed manners.

> So true is this, indeed, so creative is the novelist's awareness of manners, that we may say that it is a function of his love. It is some sort of love that Fielding has for Squire Western that allows him to note the great gross details which bring the insensitive, sentient man into existence for us.[5]

We can now rejoin Brooks and the theme of alienation. The novelists' problem was not that America lacked cultural tensions, nor that it lacked variety of manners—despite the insistence to the contrary, on the part of many critics (here Brooks was right to have insisted that Whitman had revealed that the material was there).[6] No doubt democracy had narrowed the range of manners, as foreign observers would notice: but as the American scenes of *Martin Chuzzlewit* remind us, the scene was far from flat. However, despite cultural tension and variety, despite wealth and potential leisure, America remained less civilized than Europe. The finer the American artist, the more sensitive to the life of the mind, the spirit, and the senses, the less likely, once he had discovered the impoverishment, he would be able to love American life. Or rather, although he might love it, he could not love it as a novelist. This, it seems to me, is the source of the complaints we find in Cooper, Hawthorne, and James: the common theme is the absence of the picturesque, which is, in most ways, a civilized quality—a thoughtful, yet spirited sensuality, the presence of art in the objects and actions of ordinary life. (This absence, I believe, goes some way to explain the compensatory emphasis on the natural landscape, violence, and physical energy in American life and literature.)[7] By this token, Queequeg is in some ways the most civilized person in New Bedford (as indeed Ishmail perceives): he makes a place for the mind through contemplation and his willingness to learn from other cultures, the spirit through friendship and religion (which Ishmail accepts on the grounds of natural piety), for the senses through self-adornment and uninhibited physical affection. In short, the interest in society, which American and European novelists shared, was crossed, in the Americans, by a sense of cultural inferiority, which the European novelists did not have. To the extent that substantiality depends upon love, the finer American novelists had to struggle with abstraction.

But doesn't this return us to the romance critics? Or, if not to them, to Rahv's "Palefaces and Redskins?" Am I not talking about the pursuit of the goods of a single way of life, the uniform manners of a materialistic consensus? Not quite, because this explanation can take us only so far. First, as I have mentioned, when dealing with the past, American novelists often were able to write substantially of the very society that had thwarted its contemporaries: no great novel of the 1790s in America was written by anyone of the time, but Cooper in *The Pioneers,* and Melville in *Benito Cereno* wrote novels at least touched by greatness, and chiefly American in subject, set in that very decade. There are arguably more major novels about the late 1840s and early 1850s than there are major novels of that decade, and so on. This implies a difficulty different from an absence of available society. Second, I have risked overstating the case: not all of America was uncivilized or lacked civilized promise; nor was the development of society and culture uniform. To an extent, what the novelists discovered were the regressive cultural consequences of the crisis of that pre-Civil War Old America, evoked so poignantly by Henry James in *Hawthorne,* of which I have earlier spoken, that is, the centrifugal development of the country and the "Jacksonian" overthrow of the civilized tidewater elites. The result was, on the one hand, an acquisitive "democratic" populace led by new elites (often vociferously "anti-elitist") whose mind was bent upon material gain and whose religious impulses, pushed to one side, repressed the spirit and the senses; on the other hand, the now equally inhibited old "republican" patriciates, whose enlightenment ethos undermined their ability to come to terms creatively with the romanticism that might have revitalized them culturally, if not politically.[8] This was, in fact, a perfect situation for novelists, as some of them recognized to a great extent: the contrast between Legree and St. Clare in *Uncle Tom's Cabin* dramatizes it. It was not, however, a situation flattering to American democracy, which brings me to the third reason why substantiality was not beyond the grasp of American novelists. It is this: not all substantiality in the novel depends upon love. Although it is probably true that a novel like *Pickwick* requires a novelist to love his subject, there is, in the absence of love, from the absence of civilization, another substantiality available. In fact, there is another subject: the absence of civilization itself. If it does not permit the genial substantiality of *Pickwick*, it is the source of the tauter, corrosive substantiality of *Hard Times,* the American scenes of *Martin Chuzzlewit, The Red and the Black, Madame Bovary,* and *Sentimental Education.*

Satire, in other words, as Brooks observed in *The Ordeal of Mark Twain,* was the perfect mode to treat aspects of the American scene, especially the gap between pretensions and realities. Here too we can feel the force of James' objection that Hawthorne was not enough of a realist because he was too uncritical. From a sufficiently satirical perspective, American manners would have sprung into "observable relief." In fact, to speak only of classic novels in subject both national and contemporary, I would say that the novelists knew this. *The Blithedale Romance* and *The Bostonians,* although not only satirical, are chiefly satires. To the extent that *The Gilded Age* succeeds at all, its success is built upon satire—although Sellers, like Pickwick and Micawber, is larger than the satire he inspires. Even *Pierre* and *The Confidence Man,* although they veer into abstraction, are intended as satires (I say "intended" because I think they fail). Hawthorne catches the note of *Hard Times* in the portrait of Pyncheon, and many of the effective passages in Cooper are satirical as well. With satire, novelists of minor talent like Brackenridge and Adams could fulfill themselves: the immense *Modern Chivalry,* still in parts quite funny, shows that substantiality was available through satire even in the republic's earliest years. A touch of satire might have made Brockden Brown a little more coherent; and it was perhaps Howells' unwillingness to take satire far enough that prevented him from being a major novelist. As that expert satirist (in both the novel and criticism) Gore Vidal, has written: "the satirist breaks with his origins; looks at things with a cold eye; says what he means, and mocks those who do not know what *they* mean."[9] James especially, in *The Bostonians,* shows us what could have been frequently done. The struggle between Ransom and Olive, so traditionally rooted in class and cultural differences, is overlaid by a satirical perception of the radical deficiencies in each.

What kept the American novelists from breaking with their origins more often than they did? It is not quite that, although disappointed with American life, most American novelists remained faithful to democracy. This was a difficulty that could have been overcome had they possessed an idea of democracy larger than their society's. (In fact, in their successful novels, I believe that they often did, but the subject of this chapter is not success.) Too often, however, they did not. Here Leavis' remarks dovetail with an idea of the ideological critics (and, further back, of Henry James): that the symbol of America, drawn from the ideology of the early republic, acted as an "ancestral taboo." The obstacle was this: the idea that America and democracy were one, that America so far embodied democratic possibility that its failures reflected upon democracy itself. To remain loyal to the idea of democracy, while disliking American life as the only possible fruit of democracy, to believe, as a democrat, that a satirically substantial treatment of American life would compromise the democratic ideal: this was, taken with the conviction that informed it, the "American ideology"—or rather, as I think Henry James would have called it, the American provinciality. For the belief, after all, was provincial. Democracy, because it arose from the political and social movements of the Enlightenment, belonged to Europeans as much as to Americans. Meanwhile, some of the unsettled problems of American life—the effects of the unrestrained capitalism among them—were neither specifically American nor (to say the least) democratic.

How far did the major American novelists accept this idea? Regarding their conscious views, the question is perhaps the wrong one. The idea that America and democracy are one is an American folk belief, a little like the folk belief in France that civilization ends on the west bank of the Rhine. And folk beliefs, because they exist in popular assumption, do not require conscious assent to be effective. Our idea even crops up in the attitudes of modern historians, who should and probably do "know" better: in assumption it is "believed" and "disbelieved" by turns.[10] Regarding the classic American novelists, the point is this: they sometimes behaved as if they did believe the idea. It had power over them: often, it checked or ruined their satirical impulses. The reasons for its power can be simply stated: actual, if occasional belief, fear of appearing undemocratic (or unpatriotic), and historical circumstances. The last is the most important and implies the other two. The idea was born and had its greatest currency in Old America before its crisis, when a series of events—the establishment of the republic, its prosperous expansion, the separation of America from Europe by the Napoleonic Wars, and the momentary check those wars put upon European democratic aspirations—made it seem very plausible, even to the intelligent, that America was democracy's natural, and only, home. Now the classic American novelists were children of Old America: Cooper, Hawthorne and Melville (virtually) lived out their lives in it, and the continual return to the Old America of childhood and youth in the writings of Twain and James testifies to the spell it continued to cast long after it had been swept away.

Here then, is my hypothesis for the major American novelists dilemma. On the one hand, their perceptive and anguished dissatisfaction with contemporary American life made it difficult for them to write of that life with a substantiality born of a fascinated love. On the other hand, their democratic ideals, which they associated with America, especially the promise of Old America, made it difficult for them to contemplate a realistic satire of the contemporary American scene. Their resolution of this dilemma, I believe, accounts for the directions their writing actually took.

Now this hypothesis, I want to insist, although ecumenical, is a very limited one. It is just its limited nature that appeals to me. It allows us to dispense with the consensus interpretation of American history and the triumphalist aspects of the theory of the American romance. We do not have to assume that American novelists lacked subjects, owing to the absence of cultural or class tensions in America, and that, because of this, or because of unique intellectual interests, they wrote in an exceptional and admirable American genre. In fact, they had the same subjects as novelists elsewhere (including the one less available in civilized Europe) and they used them—though some were not as well used as they certainly might have been. And although I agree with the ideological critics that the novelists sometimes yielded to something we can call, following them, the "American ideology," I do not agree that this was a relentless consensual progression extending from the Puritans to the present, or that it limited all of the novelists' work and accounted for its energy at once. As I see it, the "American ideology" was not a world view, but an idea of a particular moment—the moment of Old America—and was restricted in its influence: so far as it limited the novelists' work, its influence was wholly bad.[11] It was restricted chiefly to the major novelists who grew up in Old America itself, and it very much affected a part of their work—especially when they contemplated, directly and exclusively, the American scene. It did not, however, always prevent them from looking beyond the boundaries of their culture. In examining both the American past and international subjects, they were constantly looking beyond the boundaries of their culture. Sometimes they did this when they examined the contemporary American scene as well. It was precisely when they did *not* that we can find the influence of the "ideology."

This it seems to me, is the right emphasis when we turn to the elements of the American novel's "case." It is especially so when we consider the American novelists' preference for the past and for international subjects, for it allows me to correct an impression my discussion so far may have invited, that these subjects represented an escape from the dismal American scene. Now this is partially true—and why not? Escape, when beautiful, has its own legitimacy. It even implies a criticism of the society it has left behind. (This is one point about many of the stories of Poe and Hawthorne—to this extent Trilling was right to have defended both, especially Hawthorne, against Parrington's populist strictures.) But most of the novels on "historical" and international subjects have a purpose beyond escape—the same that animates the novels on contemporary and national subjects: the critical and reforming purpose of the novel in its classic intention. That purpose arose precisely out of the disturbance—the creative disturbance—of the major American novelists' sharp reaction to American actuality. As I have argued in other chapters, in pursuing their subjects, especially international subjects and those drawn from the American past, the American novelists were largely writing the imaginative history of their society—including its contacts with other societies. And that in this they were engaged, as major novelists everywhere, in an active quest for civilization—"culture"—in the largest sense: for ideas and manners that suggested an ideal of how life might be lived, and that reflected critically on existing societies, including their own. In the international novels especially, the satire of American manners has a large role. The internationalism itself and the charms and virtues granted other societies all indicate how little the novelists thought that the whole of civilization was to be found in contemporary America. And sometimes (in *Satanstoe* for example) the American past is evoked to the same effect. Like the Europeans, in other words, American novelists responded to the cultural tensions in their class society, but, owing to their sense that America itself was short in civilized possibility, they turned more frequently than Europeans did to a study of societies not their own—not only to celebrate them, but to examine them critically as well, for the light they could cast on the American present. Responding to the crisis of Old America, Cooper set two-thirds of the Littlepage trilogy and *Wyandotté* in the past, Hawthorne turned to the New England past and to Europe, Melville turned to the late eighteenth century in *Benito Cereno*, and to the contemporary world of the cosmopolitan sailors and the South Sea islanders ("I'll try a pagan friend, thought I, since Christian kindness has proved but hollow courtesy").

At the same time, although the study of society, in the interest of culture and civilization, was the major motive, it is also possible to discover compensatory motives. The very small number of successful novels on contemporary American subjects suggests that the novelists could most easily release their powers when they turned to the past and to the wider world. The turn from the contemporary American scene, in other words, was an often successful strategy against inhibitions imposed by the idea that to satirize America was to satirize the democratic hope of the world. Perhaps by criticizing other societies—either American society in the past or a foreign one—American novelists could demonstrate, to themselves or to their public, that it was not *only* contemporary America they wished to single out. In addition, distance in time or place may have brought an equanimity unattainable when a subject had a contemporary reference: perhaps for this reason the satire of entrepreneurialism in *Satanstoe* is more convincing than in *The Redskins*, while the satire of American innocence in *Benito Cereno* is better focused than in *Pierre*.

So much for the preference of the major novelists for "historical" and international subjects (but not for their failures in these subjects—to which I shall return). It is easy to see now why the preference, and in one sense the achievement, was different for the minor novelists. Howells is largest of these—

so large that his minor status may one day be upgraded.[12] But even if we make an exception of Howells, what is usually said of him is certainly true of De Forest, Tourgée, and the regionalists. That is, they didn't have the awareness of civilized possibility that marks the major novelists (even if we are unhappy, as I am, with what some of the major novelists made of their awareness). They are, most readers believe, too undisturbing—despite their virtues and often large interests. Talent aside, this effect most probably exists because they were a little too undisturbed themselves.

But now, as I think we can see, it was precisely because of their lack of disturbance, that they, Howells included, could have so readily treated the contemporary American scene. Had they been more aware of civilized possibility they would have been as the major novelists were, so disturbed by contemporary America they could never have approached it readily. Either this, or their impressive substantiality would have been much more difficult to achieve. Of course, nobody would say of the better minor novelists that they are simply uncritical. But the social problems they examine do not disturb them as social problems disturb major writers. *Miss Ravenel's Conversion,* for example, is a large novel with an exciting subject. But when we compare it with *Vanity Fair,* which clearly influenced it, its minor quality is evident. *Vanity Fair* itself may not quite be the masterpiece Victorian readers thought it was, but nobody would think of describing it as a Napoleonic Wars novel. The wars are an integral part of the book, but Thackeray's imagination does not stop with them. By contrast *Miss Ravenel's Conversion* really is a Civil War novel. De Forest is excited only by the war, and does not recognize, as Thackeray does, that his war is an occasion to call into question all the assumptions and conventions that characterize his world. Something similar could be said about Tourgée's *A Fool's Errand,* when we contrast it with any one of the great Russian novels that incorporate the theme of the emancipation of the serfs. In short, if the minor American novelists found it relatively easy in their work to be at once American, contemporary, and substantial, it is precisely because they were minor, in the sense that their awareness of civilization was limited. Contemporary America did not disturb them enough, and they were content with it as a subject.

This brings us to the novels of major writers that did treat contemporary subjects and failed—thus depriving contemporary readers of an imaginative portrait of American society. I mean novels such as *The Redskins, Home as Found,*[13] *The House of the Seven Gables, Pierre* and *The Confidence Man.* How do these novels fail? And how does their failure reflect on the problem of insubstantiality?

Let me summarize traditional arguments that disappointed readers (rightly, I believe) have made: that *The Redskins* suffers from a declamatory didacticism and a contrived happy ending (the improbable alliance of frontiersmen, gentry and Indians); that a similar ending (Judge Pyncheon's death) ruins the logic of the plot, such as it is, of *The House of the Seven Gables;* that the abstraction of *Pierre* leaves the hero's psychology insufficiently dramatized; and that the abstraction of *The Confidence Man* leaves the episodes insufficiently differentiated, with the result that the novel is repetitious, dull, and (luckily) unmemorable. Regarding these novels, the idea of a taboo, owing to an identification of democracy with America, seems to me an important part of the truth, if not perhaps the entire truth. Had their authors not been democrats or had they been able to detach their democratic hopes from the fate of the United States, the perception of American failure would not have shocked them as it did. As it was, they were unable to reconcile democratic hope with the perception of American failure. Either the hope denied the failure or the failure destroyed the hope. In *The Redskins* we get both results: the didacticism, from Cooper's outrage at the entrepreneurs' triumph over the gentry, the contrived happy ending, from his inability to accept (as an artist) this triumph. Something similar can be said of *The House of the Seven Gables:* Hawthorne was afraid that the logic of his story, which foreshadowed the triumph (or survival, at least) of Judge Pyncheon, would impugn the superiority of the democratic present to the undemocratic past—whose heir Judge Pyncheon is. In *Pierre* and *The Confidence Man* the failure is just the opposite. The abstraction of these novels is owing to the nihilistic despair remarked by all readers, which corroded Melville's capacity to dramatize his materials and cancelled his satire at once. (Satire, after all, requires a belief in something—while nihilism rejects belief.) Perhaps this despair was initiated, as some critics have claimed, by the American public's rejection of *Moby Dick,* which caused Melville to lose his tenuous, populist faith. (Very probably, because the style of *Pierre,* especially in the early chapters, often parodies the sentimental literature preferred by that public—the worst possible choice, however, to develop the psychology of the hero and dreadful to read besides: the object of parody defeats the parodist.) But whatever the source, the result was the same. Here, I think, Sacvan Bercovitch is exactly right: American failure became, for Melville, the failure of humanity—which led him (although Bercovitch would not want to follow me so far) to take his eye off American society and leave his characters undeveloped, especially in *The Confidence Man.* It is of course because they are undeveloped that they sometimes seem to achieve universality. But their universality is not like that of *Gulliver's Travels* (with which *The Confidence Man* has been compared), where the abstract conception has a concrete execution. We *remember* the characters and situations of *Gulliver.* (Quick now, name the memorable characters and situations in the *The Confidence Man.*)[14]

Each of these novels, then, at least partially fails because none is able to sustain the satire implied by the subject. Hand in hand with this, I believe, is the problem I mentioned in earlier chapters in connection with Cooper's work and Hawthorne's use of Chillingsworth: improbable events and abstract mythic characters—symbols of emotional safety—steer the novel away from experience the author does not want to explore, because he wants to affirm a vision without inviting ambivalence towards it. In Cooper the failure, as I have mentioned, is a simple one: the polemicist overwhelmed the novelist. *The Redskins* is a traditional novel and its social criticism is sustained, although very overwrought. In Hawthorne and Melville the failure goes deeper, and touches, much more than in Cooper, on the idea of a taboo. In *The House of the Seven Gables,* there is a notable tendency to deny the perception of American social failure. In *Pierre,* to a degree, and in *The Confidence Man* throughout, there is a tendency, through the very abstraction that leaves the characters undeveloped to implicate humanity in that failure, which then ceases to be American. In the first case, democratic hope is spuriously saved, in the second American failure merges with human nature as the cause of despair. In either case the satirical focus on American society collapses, and the collapse of the satire is the collapse of the art. So brief a comment leaves much unsaid, but I hope that it indicates how, had the writers of these novels not been bound by a provincial scruple, they might very well have realized the promise their novels contained. *The Redskins,* equanimity achieved, might have been as good a novel as Tate's *The Fathers*— an elegiac portrait of a convention-bound aristocracy that collapses before upstarts who violate the conventions upon which aristocratic power is based. *The House of the Seven Gables,* with a careful portrait of a generations-long class conflict, might have been an American *Bleak House. Pierre,* purged of its parodistic style, and with its sociological context more carefully explored, might have been a psychologically convincing satire of ineffectual, privileged innocence, a darker American *Idiot,* and *The Confidence Man,* its scenes more individualized, more vivid, might have been the American *Dead Souls.*

The success of American novelists when they treat contemporary and national subjects should now be evident and can be quickly stated. In *The Blithedale Romance, The Bostonians,* and the parts of *Moby Dick, Uncle Tom,* and *The Gilded Age* that certainly succeed, success arrives largely because the satire is uninhibited. It is possible to suppose that this was furthered by the subjects themselves. In the New Bedford and Nantucket scenes, and some of the descriptions of the crew and its work in *Moby Dick,* Melville had a warmth for his subjects: he could portray them and satirize them—and not only satirize them— freely. Twain had a similar warmth for Sellers: in Melville and Twain we get a critical substantiality mingled with love. Probably the power of *Uncle Tom,* unique in Stowe's work, was possible because slavery, of all American institutions, was the easiest to dissociate from the idea of democracy. Edmund Wilson believed that Stowe's "consciousness that the national ideal was in danger," gave her a "desperate candor," much like Dickens'.[15] Probably Hawthorne, in *The Blithedale Romance,* is comfortable as a satirist precisely because the satire is directed more at the utopian reformers than at the society they wish to reform. The book sometimes fails in quality and substantiality when the focus shifts away from them—to Priscilla for example, who is almost, like Phoebe in *The House of the Seven Gables,* an abstract symbol for the middle-class domesticity Hawthorne too often simply affirmed. (Priscilla, however, is not quite so uncritically presented.) Something similar could be said of *The Bostonians,* except that it is too large and succeeds throughout. To my mind, *The Bostonians* is the greatest of the classic American novels with an American setting. Its only rival is *Huckleberry Finn,* and it is no accident that James and Twain, ordinarily so different as artists, are, in these novels, similar in important ways: both treat subjects related to what each believed was the central event in American history, the Civil War, both invent a panoramic cast of characters, the portrayal of whose relations achieves considerable substantiality, both share a similar satirical humor—compare, for example, the charlatanry of Sellah Tarrant with that of the Duke and the Dauphin, or the effusions of Verena Tarrant with the poetry of Emmeline Grangerford.[16] *The Bostonians* and *Huckleberry Finn* (except for its burlesque resolution, which is as contrived, and for the same reason, as Pyncheon's death in *The House of the Seven Gables*) achieve the poise of the great European novels, and offer us a substantial, critical, and satirical analysis of American manners, ideas, passions, and follies. James, of course, as the most sophisticated of American novelists, was the one least likely to suffer from ideological limitation. I think it was rather a spirit of chivalry that lead him to undertake contemporary American subjects so rarely, and that also—in part— led him in his other American novels to portray with great, if critical, affection the more attractive, because more civilized, Old American subjects of *Washington Square* and *The Europeans.*

What of the question of insubstantiality? I think it has been answered, to the extent that it can be, in what has gone before. What is true for the novels of contemporary national subjects is true for the tradition as a whole. For the turn to the American past and to the wider world, although largely successful, was not completely so. In these subjects too, the American novelists found what they took to be democratic and American failures, and sometimes they retreated or collapsed before what they saw. Elsewhere I have mentioned *The Prairie, The Scarlet Letter* and *Huckleberry Finn* in this connection. In *The Prairie,* when the abstract Natty defeats the concrete Bushes and clears the way for more genteel (and also more abstract) settlers, "romance" defeats realism and softens the satirical focus. For if the Bushes are Americans, so is Natty: democratic and American honor is saved. The same could be said of the burlesque in *Huckleberry Finn:* by reducing Jim to an abstract cliché, it diminishes the force of the satirical social theme. In *The Scarlet Letter,* the abstract Chillingsworth lightens the burden of responsibility on Hester and Dimmesdale. Even clearly international novels were not immune from this problem: in *The Marble Faun,* after descriptions of Rome and expatriate life that promise to make this Hawthorne's most substantial novel, Hawthorne turns to "romance" to tip the scales from Donatello and the fascinating Miriam in favor of his priggish Americans, Kenyon and Hilda. These are all local and dramatic examples, but I believe they highlight the dilemma of the tradition as a whole: novels that do not love, and that cannot satirize their subjects, are doomed to insubstantiality.

Let one last example suffice to make the point, although here I am treading on dangerous ground. *Moby Dick* is often called the greatest of American novels, but, as I indicated in my introduction, I agree with the case made by Martin Green against the Ahab sections: that the psychology of Ahab, like Pierre's, is undeveloped (we can't imagine Ahab, as Green observed, without the wooden leg), that the Gothic aura and lavish rhetoric Ahab imports to the book are intrusions, and that, as a result of both defects, Ahab's hold on his crew is insufficiently established, thus leaving unrealized the novel's dramatic possibilities.[17] Consider the change brought about in the novel by Ahab's quest speech. Until then, in the New Bedford and Nantucket scenes and the early scenes aboard the Pequod, Melville has been writing beautifully, in a mode of satirical romantic realism, akin to Dickens and Twain, that he had developed in some of his early work. Suddenly, as everyone notices, with the speech of Ahab, which doesn't so much persuade the crew as cast a spell over it, the rhetorical temperature heats up. Since Melville was so much influenced by Shakespeare, consider the difference between this speech and Antony's in *Julius Caesar,* when the Roman populace is persuaded to revolt against Caesar's assassins. There, the populace has first-hand knowledge of the victim and of his killers: Caesar's career and Roman politics are established facts in their lives. And the action Antony urges, although extreme, is given a fitting context by the assassination itself. In that context, the course of action he urges is very plausible. In *Moby Dick,* on the contrary, the crew has little first-hand acquaintance of Ahab and none at all of the white whale. Moreover, what Ahab urges is preposterous in the context of their lives. Yet, Antony, although his task is more plausible, is given a speech that is not only long, but that also bears the marks of the most careful preparation. It also has the benefit of Shakespeare's poetry. Ahab's speech, by contrast, is much briefer and extemporaneous. And I suppose even admirers of *Moby Dick* have never claimed that its language (here) ranks with Shakespeare's: ("What do you do when you see a whale, men?"). Yet Ahab is just as successful as Antony. This is why I say he casts a spell. It is true that Melville allows reservations to Starbuck, but Ahab's response to this, if more developed, is no less inexplicable in its success ("Take off thine eye! more intolerable than fiend's glarings is a doltish stare! . . . Stand up amid the general hurricane thy one tost sapling cannot, Starbuck!"—phrases that invite the response of the Puritan children in *The Scarlet Letter:* "Come, therefore, and let us fling mud at them")—as Melville himself seems to recognize, when he calls

Starbuck's acquiescence "enchanted." Nevertheless, the Pequod's course is set. Thereafter, whenever Ahab is centerstage, the novel is transformed (into a failure, in my opinion, until the white whale saves it—in part by killing Ahab; into a great romance, in the opinion of others). This does argue, I believe, for the working of a taboo—an unwillingness, which became an incapacity, to continue in the satirical mode of romantic realism, even if we allow that Melville circumvented or transcended his difficulty. What was the difficulty? Probably the same that later ruined *Pierre*. Ahab, an American figure, is clearly rejected, but so overwrought is the reaction to him that Melville overshoots the mark, and transforms his character into a Gothic Titan whose failure implicates humanity, and lets America, no less than the white whale, off the hook. Critics who see the Ahab sections as a successful criticism of America, because Ahab is "representative" of "the American world,"[18] are, I believe (following Green), simply inventing the novel Melville might have written, but did not write. Because of abstraction, the connections are not sufficiently developed to make Ahab nationally representative. Indeed, some of Ahab's behavior (his reliance on Fedallah's black magic, for example) is arguably unrepresentative. Meanwhile, its frequent preposterousness (the blank verse soliloquies, the reliance on Fedallah again) prevents him from effectively representing a more generalized type of humanity.

The point, I hope, has been made, even if we make an exception of *Moby Dick*. Where love and satire fail, abstraction begins, and with it, at times, come more intrusive forms of "romance"—contrivance in plot and abstract, ideological symbols, both reflecting a need for emotional safety. Where abstraction alone is the difficulty, the novel is simply less substantial than it might be. When plot contrivance and symbols of emotional safety are employed, satirical criticism is either denied or spoiled when it is sustained. And although the novel may be amplified by abstract mythic characters, some positive, like Natty, and some who, like Ahab, attract the author's critical attention, substantiality, in the sense of believable manners (believable in the context of the novel) yields again. To sum up: abstraction—hence insubstantiality—is a substitute for satire and criticism of American life, associated in the democratic artists' mind with democratic possibility. If we speak of it at all we speak not of a genre, but of evasion or overwrought response in the context of traditional novels. But where art is defeated, American society triumphs, offering us one more reason why the nationalist critics of the fifties were indifferent to plot contrivance, enchanted by tendentious symbols of emotional safety, and excited by the idea of abstract romance.

My discussion is nearing an end. If the belief that America embodied democratic hope was most plausible in Old America, the obvious reason why it did not affect the novelists of the 1890s, with one exception, is simply that they had no experience of Old America itself, but had much experience of the Gilded Age. They were only tepidly democratic and very much disabused. The idea that America and democracy were one, even had they believed it, could have had no intense reality for them. This last comment connects to a limitation many readers have noticed, especially in Norris and Dreiser: it is difficult to imagine any idea that could have disturbed them as much as energy, cruelty, and suffering. But as has been often said, it was perhaps just for that reason that they were so relatively uninhibited. As a result, in their novels, intellectual and stylistic turgidity and substantiality go hand in hand.

The one exception among the novelists we can associate with the 1890s—although her best work belongs to the next two decades—was Edith Wharton. For she was connected to Old America through Old New York, and in almost every way she is closer to James than to the more nearly contemporary Dreiser. This is why she is such an exemplary figure. Not only does she succeed in novels of the American past and in international novels, in her novels of contemporary American society—*The House of Mirth,* the first half of the *Custom of the Country, Ethan Frome, Summer,* and *Bunner Sisters*—she shows what the earlier classic American novelists, allowing for their different temperaments, might have accomplished more often and more consistently. It is true that "her note of suspension in fierce irony" has made even some of her admirers uneasy. Louis Auchincloss once complained that the flaw in *The Custom of the Country* is that she hated Undine Spragg too much, while Q. D. Leavis thought that she was too bleak, not having "the richness of feeling" we find in George Eliot. Lionel Trilling, not an admirer (perhaps predictably, as an advocate of American romance) complained of a "limitation of heart" and wrote of *Ethan Frome* that it "might be understood to exemplify the thesis that love and joy do not flourish on poverty-stricken New England farms."[19] Trilling was too fine a critic not to have grasped the point while missing it. Wharton was interested in love and joy and discovered they were absent in her subjects. As a result, in the first half of *The Custom of the Country,* she employs with brilliance the method of *The Bostonians:* the barbarous, energetic new rich and the wanly cultivated, ineffectual, and equally naive representatives of Old New York struggle with each other beneath a satirical gaze. As for richness of feeling—had George Eliot been an American, her New England *Silas Marner* would have had the tone, perhaps not of *Ethan Frome,* but of *Summer.* More than any of her predecessors Wharton had the courage to sound, and the ability to sustain, the satiric note. This, combined with her other gifts, makes her, with James, the greatest of the classic American novelists and also the most strong-minded.

In most respects then, the American novelists fell short, as I have perhaps too much insisted in this chapter, of their English, French, and Russian contemporaries. Nevertheless, when they did release their powers, by not evading their subjects, American novelists did write a number of considerable novels. Partly thanks to their talent for writing of the past, they did produce something like an imaginative social history of their country, and they made the international novel very much their own. As a result, they rendered their countrymen an inestimable service by creating a cultural heritage similar in kind to that which the Europeans received from their writers, thereby providing one basis by which Americans could remain members of a cosmopolitan civilization. A limited, partial, but genuine distinction then, of a fairly traditional kind—the kind James allows Hawthorne, but with major successes, owing chiefly to James and Wharton, with a point of originality in the international novel, and major failures as well—this seems to me to be the actual achievement. It is of course the kind of achievement Americans find hardest to accept.

A final word about the theory of the American romance, the critics who made it, and those who have renewed it. My indebtedness to Trilling for many of the ideas I have used is profound, despite my sharp disagreement with him; in large measure, I have taken what I believe is the rightness of his understanding of the novel, and its relation to society, and have used it against what I believe is the consequence of his one major failure: the rejection of the Progressive tradition in the place where it joined the critical view of James. I am also indebted, in this chapter, to the ideological critics (although more to James) for much of my idea of how American novels fail. I regret that, in the end, these critics subvert their own value judgments, and appropriate from the theory of the American romance ideas that suggest that a difference in genre, instead of a difference in aesthetic power, separates the American and the European novel. It is ironic that, despite their brave call to reject the American ideology, the ideological critics lack the audacity not only of James and the young Van Wyck Brooks, but of the representatives of the now despised genteel tradition, such as W. C. Brownell, who did not shrink from stating plainly their belief that the works of American culture were inferior to those of European culture.[20] Hence, despite its radical stance, ideological criticism rejoins the different tradition studied in these pages.

Not long before his death, Edmund Wilson recalled that in the America of his youth, and until the First World War, American literature was largely ignored: "That was a time when we wanted American literature taken seriously; as was said of Noah, we prayed for rain and were deluged." The deluge, as he wrote in another place, had a political rather than a literary origin: "that the emergence of the United States as a self-righteous but not self-confident 'World Power' should stimulate a boom in our literature and history . . . and that this should, in the present period, have given rise to an exploitation which exaggerates its importance is not at all surprising."[21] Wilson, when he wrote this, was not speaking of the critics I have been studying, and would never have applied the term "exploitation" to their work. Neither do I, as I hope I have made clear, but I believe that the circumstance Wilson observed is the source of their error. America's rise to world power has been accompanied by the forging of a cultural consensus and a tradition of literary patriotism that, when fused, have given rise to the theory of the American romance. The more modest evaluations of late-nineteenth-century and early-twentieth-century critics have been drowned out by it; the ideological critics have in part succumbed to it—ironically, as I have said, but after all logically. With a belief that truth is an illusion and that ideology realizes meaning in the world, one is simply disposed, even if programmatically suspicious, to view those whose ideology makes claims to exceptionalism as exceptional—by virtue of the power of realization inherent in ideological self-estimate. Ideological criticism, which castigates those who cannot conceive that American life is "but one of the many forms of society" (and hence cannot claim exceptional virtue) in the end advances the cause of the very exceptionalism it rightly, though only fitfully, regards with scorn. In this self-subversion the theory of the American romance plays a role—which testifies to its enduring power as a vehicle of critical false consciousness and modern American self-absorption and self-promotion, leaving to an uncertain future the real, but yet unrealized, possibility that American critics, by discovering their vocation as modest interpreters of a literature of modest and unexceptional importance, will free themselves from ideological chains.

Notes

Introduction

1. Most readers now add to that short list the novels of Edith Wharton, whose neglect by the theorists of the American romance is most plausibly explained by the fact she does not conform to the thesis. Q. D. Leavis, it should be said, recognized Wharton's quality at a time when American critics such as Lionel Trilling were deprecating her work. See "Henry James' Heiress: The Importance of Edith Wharton" in Irving Howe (ed.) *Edith Wharton* (Englewood Cliffs, 1962), also in *Collected Essays*, vol. 2 (Cambridge, 1985). I should also mention that nonacademic American critics such as Edmund Wilson, Louis Auchincloss, Diana Trilling, and Gore Vidal also argued for Wharton's major status at the time when her reputation was in eclipse in the academy. R. W. B. Lewis' fine biography seems to have to have set the seal on her reputation: *Edith Wharton* (New York, 1975).

2. The first challenge, that of Delmore Schwartz, "The Duchess' Red Shoes" in *Partisan Review* for January-February 1953, was rightly rejected for its dreadful tactics, and for its willful misunderstanding of Trilling's position. Nevertheless, one point Schwartz made, that *any* culture, if properly approached, could become the subject of a traditional novel, has been taken over here, with much modification. Schwartz seems to have grasped that, if American novels were socially insubstantial, this was a problem, and not an inevitable outcome of American social and cultural conditions. However, he was so quick to defend the social dimension of the American novel that he denied the problem, thus leaving himself open for easy refutation. The essay has been collected in *Selected Essays* (Chicago, 1970). The next major challenge, I believe, came from Martin Green's *Re-Appraisals* (New York, 1967), one of the unjustly neglected critical works of the sixties. Green argued that the work of the classic American novelists stands or falls according to the standards we apply to the European novel. (He thought it falls.) While I disagree with Green in many of his particular judgments, and in much of his understanding of the motives behind romance theory (he thought it was motivated, in part, by academic dislike of America) I think he was right in this, and right also in his belief that modern critics have claimed virtues for the classic American novel that do not really exist—except as defects. See especially "American Literature as a Subject."

3. Joel Porte, *The Romance in America* (Middletown, 1969), p. ix.

4. Michael Davitt Bell, *The Development of the American Romance* (Chicago, 1980), p. xi. The following are attacks on the theory: David H. Hirsch, *Reality and Idea in the Early American Novel* (The Hague, 1971); Robert Merrill, "Another Look at the American Romance," *Modern Philology* 78-379-92 (May 1981); Nicholaus Mill, *American and English Fiction in the Nine-*

teenth Century: An Antigenre Critique (Bloomington, 1973); Richard Poirier, *A World Else-where: The Place of Style in American Literature* (New York, 1966), especially pp. 8–11. At no time, it should be mentioned, did the English critics of the Cambridge school, such as Green or the Leavises, ever accept the exceptionalist emphasis of the theory, although Q. D. Leavis was willing to use the term "romance" in relation to Hawthorne (while pointing out *The Scarlet Letter*'s similarity to *Anna Karenina*), *Collected Essays,* p. 51.

5. Bell, ibid., p. xii. Bell's doubts about the insubstantiality of the classic American novel (see note 43) and his preoccupation with postmodernism place his work outside the scope of this book, despite his title.

6. George Steiner, *Tolstoy or Dostoevsky* (Boston, 1980), p. 6.

7. For my purposes, the most relevant passage in Plato is the *Gorgias,* where he identifies poetry with the rhetoric of the Sophists, here represented by Gorgias himself and Callicles, who expounds the doctrine "might makes right." See *The Collected Dialogues*, Huntington Cairns and Edith Hamilton, eds. (New York, 1964), pp. 283–85 (560b–503d.)

8. The term is Alfred Kazin's in *On Native Grounds* (New York, 1942), p. xi. Kazin's book contains a still very useful discussion of both sociological criticism and the new criticism from an old-critical perspective: "Criticism at the Poles."

9. See Steiner, *Tolstoy or Dostoevsky* , pp. 3–12.

10. See Lionel Trilling, *The Liberal Imagination* (New York, 1976), pp. 11–21. Bewley makes only a passing, dismissive reference to Dreiser in *The Eccentric Design* (New York, 1963), p. 291, but he certainly, as Leavis' pupil, would have agreed with Leavis' estimate that Dreiser "writes as if he hasn't a native language," in the review of Bewley's *The Complex Fate* collected in *Anna Karenina and Other Essays* (New York, 1969), p. 155.

11. F. R. Leavis, *The Great Tradition* (New York, 1964), pp. 8–9. See the general discussion that envelopes this quotation as well.

12. Not everyone will recognize the moral emphasis as Aristotle's, but it is clearly indicated in *The Poetics* when he speaks of "the diversities of human character being nearly always derivative from this primary distinction [between good and bad]," and when he says that Comedy is distinguished from Tragedy because "the one would make its personages worse, and the other better, than the men of the present day," from *The Poetics, The Rhetoric and the Poetics* (New York, 1954), pp. 224, 225 (1448a3–1448a19). That is, the writer needs moral discernment— knowledge of good and bad, better and worse—in order to create characters and to discover and realize the proper forms for their activities.

13. Geoffrey Thurley, *Counter-Modernism in Current Critical Theory* (New York, 1983), p. 146. This of course descends from Aristotle's contention that (*pace* Plato) "poetry is something more philosophic and of graver import than history; since its statements are of the nature rather of universals." Ibid., p. 235 (1451b5).

14. See Thurley, ibid., pp. 60–70, and Steiner, *Tolstoy or Dostoevsky,* p. viii.

15. Robert Scholes, *Textual Power* (New Haven, 1985), p. 14.

16. For a discussion of the historicism and relativism of postmodernism, see J. G. Merquior's *From Prague to Paris* (London, 1986), especially pp. 199–209. For a discussion of the decline of one old critic's influence with the rise of postmodernism, see Gregory S. Jay's "Lionel Trilling" in Gregory S. Jay, ed., *Modern American Critics, Dictionary of Literary Biography,* vol. 63 (Detroit, 1988), pp. 288–89 especially.

17. See Geoffrey Hartman's preface in Harold Bloom, ed., *Deconstruction and Literature* (New Haven, 1980), pp. vii–ix.

18. See, for example, Denis Donoghue's "Deconstructing Deconstruction," *New York Review of Books* vol. 28, no. 10 (June 12, 1980), p. 37, Steiner's comment on the new criticism, *Tolstoy or Dostoevsky,* pp. vii, and Thurley's attempt to reconcile the critical approach of Leavis with that of formalism, *Counter-Modernism,* pp. 117–18, pp. 166–67. Thurley's entire book, in fact, can be read as an attempt of an old critic to concede as much ground to new criticism as possible, in order to present a united front against postmodernism. Lest this comment seem deprecatory, I should add that I think the attempt is admirable, although sometimes strained (as on pp. 25–26).

19. Bell, *American Romance,* pp. xiii–xiv. Bell's own glosses are often tinged with deconstruction; for example, his statement that "the very complexity of [*Arthur Mervyn*'s] narrative structure raises doubts about the reliability of all narrative," p. 57. *All* narrative? Well, complexity does nothing of the sort, unless we make "complexity" a synonym for "unreliability" (cf. deconstruction's "indeterminate meaning")—in which case we have assumed what we want to prove.

20. See Judith Fetterly, *The Resisting Reader* (Bloomington, 1978), Sacvan Bercovitch, *The American Jeremiad* (Madison, 1978) and Sacvan Bercovitch and Myra Jehlen, eds., *Ideology and Classic American Literature* (Cambridge, 1986).

21. For example, *Ideology and Classic American Literature* ignores Bewley, and makes only two brief references to Trilling (the longer by the one old critic in the collection, Gerald Graff). Only Richard Chase seems to have retained any influence over contemporary critics.

22. Key texts are the books of Scholes, Merquior, Thurley, already cited. Gerald Graff's "The Pseudopolitics of Interpretation" in W. G. T. Mitchell, ed., *The Politics of Interpretation* (Chicago, 1983), "American Criticism Left and Right" in *Ideology and Classic American Literature, Literature Against Itself* (London, 1980), and Tzvetan Todorov, *Critique de la critique: Un Roman d'apprentissage* (Paris, 1984).

23. See M. H. Abrams, "The Deconstructive Angel," *Critical Inquiry* vol. 3, no. 3 (Spring 1976). Both Lévi-Strauss and Foucault, for example, adopt self-refuting positions. For Lévi-Strauss the thought of a culture is an ephiphenomenon of that culture's structure. Therefore, the universalist claims of Western ideology are untrue. But even if all thought is epiphenomenal (which is doubtful) this conclusion does not necessarily follow—for some structures might still be more conducive to truth than others. Besides, on Lévi-Strauss' principles, his own ideology is Western: hence, if he is right, the West is right; if the West is wrong, so is he. Foucault makes a similar error (repeated by Stanley Fish—or so it seems to me) whenever, first, he criticizes discourses that lay claim to truth for being expressions of the will to power, and, second, goes on to claim that the will to power animates all discourse. His own? In any case, if we cannot escape the will to power, why criticize any discourse on these grounds? See the discussions of Lévi-Strauss and Foucault by Merquior: *From Prague to Paris,* pp. 88–107 and *Foucault* (London, 1986). For a criticism of Fish see Scholes, *Textual Power,* pp. 149–65. For a succinct summing up of American Foucauldians see Graff, "American Criticism Left and Right," in Mitchell, *Politics of Interpretation,* p. 114.

24. As when, for example, Derrida says of Heidegger that "he had to borrow the syntaxic and lexical resources of the language of metaphysics, *as one always must do*" (italics mine), *Positions* (Chicago, 1981), p. 10. See also his polemic against Foucault, chapter 2 of *Writing and Difference* (Chicago, 1978).

25. For the propositionality of language see Graff, *Literature against Itself,* and *Poetic Statement and Critical Dogmas* (Chicago, 1970). For the referentiality of language see Scholes, *Textual Power,* pp. 86–110, and Merquior, *From Prague to Paris,* pp. 229–33.

26. Steiner, *Tolstoy or Dostoevsky,* p. vi.

27. See Thurley, *Counter-Modernism,* pp. 99–109, where he discusses a point raised by V. I. Voloshinov's *Marxism and the Philosophy of Language* (New York, 1975).

28. See Todorov, *Critique,* pp. 192–93 especially.

29. "A critic must choose either the tradition of presence or the tradition of difference." Thus J. Hillis Miller in "Tradition and Differences," a review of M. H. Abrams' *Natural Supernaturalism* in *Diacritics* 2:6 (Winter, 1972). I should add that I think the dichotomy between "presence" and "difference" drawn by Miller is false, however. We do not have to insist on a transparent "presence" to be dissatisfied with the discourse of "difference."

30. Of course, both A. N. Kaul and Joel Porte, as already mentioned, argued that the classic American novel had a social concern, but that it approached society indirectly.

31. Although I would not go quite so far as Gore Vidal, who claims that the American canon, James and Wharton aside, "is a strange list of minor provincial writers grandiosely inflated into 'world classics' "—*Homage to Daniel Shays* (New York, 1972), pp. 299–300—his view is a salutary one at a time when, for example, *Pierre* is lauded as a "savage, brilliant, and sweeping attack on the American dream" (Bercovitch, *The American Jeremiad,* p. xv). "Brilliant," which implies brightness and clarity, is the last word to apply to this most muddy of classic American novels. I should add that I agree with Vidal in his ranking of James and Wharton.

32. F. R. Leavis, "The Americanness of American Literature," *Anna Karenina and Other Essays,* p. 138.

33. Ibid., p. 145.

34. Mill's *English and American Fiction in the Nineteenth Century* pairs very usefully the writers he takes to be cognates: Scott/Cooper, Hawthorne/Eliot, Dickens/Twain, Melville/Hardy. Only the last pair seems to me questionable.

35. For Hawthorne's influence on Eliot see F. R. Leavis, "Adam Bede," *Anna Karenina and Other Essays,* p. 52 especially. For Scott's influence on Hawthorne see Neal Frank Doubleday, *Hawthorne's Early Tales* (Durham, 1972).

36. Trilling, *Liberal Imagination,* p. 275.

37. This concept, discussed in my final chapters, is elaborated in *Ideology and Classic American Literature.*

38. Trilling, *Liberal Imagination,* p. 261.

39. Just as some political historians have tried to extend the liberal consensus back to a time when it did not exist, so some urban historians have tried to do the same with suburbanization. Here is a representative assertion by Prof. Joel Schwartz: "The outward rush after World War II has largely obscured the slow, incremental process which suburbanized a seventh of the population during the century before 1930." What Prof. Schwartz really tells us is that suburbanization was slow and incremental until 1930, at which late date only a seventh of the population was suburbanized. Then came the outward rush. The continuity of development he claims to perceive is in the service of the idea of American exceptionalism. In Philip C. Dolce, ed., *Suburbia* (New York, 1976), p. 31.

40. See Graff, "American Criticism Left and Right," in Bercovitch and Jehlen, *Ideology,* p. 107, and Bell, *American Romance,* p. xii.

41. Bernard De Voto, ed., *The Portable Mark Twain* (New York, 1965), p. 17. In addition, as De Voto mentioned, American publishing practices were designed to keep American novels short. Twain was obliged to cut a chapter from *Huckleberry Finn.* This De Voto rightly restored. See his note pp. 291–92.

42. Trilling, *Liberal Imagination,* p. 212.

43. See Geoffrey Thurley's discussion of nineteenth-century German fiction in *The Dickens Myth* (London, 1976), p. 52. The idea is his.

44. Henry James, *Hawthorne* (Ithaca, 1956), p. 52.

45. Henry James, "Charles de Bernard and Gustave Flaubert, " *European Writers and the Prefaces* (New York, 1984), p. 159.

46. Thurley, *The Dickens Myth,* p. 21.

47. See Green, "Melville and the American Romance," *Re-Appraisals.* Robert Merrill makes a similar point, in his fine essay on *The Scarlet Letter,* about the "romance" tradition as a whole, *Modern Philology.*

48. Van Wyck Brooks, *America's Coming of Age* in *Three Essays on America* (New York, 1970), p. 55.

49. See Daniel J. Boorstin, "Our Cultural Hypochondria," *The Genius of American Politics* (Chicago, 1953).

50. I should be clear that I am referring not to the tradition represented by writers such as Malamud, Morris, and Percy, but to the tradition represented by writers such as Pyncheon and Barth. The novels of Barth, indeed, embody the split I have noted in the classic American novel between an impressive realism and a less impressive "romance." Unfortunately, after the excellent *The End of the Road* Barth let the romance element take over his work. The same split appears in Bellow's work, although less rarely—*Henderson and the Rain King* is "romance." But in his best work, such as the first half of *Humboldt's Gift,* Bellow is impressive. For a witty (and convincing) discussion of the Pyncheon/Barth tradition see Gore Vidal, "American Plastic: The Matter of Fiction," *New York Review of Books,* vol. 23, no. 12 (July 15, 1976), pp. 31–39.

51. Quoted in Leon Edel, *Henry James* (New York, 1985), p. 87.

Chapter 1

1. Alfred Kazin, *On Native Grounds* (New York, 1942), p. 487, pp. 501–3, pp. 489, 488.

2. Two good, brief discussions of consensus history are provided by Barton J. Bernstein in his introduction to *Towards a New Past* (New York, 1968), pp. v–xiii, and in Richard Hofstadter's "Conflict and Consensus in American History," *The Progressive Historians* (New York, 1968), pp. 437–66. Bernard Sternsher, in *Consensus, Conflict, and American Historians* (Bloomington, 1975), has written an exhaustive book on the subject.

3. In fact, certain consensus historians, especially Daniel J. Boorstin, tended to discount the influence of ideology in achieving consensus (of which more later). Yet, as Sternsher has pointed out, even Boorstin, who emphasized geographical factors, was obliged to concede that a common ideology, even if it was the product of a prior cause, notably furthered consensus. Ibid., pp. 33–47.

4. See, for example, Boorstin's *The Genius of American Politics* (Chicago, 1953) whose thesis was this: "My argument is simple. It is based on forgotten commonplaces of American history. . . . I argue, in a word, that American democracy is unique" (p. 1). The contrasts Boorstin drew between the United States and Europe sustained the arguments of his book. See especially pp. 29–35 and pp. 171–89.

   My use of the terms "liberal" and "bourgeois society" is meant to be fairly strict and follows Marx via George Lichtheim in *Marxism: An Historical and Critical Study* (New York, 1965), p. 164:

   > Strictly speaking there is no such thing as capitalist society, at least if one adheres to the Marxian scheme. Capitalism refers to the economic relations characteristic of *bourgeois society,* which as a matter of historical fact has never existed outside Western Europe and the Americas, though in a rudimentary form it was beginning to develop in Eastern Europe before 1917. . . . In the following, capitalism denotes the *economic system* characteristic of bourgeois society, the latter being the fully developed form of *Western Civilization.*

   "Liberalism" is the prevailing ideology of this society and implies a commitment to both capitalist ownership and the market, and to some form of parliamentary regime, although it does not necessarily imply a commitment either to capitalism in its laissez-faire version or to democracy.

5. Max Lerner, *America as a Civilization* (New York, 1957), p. 9.

6. Daniel J. Boorstin, *The Americans: The Colonial Experience* (New York, 1958), p. 110.

7. Daniel J. Boorstin, *The Genius of American Politics,* p. 179.

8. Christopher Lasch, "From Culture to Politics," in George Fischer, ed., *The Revival of American Socialism* (New York, 1971), p. 219.

9. Boorstin, *The Genius of American Politics,* p. 184.

10. See note 2. Hofstadter's fine book discusses in detail the Progressives' economic determinism. For a brief and sharply critical appraisal of economic determinism in both Progressive and Marxist interpretations of the Civil War, and in providing a distorted populist focus on American history as a whole, see Eugene Genovese, "Marxian Interpretations of the Slave South," *Towards a New Past,* pp. 90–125. Christopher Lasch, in "The Decline of Populism," pursues a similar theme, and like Genovese is critical of both Progressive and consensus history: *The Agony of the American Left* (New York, 1969), pp. 3–31.

11. Bernstein, *Towards a New Past,* p. vii.

12. Ibid., pp. vii–viii.

13. Ibid., p. viii.

14. Cited by Jesse Lemisch, "The American Revolution from the Bottom Up," ibid., p. 31, note 12.

15. See Max Weber, *The Theory of Social and Economic Development* (New York, 1947), especially pp. 278–80, and Maurice Dobb, *Studies in the Development of Capitalism* (New York, 1947), pp. 120–23, in which he cites Marx.

16. The term, so far as I know, is George Lukacs' and provides the title for the first chapter of *The Theory of the Novel* (Cambridge, Mass., 1971). Although Lukacs argues that medieval civilization was not really integrated, I believe that in this opinion he was simply reflecting the anti-medieval bias in most central East European intellectuals of his day, who, after all, were

laboring in societies still marked by feudal relations.The same can be said of Bakhtin, who argues, in *Rabelais and His World* (Cambridge, Mass., 1968), p. 20, that the "culture of folk humor," belonging to the people, was sharply at odds with official medieval ideology until the Renaissance synthesized and transformed both. A virtual prisoner of the Soviet state, Bakhtin probably had no chance to study *The Canterbury Tales* or *Sir Gawayne and the Grene Knight*, and certainly had no chance to study, at first hand, the art of the Gothic cathedrals. His populism can be seen as a veiled protest against official Soviet ideology, rather than as a sober estimate of feudal relations, in which, as *The Canterbury Tales* show, there was constant cultural commerce between the classes. His Western disciples, however, have not this excuse.

17. George Lichtheim, "The Private Philosophy," *Collected Essays* (New York, 1974), p. 132.

18. Eugene Genovese, *The World the Slaveholders Made* (New York, 1969), p. 22.

19. Ibid., pp. 101–2. For Elkins' discussion of this subject see "The Dynamics of Unopposed Capitalism," in *Slavery: A Problem in America and Intellectual Life* (Chicago, 1959).

20. Boorstin, *The Genius of American Politics*, p. 189.

21. The term, again, comes from Lukacs' *The Theory of the Novel*, p. 73.

22. Ibid., p. 56. *The Theory of the Novel*, in its sense of the relations of the novel and culture with society, is highly traditional, and in many ways belongs to a world not yet shattered by the First World War. (It was written in 1914.)

23. M. S. Wilkins, *Political Science Quarterly*, vol. 75, no. 2 (June, 1960), p. 302.

24. This was true in the West. As Henri Peyre pointed out, the novel as it developed in the East cannot be so easily described: "Introduction," in Henri Peyre, ed., *Fiction in Several Languages* (Boston, 1968), pp. xxiv–xxv. This point, however, does not touch upon our concern, which is exclusively Western in its orientation.

25. Boorstin, *The Genius of American Politics*, pp. 172–74.

26. Ibid., pp. 173, 170.

27. Ibid., p. 175.

28. Ibid., pp. 175–77.

29. Ibid., p. 2.

30. See, for example, James E. Miller, Jr., "American Epic," in *A Critical Guide to Leaves of Grass* (Chicago, 1957).

31. Richard Chase, *The American Novel and Its Tradition* (Garden City, 1957), p. 13.

32. R. W. B. Lewis, *The American Adam* (Chicago, 1955), p. 7.

33. Cecil Tate, *The Search for a Method in American Studies* (Minneapolis, 1973), pp. 87–88.

34. There is a logical problem with the idea that an identity can be constituted by opposing ideas. If the ideas are irreconcilable, there is no identity. If there are points of agreement then these constitute such identity as the ideas share. But in that case, identity emerges precisely where the ideas are not opposed. Perhaps Lewis would argue that "the party of Irony" synthesized the other two positions. Perhaps so, but only in principle, not in fact. I doubt that the ideas of Henry James, Sr., were much shared by his countrymen.

35. Boorstin, *The Genius of American Politics*, p. 173.

36. For an account, sympathetic to Emerson, of the decline of his reputation, see Martin Green, "Emerson: The Rejected Leader," *Re-Appraisals* (New York, 1967).

37. In fact this distinction, although in a different context, descends from Van Wyck Brooks in *America's Coming of Age*, collected in *Three Essays on America* (New York, 1970). See pp. 60–61.

38. Here again Green's discussion is useful. The first citation is the title of Harry Levin's *The Power of Blackness* (New York, 1958), the second is from Chase, *The American Novel and Its Tradition*, p. xi.

39. Levin, ibid., p. 35.

40. Ibid., pp. 8–9, 7.

41. For a more recent contribution, in an even wider context, to this line of thought one can refer to Irving Kristol, who has American society in mind when he writes:

> The trouble is that capitalism outgrew its bourgeois origins and became a system for the impersonal liberation and satisfaction of appetites, an engine for the creation of affluence. Yes, it does provide more food, better housing, better health, to say nothing of all kinds of pleasant conveniences. Only a saint or a snob would dismiss these achievements lightly. But anyone who naively believes that, in sum, they suffice to legitimize a socio-economic system knows little of the human heart or soul. People can learn to despise such a system even while enjoying its benefits. *Two Cheers for Capitalism* (New York, 1978), p. 88.

42. R. W. B. Lewis, *American Adam*, p. 91.

43. See Lionel Trilling, "The Princess Casamassima," *The Liberal Imagination* (New York, 1976). This may very well be Trilling's finest essay, but the tendency of which it is a part had its less distinguished side. See especially Martin Green's discussion of the subject in "American Literature as a Subject," *Re-Appraisals*.

Chapter 2

1. Lionel Trilling, *The Liberal Imagination* (New York, 1976), pp. 212, 260–61, 262.

2. See Marius Bewley, *The Eccentric Design* (New York, 1963), pp. 13–21; Richard Chase, *The American Novel and Its Tradition* (New York, 1957), pp. 6–8, 162–67, 205–36; Charles Feidelson, *Symbolism and American Literature* (Chicago, 1953), p. xii; and A. N. Kaul, *The American Vision* (New Haven, 1963), pp. 1–6, 305–26.

3. Trilling, *Liberal Imagination*, pp. xi–xii.

4. Ibid., p. vii.

5. In "Reality in America," ibid. See discussion below and in the following chapters.

6. Alfred Kazin, perhaps a little harshly, associated the attitude of "Reality in America," Trilling's attack on the Progressives, with that of "a whole intelligentsia, post-Communist, post-Marxist, which could not look at Alger Hiss in the dock without shuddering at how near they had come to his fate, [and] now tended to find their new ideology in the good old middle-class virtues." Alfred Kazin and Charles Shapiro, eds., *The Stature of Theodore Dreiser* (Bloomington, 1955), p. 9.

7. Richard Hofstadter, *The Progressive Historians* (New York, 1968), p. 451.

8. Eugene Genovese, *In Red and Black* (New York, 1971), p. 369.

9. See Cecil F. Tate, *The Search for a Method in American Studies* (Minneapolis, 1973), pp. 10–13.

10. Trilling, *Liberal Imagination*, p. 207.

11. Ibid., p. viii.

12. Ibid., p. 212.

13. See George Lukacs, *The Theory of the Novel* (Cambridge, Mass., 1971), p. 63.

14. Trilling, *Liberal Imagination*, p. 259.

15. Ibid., pp. 260–61. The second comment, with my bracketed gloss, was a response on Trilling's part to the idea that "ethnic conflict might be the equivalent of a class differentiation." His answer was "I think it is not [because] it involves no real cultural struggle, no significant conflict of ideals, for the excluded group has the same notion of life as the excluding group." Differences in class, culture, and, ideals, then, make the essential tension of the novel: hence my gloss. My criticism has two parts: (1) there are often immanent cultural differences between classes, even when their consciously held ideals are the same, which can serve as the basis for a novel; (2) Trilling knew this (as in his use of the apocryphal Hemingway/Fitzgerald exchange about the very rich), but was inconsistent in his application of the insight.

16. Actually, Trilling does use the more precise term "bourgeoisie" occasionally. See ibid., p. 260. The proper opposition to "middle class" is provided by either "upper class" or "lower class," and different classes have occupied these positions in the course of history. When Trilling speaks of a "middle class" in opposition to an aristocracy it is always the bourgeoisie that he means.

17. See especially F. R. Leavis, *The Great Tradition* (New York, 1964).

18. Which is one reason why we still find them fascinating, in contrast to Statius and the romances Chaucer parodied in "The Tale of Sir Thopas." It should be evident from my discussion (and from the theme of my book itself) that I am uneasy with rigid distinctions in genre. I think, indeed, that part of the greatness of authors lies in their ability to transcend the conventions that govern perception and expression in their time and place. My point here is only that, in any time and place, conventions exist and, exceptions aside, do govern.

19. Karl Marx, *The Eighteenth Brumaire of Louis Bonaparte*, in *Surveys from Exile*, ed. David Fernbach (Harmondsworth, Middlesex, 1973), p. 148.

20. Trilling, *Liberal Imagination*, p. 260. The context of Trilling's remarks is a discussion of Henry James' use of the term "romance." But the "romance" in this case is not the "romance" that only the classic American novelists and a few others are supposed to have written.

21. Ibid., p. 262.

22. Ibid., pp. 212–13.

23. Ibid., p. 262.

24. Ibid.

Chapter 3

1. Lionel Trilling, *The Liberal Imagination* (New York, 1976), pp. 207–8.

2. Ibid., p. 240.

3. Ibid., p. 259.

4. Ibid., p. 206.

5. Ibid., p. 262.

6. Ibid., p. 260.

7. Ibid., p. 274.

8. Ibid.

9. Ibid., p. 275.

10. Ibid., p. 262.

11. Ibid., p. ix.

12. Ibid., p. 275.

13. Ibid., p. 292, 212.

14. Ibid., p. 212.

15. Ibid., p. viii.

16. Chase's case is curious. An exciting critic, whose readings of novels were often vividly suggestive, his discussion of the value of American novels is full of remarks about their shortcomings. Yet the final emphasis, I believe, is inflationary, as I shall try to show. Bewley, by contrast, has a more modest final emphasis, but is slightly inflationary—cf. the essays on Cooper, and his remarks about *Moby Dick*'s formal perfection: *The Eccentric Design* (New York, 1963), p. 211 in his individual readings.

17. Ibid., pp. 4, 9. Parrington's criticism of Hawthorne's failure to use New England is in *Main Currents in American Thought: The Romantic Revolution in America* (New York, 1958), pp. 444–45.

18. See Henry James, *Hawthorne* (Ithaca, 1956), and my discussion of it in chapter 8; the strictures on Chillingsworth, in W. C. Brownell's *American Prose Masters* (New York, 1909); Van Wyck Brook's *America's Coming of Age,* in *Three Essays on America* (New York, 1970). According to Edmund Wilson, Brownell, as editor of Scribners, turned down *America's Coming of Age* because "it was still 'too early' to call attention to the weaknesses of our supposed classics"—meaning, of course, that he agreed about the weaknesses: *The Devils and Canon Barham* (New York, 1973), p. 93. Once the theory of the American romance was launched, it was too late.

19. Trilling, *Liberal Imagination,* p. 9.

20. Both citations are in Bernard Sternsher, *Consensus, Conflict, and American Historians* (Bloomington, 1975), p. 5.

21. Ibid., p. 5.

22.　Ibid., p. 36. See Sternsher's discussion of the tensions in Boorstin's argument, pp. 33–47, for a further elaboration of this theme.

23.　Bewley, *Eccentric Design*, pp. 18, 14. I had better say right away that Bewley stands, in many ways, to one side of my argument; he was very much alive to cultural tensions rooted in American society, and to the American novelists' treatment of them. It is his thesis that they could not have treated these realistically, owing to the crudeness of American manners (p. 15), but found their solution in symbols that then led them away from society to the human condition, which I disagree with, as well his admiration for the symbols when they are abstract. It is just to the extent that he overestimated consensus, in other words, that his book fails. See note 17, chapter 4.

24.　Ibid., p. 14.

25.　Ibid., p. 18.

26.　Ibid., pp. 18, 23–24, 39, 40. See also Bewley's discussion of the genteel tradition itself, pp. 303–10.

27.　Ibid., pp. 24, 33.

28.　Richard Chase, *The American Novel and Its Tradition* (Garden City, 1957), pp. 6–7.

29.　Ibid., p. 7.

30.　Ibid.

31.　Daniel J. Boorstin, *The Genius of American Politics* (Chicago, 1953), pp. 1, 11.

32.　Chase, *American Novel*, p. 11.

33.　Boorstin, *American Politics*, pp. 38, 65.

34.　This is the title Boorstin chooses for a section of *The Genius of American Politics*, pp. 161–89.

Chapter 4

1.　Lionel Trilling, *The Liberal Imagination* (New York, 1976), pp. 285, 286, 288.

2.　Ibid., pp. x–xi.

3.　Ibid., pp. xi, xiii.

4.　Marilyn Butler, quoted by Gore Vidal in "Thomas Love Peacock: The Novel of Ideas," *The Second American Revolution* (New York, 1982), pp. 127–28. The suggestion is Vidal's *passim*.

5.　Trilling, *Liberal Imagination*, p. xv.

6.　Ibid., pp. 3, 21.

7.　Ibid., p. 10.

8.　Ibid., p. viii.

9.　Richard Chase, *The American Novel and Its Tradition* (Garden City, 1957), p. 13.

10.　Marius Bewley, *The Eccentric Design* (New York, 1963), p. 13.

11.　Ibid., pp. 13, 14, 293.

12. Ibid., p. 293.

13. Chase, *American Novel*, p. 13.

14. Ibid., p. xi.

15. Ibid., p. 5.

16. Ibid., p. xi.

17. This was odd in Bewley's case, because one does not have to read far in his book to find references to ideological conflict. Bewley was too quick, I believe, to assimilate Cooper's aristocratic sympathies, especially as embodied in his aristocratic characters, to a version of liberalism (*Eccentric Design*, p. 19, reference to Trilling, *passim*), and to discount the genteel tradition (whether it derived from Hamilton or not is another question): his effort to sever Cooper and James completely from it is unconvincing (p. 310). He thus missed, theoretically, an important dialectic in the making of the American novel. A fine practical critic, Bewley was at his best when he set his theoretical framework aside.

18. Daniel J. Boorstin, *The Genius of American Politics* (Chicago, 1953), pp. 30, 6.

19. Ibid., pp. 6–7.

20. Bewley, *Eccentric Design*, pp. 14, 292.

21. Charles Feidelson, *Symbolism and American Literature* (Chicago, 1953), p. 213.

22. George Lichtheim, *Europe in the Twentieth Century* (New York, 1972), pp. 90, 184.

23. See George Lukacs, *Realism in Our Time* (New York, 1971), especially pp. 19–22.

24. See Lionel Trilling, "Hawthorne in Our Time," collected in *Beyond Culture* (New York, 1965), especially pp. 197–202; and Harry Levin, *The Power of Blackness* (New York, 1958), pp. 46–47.

25. Boorstin, *American Politics*, pp. 182–83.

26. Chase, *American Novel*, p. 9.

27. Ibid., pp. 27–28.

28. This is, I believe, demonstrated by John Spiers, *Poetry Towards Novel* (London, 1971).

29. In their short stories, Poe and Hawthorne did come close to modernism, but this is just my point. Hawthorne expressed dissatisfaction with his stories' "paleness," and when he moved to the novel he was trying for something else. And not even in their stories were Poe and Hawthorne exceptionally "American."

Chapter 5

1. Marius Bewley, *The Eccentric Design* (New York, 1963), p. 16.

2. Raymond Williams, *The English Novel from Dickens to Lawrence* (Oxford, 1976), pp. 9–11.

3. That Americans attributed great importance to literature in the nineteenth century is one of the themes of Martin Green's *The Problem of Boston* (New York, 1967), and Trilling's appreciative essay on Howells in *The Opposing Self* (New York, 1955). See also the similar remarks in *The Liberal Imagination* (New York, 1976), pp. 94–96.

4. Lionel Trilling, *The Liberal Imagination,* p. 264.

5. Ibid., p. 265.

6. Ibid., p. 216.

7. Joseph Schumpeter, *Imperialism and Social Classes,* ed. Paul M. Swezy (Oxford, 1951), p. 122.

8. See, for example, James Atlas' *Delmore Schwartz* (New York, 1977), pp. 310–13, which briefly discusses the dispute between Schwartz and Trilling over the nature of the classic American novel. This dispute led to John W. Aldridge's defense of Trilling's thesis—upon which I comment in a later chapter.

9. Trilling, *The Liberal Imagination,* pp. xiv–xv.

10. E. J. Hobsbawm, *The Age of Capital* (London, 1975), pp. 140, 144.

11. Cited by Irving Howe, *Politics and the Novel* (New York, 1957), p. 15.

12. Trilling, *The Liberal Imagination,* p. 261.

13. Ibid., p. 61.

14. Actually, at times Trilling did realize this (see note 17), but does not seem to have drawn the conclusions I am drawing.

15. Many of these observations derive, I believe, from Lukacs, although other critics have made them.

16. See Henry James, "Emile Zola," *European Writers and the Prefaces* (New York, 1984), pp. 878–79 especially.

17. Trilling, *The Liberal Imagination,* p. 259.

Chapter 6

1. A. N. Kaul, *The American Vision* (New Haven, 1963), p. 64.

2. Ibid., pp. 51–52.

3. Ibid., p. 313.

4. Ibid., p. 314.

5. Ibid., pp. 313–14.

6. Ibid., p. 314.

7. Ibid., pp. 6–7.

8. Ibid., pp. 9, 8.

9. Ibid., p. 9.

10. Ibid., p. 44.

11. Ibid., pp. 39, 40, 20.

12. See Harold Bloom, *The Visionary Company* (Ithaca, 1961), pp. xiii–xxv.

13. Quoted by Kaul, *American Vision,* p. 24.

14. Alexis de Tocqueville, *Democracy in America,* vol. 1 (New York, 1945), p. 414. It is true that in the wake of 1848 Tocqueville, in the preface to the twelfth edition (pp. ix–x), had a more sanguine view of the American future, and contrasted American stability to European upheaval. Since the 1850s were to be full of civil strife in the western territories and the Civil War was only twelve years away, this later preface may be dismissed as a temporary aberration.

15. Kaul, *American Vision,* pp. 5, 67.

16. Van Wyck Brooks, *Three Essays on America* (New York, 1970), pp. 86–87.

17. Cited by Kaul, *American Vision,* p. 79.

18. Nathaniel Hawthorne, *Collected Works,* vol. 3 (Cambridge, Mass., 1891), p. 13.

19. Richard Chase, *The American Novel and Its Tradition,* p. 19.

20. Kaul, *American Vision,* p. 191.

21. Ibid., pp. 192, 307.

22. Chase, *American Novel,* p. 158. Chase does qualify the remark a little, but not enough, I believe, to eliminate the anomaly.

23. George Lichtheim, *Europe in the Twentieth Century* (New York, 1972), p. 31. See p. 25 *passim.*

24. Hawthorne, *Collected Works,* vol. 5, pp. 321–22.

25. Ibid., vol. 6, p. 15.

26. Ibid., vol. 3, pp. 15–16.

27. Ibid., vol. 5, pp. 321–22.

28. Ibid., p. 322.

29. Ibid., vol. 3, pp. 14–15.

30. Henry James, *European Writers and the Prefaces* (New York, 1984), p. 49. The precise term is "realistic romancer."

31. Martin Turnell, *The Novel in France* (New York, 1951), p. 284.

32. Hawthorne, *Collected Works,* vol. 3, pp. 13–14.

Chapter 7

1. Neal Frank Doubleday, *Hawthorne's Early Tales* (Durham, 1972), p. 54.

2. Ibid., p. 15.

3. Walter Allen, *The English Novel* (New York, 1954), p. 127.

4. Raymond Williams, *The English Novel from Dickens to Lawrence* (Oxford, 1976), p. 13.

5. Allen, *English Novel,* p. 127.

6. Ibid., p. 129.

7. Ibid., The "present as history," I believe, was coined by Raymond Williams.

8. George Lukacs, *The Historical Novel* (Harmondsworth, Middlesex, 1976), p. 42.

9. Doubleday, *Hawthorne's Early Tales,* p. 16.

10. See Van Wyck Brooks, *The Flowering of New England* (New York, 1952), pp. 7–10.

11. See F. O. Mathiessen, *American Renaissance* (New York, 1970), pp. 203–5.

12. Henry James, *Hawthorne* (Ithaca, 1956), p. 3.

13. Mathiessen, *American Renaissance,* p. 207, *passim.*

14. It is true that in *The English Notebooks* Hawthorne does show familiarity with English realism, but this probably came late, after his best work had been written, since *The American Notebooks* do not indicate a familiarity. See Jane Lundblad, *Nathaniel Hawthorne and the European Literary Tradition* (New York, 1965), pp. 188–89 especially, for a similar view.

15. Kaul, *American Vision,* pp. 307–8. Despite his commitment to the idea of the romance, Kaul gives us ample reason for disagreeing with him, as the discussion enveloping this passage shows.

16. Indeed "Actual and Ideal Society in Nineteenth-Century Fiction" is the subtitle to his book.

17. Miller has begun to come under attack in recent years, as we shall see in a later chapter. I still find him more convincing than his critics.

18. See John W. Aldridge, "The Heresy of Literary Manners," *In Search of Heresy* (New York, 1956). (Trilling's reference to the scene is in *The Liberal Imagination,* p. 216.)

19. Ibid., pp. 103–5.

Chapter 8

1. George Lukacs, *Realism in Our Time* (New York, 1971), p. 34.

2. Lionel Trilling, *The Opposing Self* (New York, 1955), p. 95.

3. Cited in Marcel Clavel's *Fenimore Cooper and the Critics* (Aix-en-Provence), pp. 339–40.

4. Quoted by Martin Turnell, *The Novel in France* (New York, 1951), p. 139. I should mention that my account of *The Charterhouse of Parma* here follows Turnell's fairly closely.

5. Ibid., pp. 149, 148.

6. Ibid., pp. 204–5.

7. George Steiner, *Tolstoy or Dostoevsky* (New York, 1980), p. 105.

8. See Judd D. Hubert, "The Devaluation of Reality in the *Chartreuse de Parme*" in Victor Brombert, ed., *Stendhal* (Englewood Cliffs, 1962), pp. 95–100.

9. See George Lukacs, *Studies in European Realism,* Alfred Kazin, ed. (New York, 1964), pp. 126–47.

10. A constant theme in James' many discussions of Balzac is how fortunate he was in his moment—"an earthly heaven . . . [when] the later part of the eighteenth century, with the Revolution, the Empire, and the Restoration, had inimitably conspired together to scatter abroad their separate marks and stigmas, their separate trails of character and physiognomic hits—for which advantage he might have arrived too late, as his hapless successors": "*Balzac, par Emile Faguet,*" *European Writers and the Prefaces* (New York, 1984), p. 145. It is true that James puts the accent of later disadvantage more on industrialization than on politics, but

politics is never far from his mind, as when he says: "half our interest in [Balzac] springs from our sense that for all the convulsions, the revolutions, and experiments that have come and gone, the order he describes is the old order that our sense of the past perversely recurs to as to something happy we have irretrievably missed": "Honoré de Balzac" (1902), ibid., p. 102.

11. "Gustave Flaubert," ibid., p. 327.

12. See Proust "On Flaubert's Style" in *Against Sainte-Beauve and Other Essays* (Harmondsworth, Middlesex, 1988) and Turnell, *Novel in France*, pp. 310–28.

13. See James' essays on Flaubert and George Sand, *European Writers,* pp. 720–22 especially.

14. See R. P. Blackmur's "Afterword" to *The Europeans* (New York, 1964), pp. 179–89, for a discussion of this.

15. Henry James, *Hawthorne* (Ithaca, 1956), p. 46.

16. Ibid., p. 47.

17. Ibid., pp. 47–48.

18. Ibid., pp. 112–13.

19. Ibid., p. 114.

20. James, *European Writers and the Prefaces,* p. 1064.

21. Ibid., pp. 158, 49, 722.

22. For James' critique of Flaubert see the articles in *European Writers and the Prefaces;* for James as an aesthete see Martin Green, *The Problem of Boston* (New York, 1967), pp. 142–64.

23. James, *Hawthorne,* pp. 48–49, 98, 52, 22.

24. Henry James, *The House of Fiction,* Leon Edel, ed. (London, 1957), p. 34. For Chase's comment see chapter 5.

25. Ibid., pp. 34–35.

26. Ibid., pp. 35–36.

27. James, *European Writers and the Prefaces,* p. 93.

28. In G. P. Lathrop, *A Study of Hawthorne* (Cambridge, Mass., 1891), p. 230.

Chapter 9

1. Gerth and Mills, in Max Weber, *From Max Weber,* Hanns Gerth and C. Wright Mills, eds. (New York, 1973), pp. 66–68.

2. Ibid., pp. 66–67.

3. Perry Miller, *Errand into the Wilderness* (New York, 1964), p. 142. For another discussion of Boston's anti-entrepreneurial bias see Martin Green, *The Problem of Boston* (New York, 1967).

4. Ibid., p. 142.

5. Marius Bewley, *The Eccentric Design* (New York, 1963), p. 69.

6. D. R. Fox, *The Decline of the Aristocracy in the State of New York* (New York, 1918), pp. 130, 133.

7. Eugene Genovese, *The Political Economy of Slavery* (New York, 1967), p. 31. For an acute (although in part ill-tempered) refutation of Robert William Fogelman's and Stanley Engerman's *Time on the Cross* (Boston, 1974) see Herbert Gutman, *Slavery and the Numbers Game* (Urbana, 1975). The classic view that the slaveholders were not aristocrats is W. J. Cash's, *The Mind of the South* (New York, 1960). Its thesis is stated on page 4.

8. Eugene Genovese, ibid., pp. 138, 142.

9. Eugene Genovese, *The World the Slaveholders Made* (New York, 1971). The phrase is the title to part 2. My summary of Fitzhugh follows Genovese: pp.125–26.

10. The phrase is Raymond Williams'. For his discussion of the concept see *The Country and the City* (New York, 1973), pp. 165–81.

11. The term "culture making" comes from Richard Chase, *The American Novel and Its Tradition* (Garden City, 1957), p. 7.

12. Raymond Williams, *The English Novel fron Dickens to Lawrence* (London, 1976), p. 9.

13. Henry James, *The House of Fiction*, Leon Edel, ed. (London, 1957), p. 36.

Chapter 10

1. Henry James, in "Charles Augustin Sainte-Beauve," *European Writers and the Prefaces* (New York, 1984), p. 672.

2. For a compendium of older criticism, with commentary, see Marcel Clavel, *Fenimore Cooper and His Critics* (Aix-en-Provence, 1938).

3. Richard Chase, *The American Novel and Its Tradition* (Garden City, 1957), pp. 54, 13, 45. Chase's discussion of the vagaries of Cooper's reputation remains very interesting (pp. 43–47). If Chase did not overrate Cooper, Trilling and Bewley, who both claimed greatness for him, did. Chase's formulation of the Cooper myth was a little ambiguous; at times he speaks of Natty's destiny as a myth that is "anti-cultural" (p. 54). My own concern is elsewhere, with the idea that Natty's abstraction and ideality should "not by any means . . . be thought of as a failure to render a character concretely" (pp. 61–62).

4. D. H. Lawrence, *Studies in Classic American Literature* (New York, 1971), p. 55.

5. Alfred Kazin on Lukacs, in George Lukacs, *Studies in European Realism* Alfred Kazin, ed. (New York, 1968), p. x.

6. Lionel Trilling, *The Liberal Imagination* (New York, 1976), p. 286.

7. Chase, *American Novel*, p. 46.

8. The examples Mark Twain gives are quite appropriate here:

> "She's in the forest—hanging from the boughs of the trees, in a soft rain—in the dew on the open grass—the clouds that float about in the blue heavens—the birds that sing in the woods—the sweet springs where I slake my thirst—and in all the other glorious gifts that come from God's Providence."

> "It consarns me as all things that touches a fri'nd consarns a fri'nd."

"If I was Injin born now, I might tell of this, or carry in the scalp and boast of the expl'ite afore the whole tribe; or if my inimy had only been a bear."

See the discussion in "Fenimore Cooper's Literary Offenses," in *The Portable Mark Twain* (ed.) Bernard De Voto (New York, 1946), pp. 553–55, especially. These concern *The Deerslayer*. In *The Prairie* the problem is, in a sense, resolved by having Natty talk in a tendentious and highflown manner throughout—even though Cooper has not yet developed the idea that the Moravians have given him an education. When Natty's speech is unrealistic—when he speaks, that is in a romance manner—it is usually because he is speaking as Cooper's polemical mouthpiece.

9. Chase, *American Novel,* p. 53. The reference to Don Quixote, just below, is on p. 55.

10. *The Great Tradition,* (New York, 1964), p. 6. Leavis later relented when Marius Bewley, who had been his pupil, began to urge Cooper's greatness—but I think this was courtesy.

11. I borrow the term "seigneurial" from Eugene Genovese's *The World the Slaveholders Made* (New York, 1971), p. 16.

12. Marius Bewley, *The Eccentric Design* (New York, 1963), p. 65.

13. Philip Rahv, *The Myth and the Powerhouse: Essays in Literature and Ideas* (New York, 1965), pp. 46, 6.

14. This also suggests why it was that the South, before the Civil War, produced so little that was worthwhile in literature. Southerners were too politicized to be interested in the human condition as such; but their political fervor excluded the satiric ambivalence that the novel of manners requires. When a Southerner such as Poe or John Pendleton Kennedy (*Swallow Barn*) did produce something of value it was because he transcended these limitations personally—and in this he was not aided by his culture.

15. Leavis, *Great Tradition,* p. 141.

16. Martin Turnell, *The Novel in France* (New York, 1951), p. 434.

Chapter 11

1. This may be a conservative estimate. Herbert Aptheker's interpretations of American history are too predictable to be interesting, but there is no reason to doubt his figures. He notes in *Colonial America* (New York, 1966) that indentured servants accounted for ten to fifteen percent of the population at any given time (p. 26), while on the eve of the Revolution slaves accounted for twenty percent of it (p. 39). However, as he points out in *The American Revolution* (New York, 1969), since the slaves began to work when very young, and since all the women worked, the slaves' percentage of the labor force was doubtless higher than their percentage of the population. See p. 207.

2. The best discussions of the initial, and substantial, power of the left and its subsequent collapse in the early twentieth century are James Weinstein's *The Decline of Socialism in America 1912–1925* (New York, 1967), his *Ambiguous Legacy: The Left in American Politics* (New York, 1975), and Christopher Lasch's *The Agony of the American Left* (New York, 1966).

3. The term occurs throughout Palmer's writings. A good summary discussion of it may be found in R. R. Palmer, *Atlas of World History* (New York, 1967), pp. 88–89.

4. The sharpest distinction is that the associations of the West were voluntary, while those of the East were not. A good treatment of this theme is provided by George Lichtheim, *The New Europe* (New York, 1963), pp. xvii–xxi especially.

5. See George Lichtheim, "Grand Old Man" collected in *Collected Essays* (New York, 1973), p. 483.

6. See George Lichtheim, *The New Europe,* especially pp. 41–64.

7. George Lichtheim, *Europe in the Twentieth Century* (New York, 1972), p. 288.

8. In saying this, however, I do not mean to argue against other ways of explaining the singularity of twentieth-century American culture. There is, for example, the simple but important point that the United States suffered far less than any other major combatant in either world war. Americans, having suffered less, may simply have learned less.

9. See note 14, chapter 1.

10. Lionel Trilling, *The Liberal Imagination* (New York, 1976), pp. vii–xiii.

11. Because Boorstin believed Americans to be without ideology it may be that he would deny having a desire to maintain a "liberal" society in the United States. Yet it is difficult to see how his admiration for the particular virtues of American democracy—as it has extended into culture, society, and economics—would not translate into some kind of liberalism.

Chapter 12

1. Sacvan Bercovitch, "Afterword" in *Ideology and Classic American Literature* (Cambridge, 1986), p. 431.

2. Bercovitch, "The Problem of Ideology in American Literary History," in *Critical Inquiry,* vol. 12 (Summer 1986), p. 639 (and *Ideology and Classic American Literature,* p. 439).

3. Ibid., pp. 639, 640.

4. Myra Jehlen, "Introduction: Beyond Transcendence," *Ideology and Classic American Literature*, pp. 11–12.

5. Ibid., p. 14.

6. Bercovitch, "The Problem of Ideology in American Literary History," p. 636.

7. Jehlen, "Introduction: Beyond Transcendence," *Ideology,* p. 13.

8. Bercovitch, "America as Canon and Context," *American Literature,* vol. 50 (March 1986), p. 107. (A variation of this statement occurs in *Ideology and Classic American Literature,* p. 427.)

9. Bercovitch, "The Problem of Ideology in American Literary History," p. 645. The nearly identical passage describing Jehlen's essay in *Ideology and Classic American Literature* is on p. 434. (I am guessing which was written first.)

10. Bercovitch, *The American Jeremiad* (Madison, 1978), pp. xii-xiii.

11. Ibid., p. 176.

12. Jehlen, "The Novel and the Middle-Class in America," in *Ideology and Classic American Literature*, p. 129.

13. Bercovitch, *The American Jeremiad*, p. xiii.

14. Ibid., pp. 180–81.

15. Bercovitch, "America as Canon and Context," p. 103.

16. Bercovitch, *The American Jeremiad*, p. 193.

17. Jehlen, "The Novel and the Middle-Class in America," *Ideology*, p. 137.

18. Bercovitch, "The Problem of Ideology in American Literary History," p. 645; and *Ideology and Classic American Literature*, p. 435.

19. Bercovitch, "The Problem of Ideology in American Literary History," p. 646; and *Ideology and Classic American Literature*, p. 435.

20. Bercovitch, "The Problem of Ideology in American Literary History," pp. 650, 652.

21. Ibid., p. 646.

22. Jehlen, "The Novel and the Middle-Class in America," *Ideology*, pp. 125, 136. The republication of this 1977 essay without modification (or qualification in Jehlen's introduction) indicates that Jehlen rejects the attacks on romance theory by critics such as Hirsch, Merrill, Mill, and Poirier. Indeed, Poirier is criticized—although obliquely, p. 139.

23. Ibid., p. 139.

24. "America, in other words, was conceived not so much in liberty as in liberalism." Jehlen, ibid., p. 127.

25. Ibid., p. 133.

26. Ibid.

Chapter 13

1. Sacvan Bercovitch, *The American Jeremiad* (Madison, 1978), p. 176.

2. Ibid., p. xiii.

3. Myra Jehlen, "The Novel and the Middle-Class in America," *Ideology and Classic American Literature* (Cambridge, 1986), p. 129.

4. Referring to herself and to her collaborators, Jehlen claims that "the tradition of Van Wyck Brooks and F. O. Matthiessen thus acquires, in ideological criticism, a sober and skeptical heir, whose interests (and perhaps sympathies) are broader for reflecting a heightened awareness of the world beyond the United States, and in the United States, of multiple Americas, none of them transcendent." "Introduction: Beyond Transcendence," ibid., p. 15.

5. See chapter 8, note 17.

6. Jehlen, "The Novel and the Middle Class in America," *Ideology*, p. 139.

7. Ibid.

8. They are opposed in this view by Jonathan Arac, who really does read *The Scarlet Letter* as if it had been written by a conservative American preincarnation of Philippe Sollers. See "The Politics of *The Scarlet Letter*," ibid. Arac's essay is rather speculative:

> *The Scarlet Letter* ends with the death of Hester, and its writing began with the death of Hawthorne's own mother. The difference is that Mrs. Hawthorne committed no crime in marrying a mariner who then happened to die in Surinam of yellow fever. Hawthorne's novel transforms his life situation by adding accountable guilt. A complex social fact—involving American trade relations in the Caribbean, the inadequacy of mosquito control, the conditions of medical knowledge—is turned into a crime. Something that might require political action—as it did to empower public health undertaking in the nineteenth century—becomes a matter for ethical judgement and psychological reflection. (pp. 252–53)

Evidently, had Hawthorne been more direct, he might have written the great novel of mosquito control. However, it is possible that the circumstances of his father's death were not germane to the composition of the novel that he did write.

9. Q. D. Leavis, *Collected Essays*, vol. 2 (Cambridge, 1985), p. 62.

10. See W. C. Brownell, *American Prose Masters* (New York, 1909), pp. 100–102, and Martin Green, *Re-Appraisals* (New York, 1967), pp. 78–80. James actually thought both male principals failed, Dimmesdale more than Chillingsworth: *The House of Fiction*, Leon Edel, ed. (London, 1957), p. 180.

11. Jehlen, "Introduction: Beyond Transcendence," *Ideology*, p. 16.

12. Jehlen, "The Novel and the Middle-Class in America," ibid., p. 133.

13. Geoffrey Thurley, *The Dickens Myth* (London, 1976), p. 21.

14. Ibid., p. 18.

15. Ibid., p. 231.

16. Ibid., p. 154.

17. In fact, when *The Gilded Age* was published, it was quite common to refer to Sellers as an "American Pickwick." I think Micawber is the better parallel, however.

18. As Michael David Bell, to his credit, notices in *The Development of the American Romance*, p. vii.

19. Jehlen, "The Novel and the Middle-Class in America," *Ideology*, p. 134.

20. Ibid., p. 137.

21. Ibid.

22. Henry James, "Honoré de Balzac" in *European Writers and the Prefaces* (New York, 1984), p. 66.

23. Ibid., p. 139.

24. Lionel Trilling, *The Liberal Imagination* (New York, 1976), p. 11.

25. Jehlen, *Ideological Criticism and Classic American Literature*, pp. 270–71.

26. Terry Eagleton, *Criticism and Ideology* (London, 1976), p. 181.

27. Ibid., p. 166.

28. Jane Tompkins, "An Introduction to Reader-Response Criticism" in Tompkins, ed. *Reader-Response Criticism: From Formalism to Post-Structuralism* (Baltimore, 1980), p. xxv. Tompkins' contribution to *Ideology and Classic American Literature*, "Sentimental Power" is wholly consonant with the position outlined here.

29. Of course, it is unlikely that any widespread radicalization, one way or the other, through the persuasive power of relativism and historicism could take place. The effects of historicism and relativism are usually not radical, but conservative. This is evident when we consider the appeal by which ideological criticism hopes to induce Americans to desert the American ideology. Americans, ideological criticism claims, are the children of the American ideology, but they ought to liberate themselves from their ideological parent by recognizing that, like all ideology, it is not universal. But, if no ideology is universal, why should anyone give up the ideology he already has—for no other, from the position of dogmatic relativism and historicism, is really any better? Children, after all, do not usually desert their actual parents when they come to realize their parents' limitations. If Americans learn that no ideology is universal, and that "there is no escape from ideology," they will probably keep the ideology they have: it is, after all, "theirs." Radical change, as I believe Marx knew, can only come from an appeal to justice, not interest. See Carol C. Gould, *Marx's Social Ontology* (Cambridge, Mass., 1980), pp. 166–78, 186–87. Gould argues, very persuasively, that Marx's conception of justice is not relativistic, although she observes that this is a subject of controversy. I think Marx rather more ambiguous on this subject than Gould makes him; I agree with her, however, that a non-relativist conception of justice can be developed from his work. He is certainly firmer than Gramsci. See James Joll's gloss of a particularly muddled passage in *Gramsci* (Glasgow, 1977), p. 32. Gramsci's equivocation is highlighted by his willingness to follow the historicism of Croce while attacking as "very degenerate" the historicism of Gentile, Croce's long-time, if erstwhile associate: *Prison Notebooks* (New York, 1976), p. 41. It need only be noted that if one draws a distinction between a healthy and a degenerate historicism, one also has tacitly assumed a position that transcends historicism and permits a just evaluation of its various strains.

30. Alain Finkielkraut, *La Defaite de la pensée* (Paris, 1987).

31. Terry Eagleton, *The Function of Criticism* (London, 1987), p. 124.

32. See Pierre Machery, "Problems of Reflection" in *Literature, Society and the Sociology of Literature* (University of Essex, 1977), p. 45. Eagleton's attempt to amend Marx by arguing that a work's "aesthetic value is an effect of the process whereby the complex ideological conjuncture in which it inheres so produces (internally distantiates) itself in a play of textual signification as to render its depths and intricacies vividly perceptible" is not only torturous, but unconvincing (*Criticism and Ideology*, pp. 177–78). As Tony Bennett, a critical admirer, is bound to confess: "quixotic in the extreme, Eagleton avoids fetishing literary value as an immanent quality of the text only to present it as an effect of the work's origins" [*Formalism and Marxism* (London, 1986)]. Bennett detects a residual humanism in Eagleton, as do I— which, however, I take to be one of Eagleton's saving graces, while Bennett condemns it.

33. Bennett, ibid., p. 137.

34. In fact, I agree with Ronald Dworkin, who argues that the idea of truth is not a metaphysical proposition, but simply a categorical imperative of the mind. The idea that there is no truth *is*, however, metaphysical, in the bad sense of the word. See Ronald Dworkin, "My Reply to Stanley Fish (and Walter Benn Michaels): Please Don't Talk about Objectivity Any More" in W. G. T. Mitchell, ed., *The Politics of Interpretation* (Chicago, 1983), especially pp. 287, 298–99.

Chapter 14

1. The prairies are beyond American settlement, in the Louisiana territory that has just been purchased. The Indians are not "domesticated" as they are in *The Redskins* and *The Pioneers*. Spanish colonial culture is present as well in Dona Inez.

2. As I have mentioned, the sailors' world, for Melville, is an international world, always contrasted to the world ashore, and so little exclusively American that *Billy Budd,* the characters of which are all European, has a natural place beside the other novels of the sea. The presence of Queequeg and Fedallah in *Moby Dick* reminds us of this.

3. Edmund Wilson, *Patriotic Gore* (New York, 1962), p. 5.

4. Q. D. Leavis, *Collected Essays,* vol. 2 (Cambridge, 1985), pp. 19–20.

5. Lionel Trilling, *The Liberal Imagination* (New York, 1976), pp. 216–17.

6. Richard Chase was the most insistent: "In America nearly everyone a novelist of manners might be interested in has been middle-class, and has very likely prided himself on manners indistinguishable from a lower class which is always incipiently middle-class itself." *The American Novel and Its Tradition* (Garden City, 1957), p. 159. Of the romance critics, Marius Bewley came closest to the view I take: "the scene was crude, even beyond successful satire, as Dickens's was to discover." *The Eccentric Design* (New York, 1963), p. 15. My point of course, is just the opposite: the crudeness of the scene was perfect for satire, as Dickens, and not only Dickens, was to discover.

7. The insight here, if such it is, owes much to John W. Aldridge's defense of Trilling's conception of the novel against Delmore Schwartz. He calls the American novel "impoverished," and mentions its reliance on violence and action, as opposed to the nuances of manners, in the narrower social sense. He does *not,* however, follow Trilling in calling the impoverished American novels romances. For Aldridge, an impoverished novel is simply that, and I agree. But it does seem to me that Aldridge (now a neglected critic), like the romance critics, underestimated the possibilities for novelists in America. Moreover, he was a little too quick to close ranks with Trilling: in some ways, his position was closer to Schwartz's—or would have been, had Schwartz thought through his position a little more clearly, and not taken refuge in populist "patriotism." See "The Heresy of Literary Manners," *In Search of Heresy* (New York, 1956), especially pp. 84–87.

8. This is one of the themes of Martin Green's *The Problem of Boston* (New York, 1967).

9. Gore Vidal, "Thomas Love Peacock: The Novel of Ideas," *The Second American Revolution,* p. 119.

10. Consider the idea, very current among historians of the fifties, and popularized by Boorstin (see note 18, chapter 4), that a major difference between the United States and Europe is that the United States has been immune from the viruses of fascism and communism while Europe has been their breeding ground. "Europe," in this connection is a misleading abstraction. The well-established European democracies did not breed either fascism or communism. They were bred in countries—not only European, as witness Japan—that lacked a well-established democratic tradition. Of course the European democracies were not immune from attack, but neither was the United States. The proper distinction in relation to the rise of fascism and communism—between countries with strong democratic traditions and institutions and those without them—was obliterated by the identification of democracy with the United States.

11. It did not always limit it. Let us consider a scene from James' *The Europeans*, which novel I have given as evidence that American novelists were very far from accepting wholeheartedly the national covenant. The national covenant is present nevertheless in the form of the Wentworth family, in 1.11. Wentworth especially, who is a symbol of that Old America evoked by James in *Hawthorne*. Wentworth embodies many of the qualities Bercovitch and Jehlen attribute to the American ideology. He is among other things upper middle-class, liberal, democratic, and provincial. Usually, in his exchanges with the cosmopolitan Baroness, with Felix, and with Gertrude (who supports them) he comes off second best. But in one great scene he does not:

> Mr. Wentworth also observed his young daughter.
> "I don't know what her manner of life may have been," he said; "but she certainly never can have enjoyed a more refined and salubrious home."
> Gertrude stood there looking at them all. "She is the wife of a Prince," she said.
> "We are all princes here," said Mr. Wentworth," and I don't know of any palace in this neighborhood that is to let."

    As F. R. Leavis long ago noted, "Mr. Wentworth at this point has his creator's backing and, opposed as he is to the Baroness, stands for an American democracy that James offers, with conviction, as an American superiority" [F.R. Leavis, *The Great Tradition* (New York, 1964), p. 140.] Leavis is right: certainly some of our sense of Wentworth's advantage depends not only upon James' dramatic skill, but upon our acceptance of the democratic principle informing Wentworth's rejoinder: if we do not think his reply just, it is simply boorish.

12. Even the beautifully appreciative essay on Howells by Trilling rates him lower than Trollope. See *The Opposing Self* (New York, 1955). More recents appraisals, such as John Updike's, have not really tried to alter the traditional evaluation.

13. I shall not discuss *Home as Found* in what follows. This is because I don't believe—and here the book differs from *The Redskins*—that it was inherently very promising.

14. If the reply is that Melville's point is that his characters and situations have no character, then there is no point to his having written a novel in the first place: *The Confidence Man* should then have been a long short story or *nouvelle*, like the much more incisive "Bartleby." Once we become accustomed to it, the scenes become predictable. Q. D. Leavis has written, in my opinion, the best argument in support of the view of *The Confidence Man* as a great novel. I think she does justice to Melville's intention (she compares Melville with Swift), but mistakes the intention for the actual achievement. See "Melville: 1853–6 Phase" in *Collected Essays*, vol. 2 (Cambridge 1985). The best brief discussion of Melville's failure in *Pierre* and *The Confidence Man* is in Bewley's *The Eccentric Design* (New York, 1963), pp. 210–19—a discussion all the more remarkable because Bewley resisted the temptation to enroll these novels into his triumphant tradition of "romance."

15. Wilson, *Patriotic Gore*, p. 8.

16. As has been often remarked, *The Bostonians* seems to have been largely inspired by *The Blithedale Romance*, with Tarrant resembling Westervelt, and Olive and Verena resembling Zenobia and Priscilla. I take this as further evidence for the centrality of satire as a means of releasing the American artists' talent.

17. See Martin Green, "Melville and the American Romance," *Re-Appraisals* (New York, 1967). The comment about Ahab's leg is on p. 104.

18. Bewley, *Eccentric Design*, p. 205. Bewley noted that there was a critical consensus here.

19. Q. D. Leavis, "Henry James' Heiress: The Importance of Edith Wharton" in Irving Howe, ed., *Edith Wharton* (Englewood Cliffs, 1962), p. 83. Louis Auchincloss, "Edith Wharton," *Pioneers and Caretakers* (Minneapolis, 1965), p. 38. Leavis, in Howe, *Edith Wharton*, p. 87. Lionel Trilling, "The Morality of Inertia," ibid., pp. 138, 143.

20. One partial late example is Ludwig Lewisohn: see *Expression in America* (New York, 1932). Although Lewisohn himself would not at all have liked being classified with the genteel tradition, he shares in its odd mixture of cosmopolitanism and patriotic piety. Despite the piety, he nevertheless concluded: "We have produced no masterpieces of a very high order . . . [and] both wholeness and high severity are lacking even to our best works" (p. 590). Lewisohn, whose sentimentality makes his work now almost unreadable and disqualifies him as a critic of poetry, nevertheless could be quite shrewd and unsentimental when piqued. See his very sharp criticism of Melville (and the Melville revival) on pp. 186–93. The comment on *Typee* is acute.

21. Wilson, *The Devils and Canon Barham* (New York, 1973), pp. 92, 189–90.

Selected Bibliography

Aldridge, John W. *The Devil in the Fire* (New York, 1972).
_____ . *In Search of Heresy* (New York, 1956).
Allen, Walter. *The English Novel* (New York, 1954).
Aristotle. *The Rhetoric and the Poetics* (New York, 1954).
Atlas, James. *Delmore Schwartz* (New York, 1977).
Bell, Michael Davitt. *The Development of American Romance* (Chicago, 1980).
Bennett, Tony. *Formalism and Marxism* (London, 1986).
Bercovitch, Sacvan. *The American Jeremiad* (Madison, 1978).
_____ and Myra Jehlen, eds. *Ideology and Classic American Literature* (Cambridge, 1986).
Bernstein, Barton J., ed. *Towards a New Past* (New York, 1968).
Bewley, Marius. *The Eccentric Design* (New York, 1963).
Boorstin, Daniel J. *The Americans: The Colonial Experience* (New York, 1958).
_____ . *The Genius of American Politics* (Chicago, 1953).
Brombert, Victor, ed. *Stendhal* (Englewood Cliffs, 1962).
Brooks, Van Wyck. *The Flowering of New England* (New York, 1952).
_____ . *Three Essays on America* (New York, 1970).
_____ . *Van Wyck Brooks: The Early Years* (New York, 1968).
Brownell, W. C. *American Prose Masters* (New York, 1909).
Cash, W. J. *The Mind of the South* (New York, 1960).
Chase, Richard. *The American Novel and Its Tradition* (Garden City, 1957).
Clavel, Marcel. *Fenimore Cooper and the Critics* (Aix-en-Provence, 1938).
Dobb, Maurice. *Studies in the Development of Capitalism* (New York, 1947).
Doubleday, Neal Frank. *Hawthorne's Early Tales* (Durham, 1972).
Eagleton, Terry. *Criticism and Ideology* (London, 1976).
_____ . *The Function of Criticism* (London, 1987).
Edel, Leon. *Henry James* (New York, 1985).
Elkins, Stanley. *Slavery: A Problem in American and Intellectual Life* (Chicago, 1959).
Feidelson, Charles. *Symbolism and American Literature* (Chicago, 1953).
Fetterly, Judith. *The Resisting Reader* (Bloomington, 1978).
Fiedler, Leslie. *Love and Death in the American Novel* (New York, 1966).
Finkielkraut, Alain. *La Defaite de la penseé* (Paris, 1987).
Fogel, Robert William, and Stanley Engerman. *Time on the Cross* (Boston, 1974).
Fox, D. R. *The Decline of the Aristocracy in the State of New York* (New York, 1918).
Genovese, Eugene. *In Red and Black* (New York, 1971).
_____ . *The Political Economy of Slavery* (New York, 1967).
_____ . *Roll, Jordan, Roll* (New York, 1976).

——— . *The World the Slaveholders Made* (New York, 1971).

Graff, Gerald. *Literature against Itself* (London, 1980).

——— . *Poetic Statement and Critical Dogmas* (Chicago, 1970).

Green, Martin. *The Problem of Boston* (New York, 1967).

——— . *Re-Appraisals* (New York, 1967).

Hartz, Louis J. *The Liberal Tradition in America* (New York, 1955).

Hawthorne, Nathaniel. *Collected Works* (Cambridge, Mass., 1891).

Hirsch, David H. *Reality and Idea in the Early American Novel* (The Hague, 1971).

Hobsbawm, E. J. *The Age of Capital* (London, 1975).

Hofstadter, Richard. *The Progressive Historians* (New York, 1968).

Howe, Irving, ed. *Edith Wharton* (Englewood Cliffs, 1962).

——— . *Politics and the Novel* (New York, 1957).

James, Henry. *European Writers and the Prefaces* (New York, 1984).

——— . *Hawthorne* (Ithaca, 1956).

——— . *The House of Fiction.* Ed. Leon Edel (London, 1957).

——— . *Selected Literary Criticism*, Ed. Morris Shapiro (London, 1963).

Jay, Gregory S., ed. *Modern American Critics, Dictionary of Literary Biography*, vol. 63 (Detroit, 1988).

Kaul, A. N. *The American Vision* (New Haven, 1963).

——— , ed. *Hawthorne* (Englewood Cliffs, 1966).

Kazin, Alfred. *On Native Grounds* (New York, 1942).

——— , and Charles Shapiro, eds. *The Stature of Theodore Dreiser* (Bloomington, 1955).

Lasch, Christopher. *The Agony of the American Left* (New York, 1966).

Lathrop, G. P. *A Study of Hawthorne* (Cambridge, Mass., 1891).

Lawrence, D. H. *Studies in Classic American Literature* (New York, 1971).

Leavis, F. R. *The Great Tradition* (New York, 1964).

——— . *Anna Karenina and Other Essays* (London, 1968).

Leavis, Q. D. *Collected Essays.* vol. 2 (Cambridge, 1985).

Lerner, Max. *America as a Civilization* (New York, 1957).

Levin, Harry. *The Power of Blackness* (New York, 1958).

Lewis, R. W. B. *The American Adam* (Chicago, 1955).

——— . *Edith Wharton* (New York, 1975).

Lewisohn, Ludwig. *Expression in America* (New York, 1932).

Lichtheim, George. *Collected Essays* (New York, 1973).

——— . *Europe in the Twentieth Century* (New York, 1972).

——— . *Marxism: An Historical and Critical Study* (New York, 1965).

——— . *The New Europe* (New York, 1963).

Lukacs, George. *The Historical Novel* (Harmondsworth, Middlesex, 1976).

——— . *Realism in Our Time* (New York, 1971).

——— . *Studies in European Realism.* Ed. Alfred Kazin (New York, 1968).

——— . *The Theory of the Novel* (Cambridge, Mass., 1971).

Lundblad, Jane. *Nathaniel Hawthorne and the European Literary Tradition* (New York, 1965).

Matthiessen, F. O. *American Renaissance* (New York, 1970).

Merquior, J. G. *From Prague to Paris* (London, 1986).

——— . *Foucault* (London, 1986).

Mill, Nicolaus. *American and English Fiction in the Nineteenth Century: An Antigenre Critique* (Bloomington, 1974).

Miller, James E., Jr. *A Critical Guide to Leaves of Grass* (Chicago, 1975).

Miller, Perry. *Errand into the Wilderness* (New York, 1964).

Mitchell, W. G. T., ed. *The Politics of Interpretation* (Chicago, 1983).

Palmer, R. R. *The Age of Democratic Revolution* (Princeton, 1969).

_____ . *The Atlas of World History* (New York, 1967).

Parrington, V. L. *Main Currents in American Thought* (New York, 1958).

Peyre, Henri, ed. *Fiction in Several Languages* (Boston, 1968).

Plato. *Collected Dialogues*, eds. Huntington Cairns and Edith Hamilton (New York, 1964).

Poirier, Richard. *A World Elsewhere: The Place of Style in American Literature* (New York, 1966).

Porte, Joel. *The Romance in America* (Middletown, 1969).

Rahv, Philip. *The Myth and the Powerhouse: Essays in Literature and Ideas* (New York, 1965).

Scholes, Robert. *Textual Power* (New Haven, 1985).

Schumpeter, Joseph. *Imperialism and Social Classes*, ed. Paul M. Sweezy (Oxford, 1951).

Schwartz, Delmore. *Selected Essays* (Chicago, 1970).

Spiers, John. *Poetry Towards Novel* (London, 1971).

Steiner, George. *Tolstoy or Dostoevsky* (Boston, 1980).

Sternsher, Bernard. *Consensus, Conflict, and American Historians* (Bloomington, 1979).

Sweezy, Paul M., ed. *Imperialism and Social Classes* (Oxford, 1951).

Tate, Cecil F. *The Search for a Method in American Studies* (Minneapolis, 1973).

Thompson, E. P. *The Making of the English Working Class* (New York, 1966).

Thurley, Geoffrey. *Counter-Modernism in Current Critical Theory* (New York, 1983).

_____ . *The Dickens Myth* (London, 1976).

Tocqueville, Alexis de. *Democracy in America* (New York, 1945).

Todorov, Tzvetan. *Critique de la critique: Un Roman d'apprentissage* (Paris, 1984).

Trilling, Lionel. *Beyond Culture* (New York, 1965).

_____ . *The Liberal Imagination* (New York, 1976).

_____ . *The Opposing Self* (New York, 1955).

Turnell, Martin. *The Novel in France* (New York, 1951).

Twain, Mark. *The Portable Mark Twain*, ed. Bernard De Voto (New York, 1946).

Vidal, Gore. *Homage to Daniel Shays* (New York, 1972).

_____ . *The Second American Revolution* (New York, 1982).

Weber, Max. *From Max Weber*, eds. Hanns Gerth and C. Wright Mills (New York, 1973).

_____ . *Theory of Social and Economic Development* (New York, 1947).

Weinstein, James. *The Decline of Socialism in America, 1912–1925* (New York, 1967).

_____ . *Ambiguous Legacy: The Left in American Politics* (New York, 1975).

Williams, Raymond. *The Country and the City* (New York, 1973).

_____ . *Culture and Society* (New York, 1958).

_____ . *The English Novel from Dickens to Lawrence* (Oxford, 1976).

_____ . *Marxism and Literature* (Oxford, 1978).

Wilson, Edmund. *The Devils and Canon Barham* (New York, 1973).

_____ . *Patriotic Gore* (New York, 1962).

Index